LOOT

INSIDE THE WORLD OF STOLEN ART

LOOT

INSIDE THE WORLD OF STOLEN ART

THOMAS McSHANE

WITH DARY MATERA

First published in 2006 as *Stolen Masterpiece Tracker* by Barricade Books. Published in 2007 as *Loot* by Maverick House Publishers.

Maverick House, Main Street, Dunshaughlin, Co. Meath, Ireland. Maverick House Asia, Level 41, United Centre, 323 Silom Road, Bangrak, Bangkok 10500, Thailand.

info@maverickhouse.com
http://www.maverickhouse.com

ISBN: 978-1-905379-37-8

5 4 3 2 1

Printed and bound by CPD.

Contents

Author's Note   VII

Introduction   IX

1 The Curse of Rembrandt's Rabbi, Part One   1

2 The Curse of Rembrandt's Rabbi, Part Two: Shuffling Off to Buffalo   18

3 A Rubens Pickup in Peekskill and Poughkeepsie Becomes the Precursor to ABSCAM   41

4 Picasso's $100 Million Purple Reign   60

5 The Russians are Coming for Tintoretto   70

6 Picasso Checks into the Motel Monet   81

7 Rubens' Spring Breakout in Florida   95

8 A Big Dog, Grandma Moses, and Van Gogh   113

9 The Boston Museum Massacre   138

10 The Peeved Pepperdine Professor   157

11 The Gunslingers Take the Gunslinger   173

Contents

12 Come Back to the Five and Dime, Remington,
Russell and Wyeth   187

13 And Away They Go   200

14 The Case of the Vanishing Virgin   223

15 Ben-Hur Hits the Swedish Embassy   247

16 Bouguereau at the Borghi   268

17 John Gotti's Henchmen Strike Out with Picasso's
Mistress   282

18 No Boston Tea Party at Isabella's   299

Epilogue   321

Index   333

AUTHOR'S NOTE

VIEWING THE ART

The internet provides the best opportunity to view historic paintings in all their colourful splendour. One of the best places to find virtually all of the works mentioned inthe forthcoming pages is *The Art Resource* at:

http://www.artres.com/c/htm/Home.aspx

Type in a search like this: Pollock, Jackson, 'Name of Painting'.

Additional web pages that provide a similar service can be found at:

http://www.artrenewal.org/index.html

http://www.wga.hu

http://www.globalgallery.com

INTRODUCTION

'YOU CAN SELL ANYTHING TO AMERICANS. THEY KNOW NOTHING
ABOUT ART ... ALL YOU HAVE TO DO IS ASK A FABULOUS PRICE.'
- *renowned forger Jean Charles Millet, grandson of 19th
Century French Barbizon master Jean François Millet*

*I*F YOU TAKE a look at Interpol's list of the top five criminal
enterprises in the world, number four might surprise you.

Art theft.

Interpol, the international police agency based in France, has
determined that stealing, copying, and reselling pretty works of art
is only exceeded by the much uglier businesses of illicit drugs, arms
smuggling, and money laundering.

In the US, the Federal Bureau of Investigation concurs. My
former employer believes that art theft now exceeds $5 billion a
year—and counting.

Make that number four with a bullet.

None of this surprises me. I've spent the past 35 years tracking
pilfered paintings across the planet, and then using various ruses
to flush them out. For 22 of those years, I was the FBI's main art
theft undercover agent. Few knew, even within the bureau, because

I operated in the shadows buried under multiple aliases and identities.

One of the things I learned early on is that there are two contrasting reasons why art theft and forgery is such a bullish growth industry. The soaring value of classic paintings has combined with a comparatively minuscule legal risk to create a landscape that has become every criminal's dream job. With the auction price of a single Picasso topping $100 million in 2004, the sky is now the limit in this crazy, highly specialised industry.

Yet the legal statutes haven't remotely kept up with the unprecedented temptation to cross over to the dark side.

Someone could snatch the *Mona Lisa* off the wall of the Louvre in Paris, sell it in New York's Central Park for a cool $350 million, get caught a week later, and expect to be given no more than 18 months or so for the 'sale and transportation of stolen property.' Lady Justice, herself a popular model for so many painters, blindly doesn't consider the value of the goods when doling out her democratic, non-prejudicial punishments.

Why not steal the *Mona Lisa* as a first time offender, and you may only walk away with probation? Or drive away in your gold-plated Hummer limousine. How many people would trade a year and a half stint in jail for $350 million? A better question is: who wouldn't?

'An art thief is entertaining, romantic,' NYPD art detective Robert Volpe lamented to *Time* magazine following some especially frustrating cat-and mouse chases we worked together. 'I've seen cases where the thief has pleaded guilty and got no sentence at all.'

Volpe and me both.

Complicating matters are the 'good faith purchase and protection laws' that were, or are, in effect in such countries as Switzerland and Japan. This means if you, wink, wink, buy some art you 'oh my gosh' didn't know was stolen, and can 'inadvertently' keep it out of sight for a while, two years or so depending on the country, it's officially yours. (In America, you must return it and you're out what you paid.)

Other countries like Russia, China, Cuba, and many of the Arab nations dispense with such annoying formalities altogether in favour of the international 'finders keepers' statutes.

Even the good ol' US of A can play this game. In recent years, the Italians and Greeks in particular have made concerted efforts to locate and repossess their stolen or looted national treasures. Many have been traced to the finest American museums, stately palaces like New York's Metropolitan Museum of Art, Los Angeles' J. Paul Getty Museum, and Boston's Museum of Fine Arts, institutions that are loath to give them back. This thorny international struggle will continue into the next decade, if not millennium.

On an individual level, while stealing the heavily secured and guarded *Mona Lisa* might be an absurd example, what about that Monet the rich guy down the street has in his study? It might only produce a mere $10 million, but most people could survive on that.

If one's personal sense of morals doesn't allow for such illegal activities, there are still millions to be made perfectly legitimately in the art theft trade. Is that same rich guy's Monet a little warm? Drop a dime and the insurance company will be more than happy to write you a cheque for a quarter of a million or so.

Farfetched? It's my estimation that every day, thousands of people gaze at the beauty of a stolen painting, completely unaware that they're hotter than the core of Mount St Helens. They're everywhere, right under our noses: big, framed, lavishly pigmented lottery tickets hanging on walls like the proverbial money growing on trees.

Consider this: every one of the 12 artworks worth a total of $300 million that were snatched from Boston's Isabella Stuart Gardner Museum in 1990 remains at large. They've no doubt been separated, scattered to the four winds, and are hanging on a bunch of modern-day robber barons' billiard room walls. Glance over the eight ball and spot one, and the reward is a nifty $5 million.

Similarly, most of the 53 Western-themed paintings and sculptures taken from the Woolworth Estate in Monmouth, Maine, nearly 40 years ago have never been recovered. That's another $50 million or so floating around. A giant purple Picasso that vanished en route from Houston, Texas, to New York, New York in 1976 remains in the wind as well. That one might be worth $50 million alone.

Take my word for it; many stolen paintings are kept in open view, and they could be anywhere. I've seen nearly $300 million worth of classics in the oddest places. A van Gogh at a grimy gas station. A Picasso in a $20-a-night roach motel. A Rubens in the back of a beat-up van. A Rembrandt in the bathroom of a small antique store. Two more Rubens spinning down from a hotel balcony, plunging to the grass below. You name it, I've been blown away by it.

Oddly enough, I never set out to become the Sherlock Homes of oil on canvas. I fell into it almost by accident. When I joined the FBI in 1968 after graduating from Fordham Law School, I didn't have a specialty in mind. I just wanted to put my legal knowledge to good use, and felt law enforcement was a noble calling.

My first day on the job was unforgettable. Two popular veteran agents were gunned down by a bank robber in a bloody shooting at an Oxen Hill, Maryland, apartment complex. The disbelief, tension, rage, and tears that swept the agency's Washington, DC headquarters were unbelievable. FBI agents are rarely murdered, so to lose two in one day was huge. The massive manhunt for the killer forced me to hit the ground running at breakneck speed. We were kicking down doors, rousting everybody in sight, crawling through the woods, and working around the clock. Helicopters churned overhead, and armies of SWAT officers combed the area like a military invasion.

I slept for three hours at a fellow agent's house, and was back at it before the sun rose the next morning. The suspect, Billie Austin Bryant, was put on the FBI's famous Ten Most Wanted list. He was captured later that day after he slipped into a randomly chosen apartment and slithered into the crawl space above the ceiling. The resident's pet dog wasn't happy about the situation, and kept looking up there and whining. Alarmed, his owner called the police. That was the end of Billie Austin Bryant. I was outside providing back-up when they found him out and brought him in.

Following that baptism of fire, things moved nearly as fast. FBI Director J. Edgar Hoover liked to expand the horizons of young agents by sending them to unlikely places. For the next two years, I played a Black Irish version of Sidney Poitier's Virgil Tibbs from *In the Heat of the Night*, only in Savannah and Augusta, Georgia, rather than Mississippi. From there, Hoover further expanded me by saying 'Go West, young man,' to Oklahoma City. I actually liked it there, and coincidently made my first art bust at the city's Will Rogers Airport. We received word that a New York hustler was coming through with a small Picasso charcoal drawing worth about $10,000 that he had pinched in Manhattan. He was planning to sell it at his next stop in Los Angeles. We nailed him at the airport and confiscated the sparse drawing without incident.

After a few years learning the ropes in Oklahoma, I was itching for more action. I ached to return home to New York and fight big bad mobsters. In 1972, my wish was granted. Ordered to pick a specialty in the bustling New York Field Office, I found myself drawn to the tiny art theft division headed by Special Agent Don Mason. The mostly autonomous niche group was one of the few at that time that was authorised to allow its agents to work undercover. Hoover had long frowned on such messy, legally blurred police work, and generally refused to allow it. I didn't share the boss' view. The prospect of getting up close and personal with the bad guys excited me.

Mason and I got along well. He decided to take me under his wing like Agent K of *Men in Black* and groom me to be his successor. Manhattan was and remains the art capital of the world, both legitimate and shady, so I was already in the heart of the fire.

The stolen masterpiece tracking dodge was so fascinating that I threw myself into the job, working all hours of the day, night, and weekends. I absorbed everything I could from Don, and bolstered that education by picking the brains of the curators, owners, appraisers, and restoration experts at New York's finest museums, galleries, and auction houses. Little by little, I transformed myself into an art expert.

Banking upon my hands-on education, broadened further by picking the more devious brains of the forgers, smugglers, and con men in the field, I created two main alter egos. They were both heavy-hitting shady art dealers willing to pay top dollar for stolen art, no questions asked.

That last part, however, was just a cliché. Flamboyant and eccentric, monsieurs Robert Steele and Thomas Bishop were prone to asking lots of questions, mostly while wearing a Nagra tape recording wire around my chest, a Walther nine-millimetre strapped inside my beltline, and a snub-nosed .38 on my ankle. I alternated between Steele and Bishop—same suave operator, different handle—to lessen the risk of exposure.

Occasionally, I was pulled into other criminal areas when manpower was short. I joined the team that hunted down the Mafia gang responsible for the $5.8 million Lufthansa robbery in 1978, the incident made famous by the movie *Goodfellas* and the book *Wise Guy*. Seven years later, I helped root out the billion-dollar Sicilian Mafia drug ring known as 'The Pizza Connection.' The following year, I became part of the squad that ended the deadly reign of the Colombo Family Mafia boss, and FBI's Top-Ten Most Wanted, Carmine 'The Snake' Persico.

In another case that was brought to life by the movies, I was drafted as a member of the surveillance team that closely monitored FBI undercover agent Donnie Brasco, the first law enforcement officer to successfully infiltrate one of New York's five entrenched Mafia families. Brasco's account of his penetration of the Bonanno clan became a best-seller, and was then made into a movie that starred Al Pacino and Johnny Depp.

When not farmed out to bust New York's endless supply of gangsters, I worked the occasional high-profile kidnapping, including the sensational Seagram's heir case in 1975. A pair of Brooklyn men nabbed the 21-year-old son of Seagram's liquor founder Samuel Bronfman and demanded a $2.3 million ransom. On that one, I ended up getting my picture splashed on the front pages of newspapers around the world while escorting one of the suspects to FBI headquarters. The guy suddenly ducked to avoid being photographed, leaving me to be captured in all my glory. Nice for my parents. Not so nice when your main job is working undercover busting art thieves.

Despite that fun and games, my true passion remained the recovery of stolen paintings, relics, artefacts, and heirlooms. Every time one of the side cases ended, exciting as it may have been, I went right back to scouring the world for missing art.

Fuelling my fascination is the all-encompassing aspect of the art field, a $100 billion annual business that is so enormous it's impossible to precisely quantify. Art is sold on virtually every street corner of the world. It's marketed in high-end galleries, and haggled over at flea markets. It goes for tens of millions at ritzy auctions, and for tens of cents at yard sales. Sometimes, in a delicious twist, the $10 million gallery piece turns out to be a worthless fake, while the ten cent yard sale find is a priceless original.

Art is by far the greatest unregulated legitimate industry in the world, one that even defies definition. It incorporates a vast array of creations from sculpture to welded iron to images burned on toast and sold on eBay. The same piece can be raved about by some and ridiculed by others.

For example, in 2005, three splashy, abstract tempera paintings by a 20th century artist named Congo were sold in London for $26,352. During that same auction at Bonhams, offerings from Andy Warhol and Pierre-Auguste Renoir received no interest. While it's not unusual for a hot, new unknown to suddenly outshine the classic *objets d'art* of their more esteemed colleagues, this sale came with a bit of a wrinkle. Congo was a chimpanzee.

A dead chimpanzee to be precise. And we all know what that means. It's universally accepted that an artist's material soars in value after his or her demise because it creates a finite market. Investors couldn't have Congo flooding the market with new masterpieces following the London sale. After all, he was noted for being a prolific craftsman who created more than 400 drawings and paintings during his brief 10-year life.

Oddly enough, the one thing that connects all art, that gives it some measure of cohesion, is its value to a crook. Whatever art is, whatever it looks like, whoever created it, man or beast, if it has a monetary value, a thief will try to steal it. And whenever that happened during the last quarter of the 20th century, it was my job to get it back.

. 1 .

The Curse of Rembrandt's Rabbi

Part One

*I*WAS FIVE years into my career as the protégé of New York-based FBI art theft pioneer Don Mason when an emergency SOS came in requesting that I catch the next plane upstate to Buffalo. The need was so dire that I had to pull rank and bump a paying passenger off an overbooked Eastern Airlines commercial flight. A paying passenger in first class no less, a necessity that was required because I needed the extra space for my specialised authentication equipment.

Police business and all that.

The rush was due to a report that an ongoing FBI sting known as Operation Tepee was about to snare its biggest catch—a small but stunning Rembrandt stolen in France that had been missing for six years.

I knew all about the Rembrandt, a vivid 10-by-11-inch portrait of a bearded, weathered old man with sad, piercing eyes known as *The Rabbi*. Finished around 1660, it was worth anywhere from

$250,000 to $1 million back then, making it one of the most valuable 'lost' paintings in the world at the time. (A decade earlier, another Rembrandt, *Portrait of Titus*, sold for $10 million.)

The notoriety of the theft itself made its price soar with each breathless newspaper headline—and that was before the extraordinary price explosion in the 1980s and '90s that rocketed the value of such masterpieces 20 to 100 times. A single painting from a Rembrandt-class artist today can be worth over $100 million.

Law enforcement agencies from Europe to the Middle East had been trying to track down the elusive *Rabbi* since the day it was snatched from the Lèon Bonnat Museum in Bayonne, France on 3 March 1971.

With no small amount of scepticism, I pulled the file. I didn't doubt that the foreign masterpiece could be close at hand. Despite the distance from France and transportation difficulties—stolen paintings aren't as easy to cart around as, say, diamonds—it wasn't unusual that such a work would end up for sale in New York. But that generally translates to Manhattan—the art theft capital of the world. Bitterly cold Buffalo was not exactly a major player in the international art trade.

Scouring the file, I found myself immersed in an ongoing story worthy of the most creative Hollywood screenwriter. *The Rabbi* had sure lived an interesting life, especially during the past six years. Among those on its trail were a crack team of reporters from *Reader's Digest* headed by Nathan M. Adams. The gaggle of journalists would later piece together the wild tale and fill in the blanks, producing a riveting book published in the late 1970s.

As is so often the case with art thefts, this was a crime of opportunity rather than precision planning. On 1 March 1971, a young French art student named Robert LeBec visited the Bonnat Museum as he often did to study the brushstrokes of the ancient masters. Europe abounds with out-of-the-way museums such as the Bonnat that, despite their relative international obscurity, can nonetheless house extraordinary collections of historic and valuable paintings. Although it doesn't have the renown of its big brother, the Louvre in Paris, the Bonnat was and remains home to nearly 1,000 works of art, including those by masters such as Rubens, Goya, and Delacroix.

In the early 1970s, these museums were reminiscent of the 'easy jug' banks American bandit John Dillinger robbed with impunity 40 years earlier. Security was lax or non-existent. Alarm systems, if present, were rudimentary and easily overcome. The atmosphere was friendly and hands-on. You could actually reach out and touch, or smudge, a priceless masterpiece.

That's exactly what touchy-feely LeBec was prone to doing. Of all the stunning pieces that adorned the walls of the Bonnat, LeBec, 25, was drawn to those produced by Dutch master Rembrandt Harmenszoon van Rijn. Like most visitors, his favourite was *The Rabbi*, known among connoisseurs for the old man's soul-mirroring eyes. After bouncing among various private collections and museums for 250 years, it was eventually donated to France and placed on display at the Bonnat in 1923.

Without thinking, LeBec reached out and touched its heavy frame. To his utter surprise, it moved. Instead of being bolted tightly to the wall as it normally was, the painting was hanging free on a nail like a velvet Elvis in a Tennessee trailer.

Instantly, a dark side he never knew existed overpowered LeBec's peaceful artistic countenance. His mind filled with visions of francs, millions of them. So many, in fact, that *The Rabbi* wouldn't be enough. He deftly sidestepped, first left and then right, and similarly tested the two other Rembrandts on display, *Christ on the Cross,* and a portrait known as *Burgomaster Six*. The pair hung on either side of *The Rabbi*, ironically enough, like the two thieves crucified with Christ.

Circumstances beyond LeBec's control or knowledge conspired to make the task easier than he might have imagined, even in those 'easy jug' times. The museum was in the process of photographing its collection, and workers weren't diligent about reattaching the paintings after they faced the cameras. At any given moment, more than 100 hung loose on a single screw or nail, waiting to be officially re-bolted when someone got around to it. Similarly lax, the museum only had two security guards, one of whom had been on sick leave for months. With all the rooms, nooks, and crannies, it was impossible for the remaining guard to watch the shop closely.

On 3 March, three days after discovering the flaw in the attachments, LeBec arrived at the museum wearing a laughable disguise that should have screamed his intentions to Stevie Wonder, much less to the ticket taker, curator, and lone security guard. He was draped in a large, loose, long beige raincoat right out of any low budget movie's 'wardrobe for spies and crooks' rack. LeBec additionally sported sunglasses, which covered the murky eye shadow he dabbed around his eyes. His face was further darkened by cheap tanning cream. Gloves covered both hands, even when he dug into his pocket for the two franc entrance fee. Getting the jump on Marlon Brandon's Oscar-winning performance in *The Godfather* a few years later, LeBec had stuffed cotton into his cheeks to lend a chipmunk quality to his normally narrow face.

France was full of colourfully dressed characters in those days, so the female ticket taker thought nothing of giving the strange youth his ticket and waving him inside. The security guard should have been more alert, that is, had he been there. Incredibly, he had called in sick that morning. By dumb luck, Robert LeBec's half-baked plan to steal three of the most valuable paintings in the world was destined to be carried out without any security whatsoever.

Unaware that he was already home free, LeBec scurried to the Rembrandts and got down to business. With gloved precision, he lifted them one by one from the wall, flipped them over, bent up the 'brads' that secured them to their decorative frames, freed them, then hid the empty frames under a wooden bench nearby.

The great Dutch artist had painted these three pieces on wooden panels instead of canvas or paper, so they couldn't be rolled up and stuffed into LeBec's back pocket. He had to slap the stiff boards together and push them up against his hip and hope nobody noticed a weird-looking character in a cheap disguise leaving an art museum with three bulky square objects protruding from under his raincoat.

Not only did nobody at the museum notice, neither did a police officer LeBec passed outside. In fact, when the dutiful security guard sucked it up and came in for a half day that afternoon, he failed to detect that a wall was barren in one noteworthy spot, and that the museum's prized Rembrandts were long gone. His boss, curator Paul Bazé, had not passed that way all day either. It wasn't until after the museum closed at 5 pm—seven hours later—that the theft was finally discovered.

By then, LeBec could have been in Moscow, London, Saudi Arabia, Fiji, or practically anywhere else. Instead, he was still a mere five miles away at his apartment in Biarritz, busy packing and preparing for the first stage of his less-than-speedy getaway.

LeBec's plan to distance himself from the scene was a smart move. Unbeknownst to him, his incredible streak of good fortune had become tainted the moment his hands touched *The Rabbi* and he left the museum. The frantic police already had him tapped as the prime suspect. Actually, he was the only suspect. LeBec had been the quiet museum's sole visitor that entire pretty spring day!

The first-time thief had apparently awakened The Curse of the Rabbi the moment he ripped the grumpy old man from his frame.

Fortunately for LeBec, his silly disguise had accomplished its goal. The ticket taker had not recognised the attractive young art student who had been in the museum so many times before. She thought he might have been some kind of weirdo foreigner.

The alarmed Bayonne detectives immediately suspected an inside job. A security guard calling in sick the morning of a huge, headline-grabbing theft? Even in bad heist movies that was too much of a cliché. Yet, that screaming clue did nothing but lead the cops down a cold trail. The hapless guard had indeed been sick, so much so that he'd visited a doctor that morning. A loyal employee, he had no connection to the theft.

The following day, a team of more artful detectives from Paris arrived to scour the scene and take up the hunt. They quickly saw it for what it was, an understaffed, underfinanced, grossly unsecured museum that was a sitting duck for such a theft. A wave of Bonnie and Clyde-like thieves had hit such places all across France— museums, galleries, castles, and private homes—and the harried Paris art theft squad was growing weary of trying to educate the curators and owners on the need for better security.

Meanwhile, LeBec's extraordinary luck continued to battle with The Curse of The Rabbi for the upper hand. Since the Rembrandts were the property of France, they weren't insured by a private company like Lloyd's of London. That meant the chase would be left to a disconnected group of poorly motivated cops with severe jurisdictional issues rather than a team of highly paid, highly skilled, highly motivated insurance investigators who would put their nose to the trail, throw money around, bribe, beat and torture, and stick to the case like glue from one end of the earth to the other until the Rembrandts were back on their rusty nails at the Bonnat. The insurance tracker's singular aim is to recover the paintings before their tight-fisted bosses have to fork over millions to cover the loss.

Instead, it was up to the Paris Police Nationale to notify the 'usual suspects.' These were: Interpol, the famed borderless police agency headquartered, ironically enough, in France; the European art dealer, gallery owner, curator fraternity; and more importantly, the snitches, wannabes, hangers on, and other ne'er-do-wells that infest the burgeoning art underworld.

Officially, Interpol had the ability to alert hundreds of police departments around the world, including the FBI. That's how the theft first became a blip on my radar.

'Ummm, a trio of Rembrandts,' I thought as I read the wire. 'Somebody hit the biggest trifecta of all time. Wonder how long it will take these babies to reach New York?'

At that point, all I could do was observe the news with a casual interest and start a 'just in case' file. It wasn't the FBI's duty to concern itself with internal French problems. That, of course, would change the instant the paintings crossed the US border, but there was no guarantee that would happen. The oil-rich Arabs were cultivating a taste for fine art, and, as with their American, European, and Asian competitors, they didn't care if the paintings were hot. It's amazing how ego, ambition, one-upmanship, and competitiveness are such universal traits.

Back in France, Robert LeBec was experiencing the same problems every small-time thief encounters when he stumbles upon the theft of a lifetime—how to reach the upper echelon of ask-no-questions buyers and convert the goods into cold hard cash. In the art world, which already views the uninitiated as blind troglodytes, that can be an extremely difficult bridge to cross.

LeBec's initial move was to venture right into the heart of the fire. Paintings in hand, he travelled 500 miles to Paris and stashed himself and the Rembrandts in the cheap apartment of a lady friend. Figuring he needed to lay low for a while, his cabin fever soon got the best of him. He decided to take the train to Amsterdam and visit an old pal who was making a name for himself in the city's exploding recreational drug business.

LeBec's childhood buddy, Jacques Faidit, also 25, had established a drug pipeline from Europe to Bolivia, Colombia, the United States, Canada, and interestingly enough, the Middle East. Despite his impressive reach, the longhaired, flower child Faidit still lived modestly in a ramshackle apartment building in one of Amsterdam's meaner neighbourhoods.

If the case wasn't already littered in ironies, Faidit's pad provided another. It was located around the corner from Rembrandt's famed studio—the same workroom where he had painted the three pieces of art in question. *The Rabbi*, whose bearded image was provided by a member of Amsterdam's 17th century Jewish community, had come home.

The two boyhood friends, now grown up into world-class criminals, wrapped their prizes in plastic sheets and tossed them in the attic for safekeeping. They later wised up and placed the art in a large safe deposit box at the Amro Bank in Amsterdam where Faidit frequently kept his drugs.

Changing into hot art dealer mode, Faidit put out feelers. While everybody was interested—mostly in trying to steal the art for themselves to finance their next high—Faidit discovered that the divide that separated the low class, junkie-infested drug world from the starched upper-crust noblemen who populated the art scene was as wide as the English Channel. He wasn't having any luck finding a buyer either.

One particular problem LeBec and Faidit encountered was that the paintings weren't signed. While this is of no consequence to the knowledgeable experts, it was a huge deal with the nouveau riche drug barons who lived in constant paranoid fear of being ripped off and/or exposed as phoney aristocrats. These scrubbed-up farmers and thugs wanted their art to have the creator's signature sprawled across it in letters as large as John Hancock's courageous scribble on the Declaration of Independence.

By July, according to the Interpol files and to the *Reader's Digest* investigators, LeBec was so desperate to turn the wood into gold that he agreed to one of the lamest schemes imaginable. His roommate in Paris turned him on to a German who claimed to have the contacts in Frankfurt needed to fence the art to the appropriate wealthy buyers. LeBec soon discovered that the German, Michael Jurgen Klötzke, travelled in the same low-rent circles that he and Faidit did. All they accomplished was to increase the number of cutthroats who knew about the paintings and would either try to steal them, or would rat LeBec out to the authorities to save their skin during their next arrest.

Panicking, LeBec agreed to Klötzke's backup plan—to sell the paintings, along with the story of the theft, to the high-octane German newspaper *Bild*. Klötzke claimed *Bild*'s fierce competitor,

Stern, had once paid for a similar story, so *Bild* would be sure to go for it.

They went for it, all right. They agreed to play ball with Klötzke, lured him in, then had the police pounce on him and snag two of the three paintings. LeBec, in a rare moment of clarity, had held back *The Rabbi* in case something went wrong.

Something had indeed gone wrong. Not only were *Christ on the Cross* and *Burgomaster Six* recovered without a fight, but the aptly named Klötzke instantly rolled on LeBec, leading the German police to where the Frenchman was staying. The cops swarmed in like they were invading Paris and caught him by surprise.

However, in the confusion over who was the thief and who was the dupe—both LeBec and Klötzke pointed the finger at each other—LeBec was briefly released. That gave him the window he needed to phone an artist friend of Faidit's in the Bussum suburb of Amsterdam and warn him to make *The Rabbi* vanish. LeBec had stashed the remaining masterpiece with the painter after he had withdrawn the three works from the Amro Bank vault.

Klötzke, singing like Pavarotti, ratted this friend called Vincent as well. Previously warned, Vincent deftly withstood the subsequent police interrogation. He claimed the package, which he had never opened, had been removed from his home days before by LeBec and 'some German guy'. Vincent even backed up his fellow countryman LeBec regarding his phoney cover, telling the cops that it was Klötzke who was Mr Big in the operation and that LeBec was just an innocent patsy.

The no-nonsense German and Dutch detectives weren't buying it. They went over LeBec's modest place with both a fine tooth comb and a rough edged sledgehammer, tearing up the floor and walls, all to no avail. So where was *The Rabbi*? Buried in the ground less than 300 feet away in a vacant lot. Vincent, no dummy, had sealed it in what he hoped was air and watertight packaging before doing so.

Despite the indignity of it all, it wouldn't be the last time *The Rabbi* went to a premature grave. If there indeed was a mysterious curse associated with the painting, such disrespectful treatment only made it grow more powerful.

Not surprisingly, Jacques Faidit was also feeling the heat in the form of rodents of a different breed. Weeks earlier, some of Faidit's drug contacts in Holland had engaged in a *Miami Vice*-style shootout over territorial rights. When the dust had cleared, two men were shot full of holes, but were still talking. The Dutch police started squeezing them for their contacts, and someone fingered the long-haired Frenchman. Within days, Amsterdam Vice's version of Sonny Crocket and Rico Tubbs were all over Faidit, busting into his grimy pad and turning it topsy-turvy searching for drugs. Anticipating such a move, Faidit had cleaned the place out. Figuring the jig in Amsterdam was up, he jetted to London to lay low and formulate a new plan.

That was why the more-astute Faidit hadn't been around to dissuade LeBec from swallowing Klötzke's disastrous scheme.

True to the curse, things got hairier from there. Vincent was strolling home one day and nearly suffered a cardiac arrest when he spotted a bulldozer chewing up the burial lot preparing it for development. He watched in horror as the angry machine chewed the ground closer and closer until fate and the art gods stepped in and saved the day. The driver, no doubt a union man, quit at the stroke of five and hopped off the beast within spitting distance of where the old man lay buried. Vincent scurried out after dark, shovel in hand, and saved *The Rabbi* from the machine's morning roar.

Following Faidit's instructions, he dusted it off and brought it to the flat of one of Faidit's drug couriers, a pretty young woman living in Amsterdam. There it sat in relative comfort while Faidit contemplated his next move. He dreamed up a laundering scheme so bizarre only an economics professor could appreciate it. Knowing he'd have to sell the hot painting short, 10 to 20 cents on the dollar, franc, mark, boliviano, krone, peso, or whatever, he could recoup his loss by buying drugs in South or Central America with the cash, then selling the dope for ten to twenty times what he paid for it in

Europe. That way, when all the globe-trotting dealing was done, he could end up with something close to face value for a million dollar Rembrandt!

Before he could put that complicated plan into place, Faidit received word at the end of the summer that the Amsterdam police were on to him and had searched his place again, this time for the Rembrandt.

Eager to make deals to ensure their own freedom, LeBec, or most likely Klötzke, had given him up as the holder of the final piece of the stolen Rembrandts puzzle. Feeling the world closing in all the way from London, Faidit decided to put a big salty ocean between him and the various European police agencies. Considering his options, he concluded that Vancouver was not only a bustling city with a healthy drug trade, it was British/French enough to make him feel right at home. Better yet, he had friends, associates, and contacts there and could hit the ground running.

Faidit made the leap in October, then summoned the pretty lady from Amsterdam shortly thereafter. She brought him a nice gift, a small wooden crate carefully packed with individually wrapped pieces of fragile Oriental statues, the kind of porcelain and china junk any Customs inspector dreads having to gingerly search through. Had one done so, he or she might have noticed that the bottom seemed a wee bit high for the outside depth of the box: just high enough to hide something 10-by-11-inches between the sheets of wood.

The Rabbi had been freed from his shallow grave—only to be hidden away in what appeared to be a homemade infant's casket. It was an appropriate description, because the old man was about to go underground again.

Faidit was bedding down on a small farm he had leased in Mission, British Columbia, a lumber mill town about an hour's drive east of Vancouver. There, he promptly buried the old man a second time, sealing it in yet another 'airtight' container and planting it in the frozen Canadian soil like a kernel of corn.

The Rabbi was now so close to my coast-to-coast American jurisdiction, I could almost smell the varnish. Sensing that it would eventually come my way, I was all but chomping at the bit to get into the game and take down these nitwits.

Unfortunately, it wasn't close enough. Although the United States and Canada are bosom buddies with generous extradition treaties, Vancouver was not quite in my gun sights.

As the months turned into years, the lure of the great capitalist giant to the south proved to be a tempting apple for the nimble but ever-cautious Faidit. Periodically, the French consulate in a big city like Los Angeles would field a call from a mysterious voice offering to ransom the national treasure back to the homeland. Thankfully, the French have a zero-tolerance, zero-cooperation policy when it comes to their paintings. They refuse to negotiate with art kidnappers. The calls were referred to the FBI.

Bingo. Thomas McShane, aka Thomas Bishop, aka Robert Steele, was now officially on the team. More accurately, the FBI was on the team. The initial leads were centred around the Los Angeles area. A stoner surfer dude type from Seal Beach had met Faidit in Canada and was making noise around town about being able to 'hook you up with a million dollar Rembrandt, man.' A team of California special agents interrogated the yo yo, who changed his story with every new wave that crashed the shore outside. Although the dude eventually was persuaded to cut the crap and give up the true story, his inability to translate French Canadian into Beach Boy lingo led the agency down a snarl of dead ends. Jacques Faidit became Jock Saddit, a name that didn't appear on any police agency's wanted list.

Surfer boy did have a blurry snapshot of 'Jock', but that didn't help either. The FBI's decision to let the local agents handle the investigation and not authorise the expense of flying me out to Los Angeles proved costly in the long run. The LA troops were not art experts, and didn't know that world.

Had I been involved, I'd have forwarded the photo, along with the variations of the California translated name Jock Saddit to

Interpol instead of the French and Canadian police. There, our astute European counterparts most assuredly would have connected the dots to determine that a Frenchman named Jock Saddit believed to be in possession of a Rembrandt in a British part of Canada was the one and the same Jacques Faidit thought to have absconded with the painting from France and England.

Patience, I told myself, betting that the mountain would eventually come to Mohammad. Until then, I couldn't step on anybody's toes. Despite our tiny New York art division's decades of success, including the recovery of millions of dollars of stolen paintings, we were still regarded as weirdo *X-Files'* Fox Mulder types by the rest of the fraternity.

Errors aside, the LA crew had uncovered a critical piece of information that they included in their report. Surfer boy said that Jock's latest scheme was something torn from the pages of the Frenchman's pirate hero Captain Pierre Le Picard. To make sure he wasn't tripped up as LeBec had been in Germany, Faidit wasn't going to sell the painting itself. He was going to sell the location of the painting. A 'treasure map' so to speak, complete with a big X over *The Rabbi*'s latest grave.

Shrewd. Only trouble was, guys like Jacques Faidit tend to hang around with a sleazy set of folks who would rip off their own mothers for their next fix, or kidnap their fathers for that proverbial big score. It's not the kind of environment where one can easily sit on a million-dollar treasure map.

Hanging out in the *Star Wars* cantina-like Gastown district of Vancouver, Faidit came into contact with a deadly Yankee gangster named Johnny 'Rio' Gandolfo, a hot-headed Italian with New York Mafia ties. Rio was on the run in Canada for various and sundry criminal offences, including weapons charges, bribery, transportation of stolen cars, and cracking safes. The dark, temperamental Johnny Rio wanted a piece of Faidit's lucrative drug business, and Faidit was having none of it. The Frenchman feared that the central casting

American gangster would not be content taking a secondary role in his operation.

Push came to shove when Johnny Rio began shadowing Faidit's dealers and ripping off their soft yuppie clients. To retaliate, and to show the city who was boss, Faidit and two armed associates staged a hit on Rio's house. It didn't go well. Faidit and Rio traded shots while their associates beat each other up. Faidit, no whiz with a weapon, sprayed Rio with a shotgun blast from far enough away to sting but not kill; a factor Faidit overlooked. He fled without finishing off his dangerous enemy—always a disastrous business decision.

Johnny Rio holed up, healed, and bided his time. The passing months cooled his vengeful rage and enabled him to formulate a more profitable way to exact his revenge. He waited patiently for six months until Faidit left the country on one of his drug buys. While the French cat was away, Rio was going to play. He paid a friendly visit to the farm where he knew one of Faidit's countrymen was crashing with his girlfriend. Rio gambled that the passive Frenchman knew nothing about the shootout and bad blood, and would welcome him as a friend. That's exactly what happened.

Once inside the enemy camp, Rio merely had to smoke some hash with his newfound friends to get them to talk. The stoned pair not only confirmed the existence of the valuable painting, they giddily told Rio that it was buried outside!

72 hours later, Johnny Rio came back for another visit. This time he wasn't so friendly. Accompanied by two armed thugs, the trio tied up Faidit's friends, tore apart the house just for kicks, then began beating the male prisoner demanding the exact location of the painting. The Frenchman held firm, claiming not to know. His memory cleared when Rio chivalrously threatened to blow the long, pretty legs off of the guy's girlfriend one .357 Magnum slug at a time.

Rio quickly dug up the old man, tossed him into the back of Faidit's car, and vanished into the night.

Like the cursed hot potato it was, *The Rabbi* had now completely left the circle of its original thieves. None of those who possessed it from France to Germany to England to Canada had made so much as a dime. On the contrary, it had brought them all nothing but major grief.

Johnny Rio didn't care. Figuring he'd hit the jackpot, he was all rebel yells and high fives as he headed to Beverly Hills. Rio was counting on a future full of movie stars and cement ponds in the famous Hollywood area enclave. The whispered Curse of the Rabbi was nothing but an old wife's tale, he insisted, and he was having none of it. The previous owners were unsophisticated Eurotrash idiots and wimps, and that's why they had botched things so badly. A street smart, American tough guy like him would have no trouble turning the old man into thick stacks of green.

Or so he thought. Truth was, Johnny Rio was yet another in a long line of low-life thugs who had no clue how to fence something so high class and historically valuable. Similarly, he had zero chance of getting close to anyone who bathed on a regular basis, much less to infiltrate the ritzy art scene. His method of cashing in, going from bar to bar, fellow low-life to fellow low-life, and spreading the news in the criminal grunge circles that he had a now-inflated '$5 million' Rembrandt, was no different than the others. Nor was it any more successful.

Years passed. Desperate, Rio systematically dropped the asking price from $5 million all the way down to $25,000, and still he couldn't unload it. His only accomplishment was expanding the ever-widening circle of people who knew he had it. Eventually, a female petty thief acquaintance traded the information to escape a bust. She didn't know where he was, but she did know something nearly as valuable—his real name. My counterparts in Los Angeles were able to ID Johnny Rio as John Joseph Gandolfo, and placed that into the fattening file.

Johnny Rio Gandolfo added his own bizarre irony to the long trail. He had a brother who lived on Third Avenue and 61st Street in

Manhattan. That was spitting distance from Flannigan's, a famous pub on First Avenue near 66th Street that was the main FBI special agent after-hours 'cop bar'. (It's now called O'Flannigan's.) New York's FBI headquarters back then was nearby on Third and 69th Street. (It moved to its current location at 26 Federal Plaza in 1980.) I half-expected Rio and his brother to waltz into the place one night and unsuspectingly try to sell the Rembrandt to a table full of J. Edgar Hoover's finest.

No such luck. The information trickling in pointed to Rio remaining in sunny California and other warmer climates. In 1974, an FBI informant tried to set up a buy in Los Angeles, but Rio spooked and didn't appear. Instead, he beat it to New Orleans, where he was arrested for possessing a .357 like the one used to threaten a French girl with amputation. Confusion over his latest alias enabled him to gain release on a cheap bail and vanish into the wind yet again.

In 1975, the hunt for Symbionese Liberation Army terrorist William Harris and his prized kidnapee-turned-accomplice, Patty Hearst, bizarrely led to *The Rabbi*. The suspects from a phoned-in tip turned out to be an exceedingly less-glamorous movie studio security guard and his exceedingly less-rich girlfriend. Shaken by the army of police who swarmed them, the guard suddenly spat out that his brother back in the famed hippy paradise of Woodstock, New York had been offered a Rembrandt by a gangster named Johnny Rio. An attempt to re-establish the connection failed when Rio spooked again.

The latest sighting galvanised my attention. As I suspected, Rio was back in New York. He was getting close. I alerted my bosses and they authorised me to start working my contacts in all facets of the art world to see if we could flush him out.

Meanwhile, FBI founder J. Edgar Hoover's death on 2 May 1972 enabled the bureau to evolve beyond its outdated crime-fighting techniques. The legendary boss disliked undercover agents and operations, preferring that his legion of investigators remain above board in their bland 'Men in Black' suits. With Hoover out of the picture, the FBI was able to catch up with local police departments and attempt more innovative activities. The loosening of the symbolic chains was a boon to my art theft operation because it enabled me to create my various undercover identities as unscrupulous art dealers, and smoke scores of hot paintings, relics, and artefacts out of the shadows.

It also enabled the FBI to set up successful storefront fencing operations. One of the earliest and most profitable was Operation Tepee, a bustling pawnshop known as the House of Tasha that specialised in antiques. It was established by the Bureau's Buffalo Field Office in the summer of 1976, and targeted organised-crime families, crooked politicians, and run-of-the-mill thieves in Buffalo, Rochester, and Syracuse.

A crafty, fast-talking local cat burglar and safecracker named Charles 'Chuckie' Carlo was the front man, and he was doing a bang-up job. Within months, Chuckie had purchased hundreds of thousands of dollars worth of high-end merchandise while the FBI's microphones and cameras recorded it all. (Carlo had previously owned a store that sold Native American artefacts, thus giving Operation Tepee its name.)

A frequent customer was a mob associate named Gennarino 'Jerry' Fasolino, a heavyset man in his sixties. Chuck had known Jerry for years. Hanging at his house one cold winter day in January 1977, Fasolino dropped a bomb. He knew where he could get his hands on 'a five-million-dollar Rembrandt'. He wanted to know if Chuck was interested.

Chuck most certainly was. He quickly agreed to the asking price of $200,000, of which half was to be Fasolino's broker's fee.

'I'll be in touch,' Fasolino said.

Chuckie wasted no time relaying the information to his FBI controllers. They advised him to make it a top priority.

The mountain, and the curse, had indeed come to Mohammad.

. 2 .

The Curse of Rembrandt's Rabbi

Part Two
Shuffling off to Buffalo

*I*T TOOK AN additional three frustrating months to set up the buy. Johnny Rio Gandolfo, as cautious as ever, wasn't easy to pin down. He had lived with the Old Man for more than four years, his dreams of wealth shattered one busted deal at a time, his personal fortunes plunging with each passing month. Now in his forties, he had been ravaged by a curse he vowed never to acknowledge. Yet, like Gollum's obsessive quest for 'my precious' in *The Lord of the Rings*, he refused to let go of that which was destroying him.

The Rabbi himself wasn't faring much better. He'd been at the mercy of a string of bungling, ham-handed kidnappers for six years. He'd travelled around France, then returned to his place of birth in Holland, only to be shamelessly buried alive, proving rather emphatically that Thomas Wolfe was right when he said, 'You can't go home again.'

Nearly freed in Germany, *The Rabbi* instead remained in various forms of bondage. He crossed the Atlantic in a false bottom, was buried alive a second time in Canada, then was unearthed not by white-hatted rescuers, but by violent Yankee thugs. Back on the run, he was carted across another border to America and began criss-crossing a world power that didn't even exist for the first hundred years of his life.

And now, if a gangster and a reformed cat burglar were to be believed, he was coming to Buffalo, New York, in the springtime. Why Buffalo? Seems that somewhere in his travels, Johnny Rio hooked up with a Buffalo girl, Toni Sartori. Eagerly hopping aboard *The Rabbi* dream train, she convinced him that her dad back in Buffalo, John Sartori, knew some mobster types who could hook them up with a buyer. It was the same old roundabout friend-of-a-friend-who-has-connections story, but Rio was at his wits end and ventured to the cold north to give it a shot with his lady.

Chuckie Carlo, the thin, pale, 32-year-old ex-cat burglar turned FBI sting front man, was summoned to Jerry Fasolino's home on 3 April 1977. There, he was introduced to one Johnny Rio, aka John Joseph Gandolfo, and his pretty Italian girlfriend, Toni Sartori, a home girl from the 'hood. Rio, packing heat in his waistband, grilled Chuckie about his criminal pedigree and underworld connections for half an hour. Duly impressed, he agreed to cough up the Rembrandt. The buy was set for 11 April.

The FBI's Buffalo team knew they were in over their heads and finally reached out to me. I had gone undercover more than a hundred times by then, dating back, coincidently, to the day when the Rembrandt was originally stolen a continent away. In yet another irony, I had spent the past five years being tutored by my own 'Rabbi', legendary FBI art sleuth Don Mason. 'Rabbi' is a slang term young police officers, detectives, and special agents use to describe their grizzled veteran partner who teaches them the ropes. The previous years had been particularly busy as I'd already recovered more than $5 million in stolen art and artefacts. Aside from posing as my main alter egos, shady art experts Robert Steele and Thomas Bishop, I'd donned the guise of a taxi driver, a gallery owner, a lawyer, a chauffeur, a bodyguard, an art appraiser, a wealthy collector, and a dozen other aliases.

Suffice it to say, while there's always a measure of fear involved in such dangerous situations, I was long over the flop sweat jitters that normally grip a person in such life-or-death situations.

Around the same time I was bouncing the hapless businessman out of first class in order to catch the flight to Buffalo, Johnny Rio and Ms Sartori showed up at Fasolino's and promptly dropped off the long-sought after, cloth-wrapped painting. It was scheduled to be inspected later that afternoon by Chuck's expert—me. Apparently, Rio felt he was in good hands on his girlfriend's home court, especially with the menacing Fasolino and his alleged Magnalina Family Mafia pals covering his back. Rio believed they could be trusted with his 'precious'.

To keep Rio on the hook, Carlo was given $10,000 in taxpayers' money to offer him as collateral. Rio snapped it up with great relish. Finally, as he'd been insisting from Vancouver to New Orleans, he'd made some money on the painting. The deal was done totally 'in the dark' police-wise because Carlo was too afraid of Rio's big gun to agree to be wired during the exchange.

It was definitely a high-wire act from all angles. Rio could have taken the money and run, never to be seen again. In turn, Carlo could have taken the Rembrandt and run, with or without Rio and Fasolino's knowledge. That would have left the FBI with an ostrich-sized egg on its face. Had it been a decade later, when the price of Rembrandts soared to more than $10 million and counting, one of those probabilities might very well have occurred. Heck, you'd even have to toss in the possibility of one or more of the FBI's agents deciding 'to hell with it,' grabbing *The Rabbi*, and taking off for Tahiti. I can assure you that although few special agents will ever openly admit it, we have all had those thoughts—me included. Many, many times. And we could get it to the right buyers.

Alas, everybody was playing this one straight—as straight as a bunch of criminals and underpaid Feds can.

Before leaving Fasolino's house, Rio let down his crusty guard and expressed a sentimental attachment to the brush-stroked companion that had shared so much of his recent life. 'It's in the same shape as when I got it five years ago,' he said barely above a whisper. 'It's been cared for.'

For a moment, the three hardened career criminals stared at the painting, each one deeply taken by the simple but moving image the great artist had created.

'You can see why it's so valuable,' Rio said. 'The man had a magical talent.'

Chuckie, snapping out of his fog, marvelled at how light it was, apparently unable to comprehend how something so weightless could be in turn worth so many pounds of gold.

As if to regain their critical macho facades, the trio quickly shook off their 17th century trance and got back to business. Chuckie told Rio that the 'expert' would need about three hours to study the painting and verify its authenticity. He promised to call Fasolino the moment the expert gave the go-ahead to make the purchase.

Special Agent Gregg McCrary picked me up at Buffalo airport and immediately began updating me on Operation Tepee. He spoke in the hyper, warp-speed manner of a man who was overworked, overtired, pumped on caffeine, and filled to the brim with a year's worth of exciting information. Trouble was, even if I could download such an ocean of names, places, and details, virtually none of it had anything to do with the task at hand. Yes, Operation Tepee was a historically successful sting. Yes, they were taking in furs, coins, jewels, gold ingots, ritzy silverware, and high-end electronics. Yes, they had mobsters, politicians, and major thieves on film ready to feed to a prosecutor. Yes, it was the case of a lifetime, the thing of books and movies. All fine and dandy, but how was this going to help me retrieve the Rembrandt? When I kept trying to steer the case to that, McCrary looked at me like I was crazy and told me about a bronze statute that had come in last week from a guy name Mario who was the cousin of a guy named Tony who was hooked up with the sister-in-law of a Gambino Family soldier who had once dated John Gotti's daughter.

At the FBI's stakeout office around the corner from the House of Tasha, the situation was the same. Special Agent Jack Poerstel, Chuckie's handler, was even more exhausted, wired, and overflowing with information than McCrary. I wasn't able to get much of anything useful out of him either.

I understood their conditions perfectly and wasn't blaming the agents at all. Undercover stings can be all-consuming, and one can quickly go in so deep you lose all sense of the outside world. There's so much information to mentally assimilate, it's natural to assume that everybody knows everything you've been through during the past hectic and highly stressful year. In reality, nobody could ever have the slightest inkling.

The funny thing is that because I was struggling to immediately tune into their special wavelength, the Buffalo gang thought I was thick. On top of that, most of the special agents Bureau-wide were suspicious of our art theft division to begin with, and felt we were a bunch of weirdoes and eccentrics, so that played into their perception of me as well. Complicating matters was the fact that I was in my Robert Steele clothes, meaning colourful and flashy, and sported long hair, a thick moustache, and sideburns. For the staid, clean-cut FBI, I must have looked like one of the Manson Family.

In typical boys' club, locker room style, the Buffalo crew took to privately, and then openly, referring to me as 'Inspector Clouseau,' the wacky French detective played by Peter Sellers in the *Pink Panther* movies.

Though humorous and stress-relieving, the tangential briefings and silly labelling came at the expense of telling me some critical details, like the fact that the House of Tasha was hooked up to a live feed. And even though they showed me a previous tape, they never identified who was who. They didn't even tell me which guy was my contact, Chuckie, and if he could be completely trusted. Nor did they tell me what had happened earlier, that Johnny Rio had given the painting to Chuckie, and that Fasolino was the muscle.

When I asked who was who on the tapes, they looked at me like I was Forrest Gump. After playing 'Who's on First?' and 'Who's got the painting?' for a few maddening rounds, I just gave up and decided to wing it.

At that point, I saw a man on the screen walk into the House of Tasha carrying a square object. I assumed it was another tape, but it was actually the live feed. After another session of 'Who's on First?' I was given a vague explanation that Johnny Rio had already given the painting to Chuckie. Why? Who knew?

On one of the screens, I noticed the man holding a painting over his head in front of a camera hidden in the ventilation grill. Poerstel and McCrary asked me if it was legit. Completely flabbergasted, I nearly went off on them.

'I can't make that decision from a television image! I need to see it in person, up close!'

After emotions subsided, they explained that the close-up was just for evidence, and that I'd be going over to the House of Tasha shortly. Before leaving, they gave me $13,000 in cash and told me not to lose it on the way over. Nice of them to add that. The money itself was disconcerting because I was told the buy would be for $25,000, and had prepared my presentation based on that figure. Even at that price it was going to be a chore, a potentially dangerous chore, because they were expecting $200,000—an amount the tight-fisted FBI would never put up. The agents impatiently explained that Johnny Rio had already been given $10,000, which for the life of me, I couldn't understand why. I'd never known the Bureau to part with money so easily.

Finally, they led me down the stairs carrying all my equipment, and wished me luck. Trouble was, they didn't give me a clue as to where I was going. McCrary shot back that he had, but it had been just a general description of Chuckie's antique shop with no specific address. Exasperated, McCrary gave me the directions in a slow, precise manner that appeared terribly condescending. I later learned that he thought by my perplexed behaviour that I might have been deaf and was a lip reader. Total insanity—and not the way one wants to venture into a potentially deadly undercover sit-down with an armed and dangerous criminal.

Fortunately, the agents called ahead and advised Chuckie to be on the look out for 'Inspector Clouseau'—an absentminded professor type. The agents also expressed misgivings to their informer as to whether I could be trusted to meet with Rio. The heads-up, minus the disrespect, was critical because the directions, a right, two blocks, then another right, led me to a general vicinity, but not to 'Chuckie's Antique Store'.

Finding the appropriate street, I was dismayed to discover it was in an 'antique' district, meaning there were many such stores in a row. Oh boy, was this turning into a disaster. Further, they never told me Chuckie's joint was called the 'House of Tasha'. Since his place was closed, with the shades drawn, I passed it by and headed for another one. Chuckie spotted me, came out, and waved me over.

Precision undercover police work at its best!

Chuckie was actually pleased with my appearance and scattered, absentminded manner. To him, I was the perfect art geek, one who didn't reek of the FBI.

Following our initial small talk. Chuckie brought me over to a chair. There it was, the elusive *Rabbi*. Although I had seen many pictures and had studied Rembrandts up close at the Met, Frick, and other famous New York City art museums, there's nothing like seeing such a historic painting live for the first time. There was something about it that instantly told me it was genuine. Of course, I couldn't rely on instinct. Some forgers are nearly as talented as the original artist, and their works can date back hundreds of years as well. It was time for me to get to work.

The biggest problem with authenticating such paintings is the wealth of bad or sloppy information recorded about them. I instantly hit the first snag when I noticed it was painted on wood, not canvas. That wasn't in the Interpol file, nor any of the research books. However, knowing how imprecise such reports can be, I powered on. A major hit was the marking on the panel, a 'B' and a '40'which were indeed the correct inventory marking of the Bonnat Gallery in France. I took out a tape measure and gently spread it across. Red flag number two. The panel measured 101/2-by-11, a half-inch larger than the records stated. A small difference, but critical when exposing a fake. Was this a masterful copy, or another example of sloppy recordkeeping? I felt myself starting to sweat. This wasn't going to be easy.

At that point, I was leaning toward dubbing it a dupe and wanted to record it as such. As with originals, great fakes need to be detailed and filed as well. For example, in August 2000, officials at San Francisco's de Young Museum went through an emotional rollercoaster when another cursed *Rabbi* stolen from them 22 years before was first recovered, then branded a fraud. The battered 'Rembrandt,' taken on Christmas Eve, 1978, was treated roughly and returned looking like a once-pampered housecat who had lived in a back alley for a few years. The Netherlands-based Rembrandt Committee said not to fret because, although the age and paint were right, they concluded that *Portrait of a Rabbi* was actually the work of one of Rembrandt's students.

Even more deflating; not only wasn't it a Rembrandt, its ceremonious demotion meant it had to be officially renamed. *Portrait of a Rabbi* thus became *Portrait of a Man With Red Cap and Gold Chain.* That sounded more like a pimp jive walking around the Tenderloin district than a once-great work of art.

Mindful of similar reclassifications over the centuries, I pulled out a 35 mm camera and asked Chuckie where I could photograph the panel without being noticed. I didn't want the flashes to bleed through the shades in case Rio or any of his scouts were lurking nearby. Of course, I still had no idea how many pairs of eyes were actually on my every move, i.e., that the Buffalo agents were watching me live on their monitors.

Chuckie suggested that I retreat to the bathroom. Within minutes, the Old Man was propped on the toilet seat. The indignity was never-ending.

Thankfully, the stolen Rembrandt wasn't a nude of a beautiful woman or the suspicious agents would have been beside themselves, wondering what the hell I was doing with it alone in the bathroom. Either way, I quickly flashed a roll and brought it back out front to continue my inspection.

Getting down to the basics, I took out a lighted magnifying glass and a long, portable ultraviolet fluorescent light equipped with a handle and cord. Firing them up, I waved the purple light over the painting, revealing an intricate pattern of blue tinted spider-web cracks covering the surface. There were also reams of microscopic blisters. I suspected that much of the damage had occurred during *The Rabbi*'s recent travels. Blisters form when a painting is exposed to water, either purposefully or through high humidity and bad storage. In this case, the blue blisters were so fresh I was certain that the knucklehead Rio had attempted to wash the painting with soap and water to freshen up the colour shortly before presenting it for sale.

Chuckie began speaking as if he had a giant invisible rabbit as his best friend. Naturally, I found this extremely disconcerting. He was actually offering updates to the agents watching and listening in, but no one had informed me that I was giving a live performance, and that the House of Tasha was wired to such an elaborate degree. I remained under the impression that buys were recorded on an audio tape machine, and the reels were collected at the end of each day. Since I was one of the good guys, there was no need to have a camera rolling then. Lucky for me, I didn't start ripping my fellow agents for their imperfect briefing, or give them 'colourful' nicknames.

Aside from leaving out the detail of the live feed, I had not been updated on the extent of my backup. There was a monitoring radio and film room three doors away, which was now populated by Poerstel, McCrary, and a young electronics whiz named Tim

Almon. Outside, there were 11 more agents surrounding the area in various cars.

It would have been nice to know all that. Instead, this unknown army of backups were itching for some kind of action, and unbeknownst to me, they were growing frustrated and weary of my 'clownish' painstaking activities.

The phone rang. It was Poerstel asking for 'Inspector Clouseau'. He wanted to know my decision. I explained that it was going back and forth, and I still needed to do some work. Poerstel alerted the teams that the decision would be forthcoming.

Pulling out a lighted magnifying glass, I checked the brushstrokes. I was looking for the long, confident marks of a master artist, something often referred to as 'the sweep of freedom'. A forger trying to copy this unrestrained manner could not possibly follow the exact lines as the original. In contrast, a fake reeks of short strokes and a sense of hesitation, telegraphing an almost painful effort to reproduce instead of create. There's a tightness and restraint in duplications that can almost be sensed as much as observed.

In this critical area, the painting passed. There was a definite creative flow to it that spoke of an unchained hand.

After that, I really put on a show for the stakeout boys. Needing total darkness, I shrouded myself and *The Rabbi* under a large black cloth. Poerstel, McCrary, and the gang thought I'd gone totally nuts, but the darkness was essential to block out all external light and go with nothing but my purple wand. I needed to visually penetrate the protective varnish over the portrait so I could study the ancient paint underneath.

The pitch-black darkness made the blue reflection give off a more greenish hue now. I had to angle the light and my eyes in a manner that cut through the reflections to reveal a submerged level. I was looking for shiny pigments, indicating the lead whites, often mixed with chalk, and lead tin yellows, azurite, and smalt that were infused in paint during Rembrandt's era. With my head turned sideways, I could see the minerals dancing on the surface like the sun sparkling off the ocean. There was also a section around the *Rabbi*'s face that was totally black. This meant the painting had undergone restoration work with a more modern paint that replaced the ancient lead whites with zinc or titanium.

Next, I studied the panel itself for the elaborate processing masters like Rembrandt did before getting started. Rembrandt was a student of the Venetian technique of sealing his medium with animal glue for preservation, then using brown ground backgrounds to start. That forced him to work from dark to light as he created instead of the usual other way around. The glue seals and brown background were present.

Another indication of an authentic Rembrandt is the elaborate under-painting. Instead of working from sketches, Rembrandt was known to build a scene from back to front, starting with a basic monochrome tonal design, then adding colour and texture as he went along. Similarly, he dressed his subjects in a natural order, meaning he would paint a shirt in its entirety before covering it with a coat.

Inspecting more closely, I spotted some curious tears around the edges. I suspected that they resulted from original thief Robert LeBec's haste in removing the panel from its museum frame. A series of tacky glue dots on the back had me puzzled until I surmised that one of the thieves, LeBec, Faidit, Faidit's female friend, Rio, Rio's girlfriend, or whomever had probably adhered it to something to sneak it over a border. Very uncool treatment.

After 30 minutes under the shroud, I began sweating profusely and became fearful that my salty body fluid might damage the painting further. I emerged from the 'nun's outfit' and wearily mopped by brow.

Chuckie wasn't looking very well himself. His year undercover selling out all his criminal associates had produced a stressful stomach that was eating him alive. He was smoking and clutching his painful belly. His complexion was as white as some of Rembrandt's hues.

'It'll only be another 10 minutes and I'll have my decision,' I announced, much to the joy of all those openly and secretly observing.

At this juncture, I was convinced that the age of the painting was a match. The only question that remained was whether it was done by Rembrandt's hand, one of his students, or an independent artist who had copied it within a half century or so of its creation in Holland. Even if any of the above were the case, it could still be the painting stolen from the museum. Great fakes have proudly hung in many a snobby gallery, some by design, to protect the originals. Regardless, if this were an ancient reproduction, I wanted it on record that it was not the original, and that the real *Rabbi* was somewhere out there. With so much imprecise information floating around, I aimed to make things easier for the next 'Inspector Clouseau' who was in my loafers. Or possibly, myself 10 years down the road if the painting was pinched again.

The final inspection involved memory work based upon my study of other Rembrandts as to brushstrokes, the thickness of the paint, and the size of the three-dimensional crests. Rembrandt is known for a robust impasto style, meaning thick creamy coats that reveal individual brush marks. Additionally, Rembrandt often substituted flat knives for brushes, delicately spreading and swirling the paint like he was icing a cake or putting peanut butter on a slice of bread. The resulting rough surfaces and raised peaks, while worn down over time, could still be seen with the proper equipment. All were present in a perfect match on this painting.

The closing determination went back to pure instinct. Was this, from my intensive study, the colour, personality, aura, and style of the great master whose brilliance, among other traits, was the vivid capturing of expression and emotion in his portraits, and how he recreated light and shadow in his landscapes and historical scenes? Did *Le Rabbin* radiate Rembrandt's unique artistic spirit?

I could only respond with a resounding yes.

'I think we've lost the inspector,' I heard Chuckie say to the invisible rabbit.

'He's back in the 1600s.'

Something about his words cleared the fog from my brain. He didn't sound like he was talking to ghosts and goblins. I asked for an explanation. Chuckie responded that we were broadcasting live, nodding toward the cameras and hidden microphones.

'I thought you knew?' he shrugged.

'News to me. I thought you were talking to the spirits,' I said.

Just then, the impatient spirits called again. They wanted a verdict. 'It's an ancient work,' I sighed, drawing out the drama and baiting the bulls.

'The craquelure, impasto, cresting, chemistry and chiaroscuro appear authentic.' I knew the technical terms would throw the weary, strung-out agents over the edge. Poerstel swallowed the bait and nearly crawled through the phone.

'Is it a Rembrandt?' he demanded.

'I'm 95% sure,' I hedged, knowing the dinosaur-sized crap that would hit the fan if I was wrong. 'I'll authorise the buy.'

That's essentially all they wanted to hear. They could now swing into action, and had a fall guy to blame if something went wrong. The news quickly spread among the troops that 'Clouseau' had verified the target.

Poerstel asked to speak to Chuckie. He wanted to know if the burglar felt he could work with me on the actual buy. Chuckie, who was in my corner all the way, firmly stated that it was probably the only way the deal could go down. That was good enough for the troops. Poerstel alerted Buffalo case supervisor and organised crime chief Don Hartnett that it was a go, and inquired as to whether Hartnett wanted to be in on the action. Not surprisingly, the well-respected Hartnett left, confident that his men could handle the situation. He said he would be available at home if they needed him for anything, and was prepared to carry the ball the following morning when everybody else burned out. Poerstel found that unusual because he,

McCrary, and the younger agents had transformed into adrenaline junkies over the course of the entire Operation Tepee sting, and wouldn't have missed the biggest buy ever for love or money. They couldn't believe that Hartnett had the discipline to sit it out.

Then again, the paranoia of J. Edgar Hoover's ghost still hung heavy over the Bureau. Poerstel and his gang knew that they were out on a limb. If anything went wrong, say a fistfight over the money offered resulted in an errant punch being thrown clear through the Old Man's zinc-infused mug, the onus would be on the field agents. They, of course, would immediately shake it off on me.

This kind of internal FBI fraternity politics no doubt ticked off Chuckie. Not that he wanted to get hung with the blame, but he did want to be included in the circle. Although he was the face and front-line soldier of the operation—and the person most likely to take a bullet between the eyes—he wasn't fully accepted into the close-knit Fed family.

I noticed that my new best friend Chuckie was now chain smoking like a Hoover—the vacuum cleaner, not the FBI boss— and was clawing at his gurgling tummy worse than ever. The once cool cat burglar had been on the front lines for more than a year, and the constant do-or-die tension was eroding his nerves. His latest stress out was due to his understanding that my verification meant the game would go on, and he'd soon have to sell the deal to the twin trigger fingers, Johnny Rio and Fat Boy Fasolino.

After all the technical tricks, we still had the little matter of the painting's value to discuss. Rio was convinced that it was now worth at least a million, that the notoriety of the painting itself had upped its value tenfold. In warped criminal logic, he felt partly responsible for that inflation and wanted the payoff.

There was a method to his madness. It would not have surprised me in the least if at the next auction after the recovery, *The Rabbi* went for such a price. However, it was my job to lowball these Neanderthals, not reward them for their crime. To do so, I'd stick to the quarter-million-dollar figure most often bandied about before its theft. Subtract fifty or so thousand for the poor current condition and need for restoration, and figure in the standard ten cents on the buck fencing discount, and that amounted to $20,000 to $25,000—which just happened to be the price the pencil pushers in DC had authorised.

Chuckie, the resident expert on fencing discounts, agreed with the computation and relayed to the listening ghosts that the offer was acceptable—with one major caveat. I was to be the one to give the armed thugs the bad news.

I expected as much, I assured him. 'That's why they pay me the big bucks.'

To ease his mind, I told Chuckie that Rio was probably speaking in terms of francs, not dollars, and that's why he was reaching so high. Chuckie did not question why a dumb-ass New York crook would be talking in terms of French currency. I smiled to myself and noted that I was already starting to feel the jazz of the undercover juices, the art of being able to whip out intellectual-sounding BS at a moment's notice, and praying that the tension in the room is thick enough to mask it from anyone's logical thought process.

In this case, Chuckie was so worried about me ignorantly showing the money too soon that the francs to dollars conversion table instantly vanished from his thoughts. That's because as Chuckie and I both knew, if you flash your cash to a killer thief at the wrong time, he may be prompted to make an instant, ad-libbed decision to turn a buy into a deadly rip-off. The plan was that after the tense negotiations were completed, and we were all still alive, I'd give Chuckie the money to make the buy.

The Chuckster then said something extremely disquieting. He advised me that should we find ourselves looking down the barrel of Johnny Rio's infamous .357 Magnum, I was to distract the man so Chuckie could make his move. With the cameras rolling and the ghosts listening in, Chuckie wasn't about to explain just what that move was. I knew enough by then not to ask. As it turned out, I'm glad I didn't. The Pepto Bismol swigging ex-burglar had a .22 calibre single-shot pea shooter disguised as a fountain pen that he liked to use in such situations.

With my technical mind, I would have pondered the 'artistic' ramifications of that. Let's see, the bad guy had a .357 Magnum with a massive slug that could blow the gams clear off a bony French chick with a single shot. My partner and protector had a little pen from an *I Spy* episode that was just as likely to blow up in his face as to fire its mosquito-like projectile in a remotely accurate direction.

Yep, we were ready to start dealing with the cutthroat gangsters!

Chuckie's agitation soon rubbed off on me to the point where I took the phone during the next call and asked the ghosts if I needed to be packing myself. They alerted me to the backup surrounding the House of Tasha and assured me I could go in naked.

'Roger,' I said, playing with their heads again. 'If something goes awry, I can always clobber the guy over the head with the painting.'

The ghosts didn't laugh. I could imagine them envisioning Inspector Clouseau doing precisely that, using a million-dollar Rembrandt as a billy club. To avoid such a faux pas, I tucked a slender German-made .38 under my belt.

Things now moved fast. Calls were made, and Chuckie left to consult with Rio at Fasolino's. When they returned to the House of Tasha, I was surprised that only Rio showed. Fasolino apparently had something better to do. The dark and sexy Toni Sartori was no doubt left out for her own protection. Rio's lack of an entourage turned things in our favour. It would be two against one, both psychologically during the negotiations, and physically if things got violently hairy. That emboldened me to take a firmer approach with him.

Cutting to the chase, I brought up the issue of the price right off. Rio naturally was upset, insisting that he had researched the market himself and felt it was worth a minimum of a million. He claimed that the painting was actually on loan to the Bonnat from the Louvre in Paris, probably the most famous and prestigious art museum in the world. It was an impressive factoid, one that forced me to counter by saying the value of a work is the same whether it's on display at the Louvre, or in the washroom of Teddy's Art Emporium next to the local Wal-Mart. To hammer home my point, I calmly showed him some books that showed similar Rembrandt 'studies' to be worth only $22,000. I explained that a study was a smaller painting that was done in preparation of doing a larger work. It was essentially a practice painting. The real *Rabbi*, I went on, was part of a bigger work, *St Matthew Being Inspired by the Angels,* which was hanging in the Louvre at that very moment.

It was part truth, part well-played BS. The photos in the book going for a mere $22,000 were preliminary sketches, not actual paintings like *The Rabbi*. Rio's prized possession, although technically one of four done in preparation of starting the larger work, was nonetheless a full-fledged painting in its own right, and would one day be of almost immeasurable value.

My matter-of-fact, firm, but non-confrontational manner put Rio at ease. We went back and forth, arguing our positions. He admitted that he had gently dabbed the surface with a damp cloth to spruce it up a bit, and my citing him on that let him know I knew my stuff.

'And nicks, there's about a million nicks,' I scolded. 'Did you throw it in the back of a car?'

'No, no, no. I treated it like a baby,' he claimed.

I could feel the air being sucked out of him. I could almost sympathise. He had lived with both the enticing dream of *The Rabbi*, and its curse, for five years, only to be told that it was nothing more than some practice doodling.

At one point, the hardened criminal tried to appeal to me on a sentimental level. 'I'm going to tell you what I'll do or not do [price wise],' he said, slamming down one of my computer printouts. 'It's been a part of me. It's influenced a lot of things I've done. It's what this means to me!'

'It's about what I can get for it,' I countered, cutting through the violins. 'I don't care what it means to you.'

Just as emotions were heating up, a police siren could be heard in the not too far distance. It was heading right for us. Rio, ever the nervous felon, went to the door, ready to jump out of his skin. For a moment, I thought the unrelated local police call was going to ruin the whole scene. The siren blew by and Rio regained his composure.

Relieved, he came back and let down his guard. In the process, he added a startling new chapter to *The Rabbi*'s curse.

'This has caused the death of a good friend of mine, two years ago,' he revealed. 'By trying to possess it, by exchanging something for me, to pay me. But nobody knows about that. That's your knowledge. You can tell them [the eventual buyers], if they're freaks about paintings.'

From what Rio was saying, I surmised that his friend had arranged a drug deal to raise the money to buy *The Rabbi*. Unwilling to change hands yet again, the crotchety Old Man had apparently cursed the deal and Rio's friend was killed in a rip-off attempt. It was a fascinating tangent, but nothing I could pursue at that moment. My job was to get possession of the cursed portrait, not solve drug murders half a continent away.

Despite his emotional deflation, $23,000 wasn't chump change in 1977. Rio wasn't going to walk away empty-handed. A rare nuance in the case worked in his favour. Since the Rembrandt purchase was swept into an ongoing FBI operation, we couldn't arrest Rio at the moment. He was going to be allowed to 'walk' with the money in order to protect Operation Tepee and keep the extraordinary sting going. Although getting our mitts on the Rembrandt was critical, arresting the seller was not. There were bigger fish to fry at the House of Tasha, including high-level gangsters and politicians, and the bureau wasn't going to jeopardise a year of intense, gut-wrenching work just to arrest one dirt bag who had stumbled upon the score of a lifetime.

Rio, unaware of his bizarre good fortune, poignantly expressed his overall frustration with the entire *Rabbi* ordeal when he gazed at the magnificent work of art for the last time and said almost wistfully, 'I never want to see that face again.'

The poor guy then related that he'd once had his hand on The Star of India, the 563.35 carat sapphire that's the largest in the world. He couldn't move that either.

'It's too big,' I said truthfully. 'It's like stealing the *Mona Lisa*. What are you gonna do with it? You can't sell it. You can't show it. Hey, if you came in here with the *Mona Lisa*, I'd tell you to get lost.'

'Yeah, I nearly went crazy. I'm the one who gave it back to the pigs. Honourable me, right. And he (an accomplice) got out and ratted everybody out. It's a beautiful stone. Madonne, you ought to see it. It's like an egg.'

Rio's bizarre tale didn't ring any bells. I knew the Star had been stolen from New York's Museum of Natural History in 1964 and ransomed in Miami by famed suntanned bandit Murf the Surf. I wasn't aware of anything more recent. Rio was probably referring to a lesser Star, or a fake.

Before leaving, Rio dropped another little bomb that raised my eyebrows. 'There's a Picasso floating around out there. Would you be interested in that?'

I had to restrain myself. A year earlier, a huge Picasso worth multiple millions had been pinched from the Jasper Museum in Houston, Texas. I was working the case, and the trail had gone ice cold (see Chapter 4). I was aching to delve into this with Rio, but didn't want to press our luck. The quicker he left, the sooner we could all breathe easy, take the Rembrandt, and run.

Rio, in no mood to stick around, did just that. He shook my hand before exiting. I had just mentally wrestled the guy out of his million-dollar retirement plan, and there we were rubbing palms like brothers. The agents watching on the screens couldn't believe it. They were praising me with the same amount of fervour that they had been deriding me with earlier.

Within the hour, the Rembrandt was professionally wrapped and sealed inside a temperature- and humidity-controlled vault. High fives were given everywhere, and just like that, the bungling Inspector Clouseau was transformed into a steely nerved Sherlock Holmes in the eyes of my peers. While celebrating later that evening, I brought the house down when I only half kiddingly informed the Buffalo agents that the deadly thug Rio turned out to be 'the nicest guy I met all afternoon.'

The brass in Washington was alerted, as were the French. The story made headlines around the world, including the previously mentioned *Reader's Digest* book by Nathan M. Adams.

The Buffalo FBI bosses ordered a 24-hour shadow on Rio, an expensive and untenable proposition that became moot when the wily gangster slipped it within two days. He vanished with his government issued dollars.

Three months later, the plug was pulled on Operation Tepee. In a massive sweep, 42 people were arrested, including the majority leader of the Erie County Legislature, an assistant district attorney, local mob boss Joseph E. Todardo Sr, and one Gennarino Fasolino. With Johnny Rio on the run, Fasolino and Rio's girlfriend's father, John Sartori, were left to take the fall for the Rembrandt, proving that the Old Man's curse was still in play. Fasolino, who had only received $3,000 for his efforts in setting up the deal, was convicted and sentenced to three years. John Sartori cut a deal to testify against Fasolino and received probation.

Two years later, Rio was finally tracked down by police in Calgary, Canada, arrested on a drug violation, and extradited to the US, where he was charged with the Rembrandt sale, among other outstanding warrants. Ever the tough guy, Rio clammed up and refused to trade information on what he claimed to know about the missing Picasso. He negotiated a plea, served a short incarceration, then vanished back into the wind.

Two French detectives and the Bonnat Museum's elderly curator, Paul Bazé, flew in for the trials. The poor Frenchmen nearly froze to death during a hellacious Buffalo snowstorm. We had to literally dig them out of their hotel to get them to court. The trio had arrived with nothing but paper-thin, haute couture French suits, and were in a world of North American hurt until we bought them some coats, gloves, and wool hats. It was so cold that week that even with the heat on full blast, we could still see our breath inside the prosecutor's office. Outside, there were ropes strung along the walkways so people could hang on and not be blown away by the fierce winds. On the way to court one morning, we spotted an old woman skittering across the ice and snow like a witch on a broom— only she had no broom!

When the elements subsided, I was able to take our esteemed visitors to their sister city, Bayonne, New Jersey. It was their idea, not mine, as I suspected the gritty, smokestack-blighted industrial pit was hardly a clone of its lovely French namesake. The Frenchmen, snug in their new coats, didn't seem to mind. Bazé took particular pleasure in pointing out a large mural on a wall at the town hall that he had painted many years before.

As for *The Rabbi*, there's a semi-sad epilogue to virtually every happy art recovery story, and it invariably involves lawyers. Legal entanglements surrounding insurance companies and the original owners often take years to resolve, especially if the painting has increased substantially in value during its time on the loose—which is usually the case. Owners are often eager to return the insurance settlement to retake possession of the work—that is, if they still have the money and the insurance company is willing to 'sell' it, which they are generally under no obligation to do. You can see where it can get messy.

In this case, there wasn't an insurance company involved, so that wasn't the sticking point. The delay here was the criminal prosecutions of Fasolino and Rio, and the Operation Tepee sting. Those entanglements dragged out for two years, forcing *The Rabbi* to suffer the indignity of being tagged as evidence and left to languish in a dark storage vault in the frozen tundra of upstate New York.

Finally, in April 1979, eight years after it was taken off the wall in Bayonne, France, Special Agents Poerstel and Hartnett escorted the weary Old Man to FBI headquarters in Washington, DC. From there, new FBI Director William Webster officially presented it to Francois de Laboulaye, the French Ambassador. The elated Laboulaye referred to it as 'a treasure returning home.'

As part of the ceremonies, Webster agreed to let the dignitaries and media view the tape of my undercover negotiations with Johnny Rio. Trouble was, nobody had alerted me. When I came home from the office that day, a neighbour was babbling that I was all over the national news on television. I thought he was nuts, but he specifically mentioned the Rembrandt case and said it was on all the networks. Any remaining doubt as to my blown cover was erased when I stepped inside the house. My wife was absolutely hysterical. 'The Mafia is going to kill us all!' she screamed, terrified out of her mind. 'We're all going to die! We've got to move now. I'm going back to Oklahoma!'

We had two small children, so her concern was intensified. I sent them to my brother's a few miles away until I could sort things out.

This wasn't the first, nor would it be the last time my cover was blown by a superior in DC. Fortunately, surveillance videos are pretty grainy, and I had my back to the camera most of the time. Assessing the damage, I determined that the only person I dealt with directly was Johnny Rio, so Buffalo's Magnalina Family really didn't have a personal score to settle. My hometown New York gangsters, the Gambinos, Genoveses, Luccheses, Bonannos, and Colombos of the world, wouldn't care either, as those guys tend to be very provincial. Plus, hardly any of them were big fans of Walter Cronkite, Harry Reasoner, Chet Huntley, and David Brinkley. The Italians were far too busy bustin' heads, breaking legs, making book, and extorting people. I concluded that it would all quickly blow over, and we wouldn't have to go in hiding out west. Similarly, I was so reluctant to bring the curtain down on my alter egos Robert Steele and Thomas Bishop that I let them live on as well.

The Rabbi was flown to France in May, and found its way back to the newly secured Bonnat Museum that October. It has rested quietly there ever since.

. 3 .

A Rubens Pickup in Peekskill and Poghkeepsie
Becomes the Precursor to ABSCAM

*T*HE OVERWHELMING SUCCESS of Operation Tepee in Buffalo in the late 1970s left the FBI brass salivating for similar stings. New Director William Webster was eager to bring the bureau out of its lowbrow cops and robbers past into the high-tech world of white-collar crime. Webster took to heart the old cliché that, 'You can steal more with a pen than with a gun.' He felt that his starched, highly educated Federal agents should be focusing their efforts on the growing breed of high-class criminals rather than engaging in bloody shootouts with run-of-the-mill thugs.

In a way, that mindset actually returned the bureau to its roots. J. Edgar Hoover's inaugural squad of special agents were lawyers and accountants who weren't even authorised to carry weapons. He envisioned a 'clean' force of suited men who fought crime through the courts and other legal means.

Unfortunately, the criminals had other ideas. The wave of Tommy-Gun wielding bank robbers like John Dillinger, Pretty

Boy Floyd, and Baby Face Nelson in the early 1930s combined with advances in high-speed automotive technology to enable local menaces to go national. It wasn't unusual for Depression-era crooks to rob a bank in one state and beat it across the border to another in a matter of minutes, all thanks to their eight-cylinder Fords, Chevys, and Hudsons, road rockets that could reach 90 miles per hour. The state-to-state hop scotching brought them under the jurisdiction of Hoover's Federal police force.

With the public screaming for justice, Hoover had to arm his legion of 'pencil-necked geeks,' and teach them to shoot. When that mostly failed, he was forced to hire a different breed of agent— ex-military men who could shoot, punch, spit, scratch, and play hardball with the likes of Dillinger and Co.

The public readily took to this new breed of bulkier and nastier Elliot Ness-type superhero Fed, so Hoover went with it for the rest of his reign. By the late 1970s, times had changed again. The new John Dillingers worked on Wall Street, pounded the keys of computers, and were employed by the banks they quietly pilfered. Their borderless crimes were way over the heads of the local beat cops, so it was up to the FBI to keep pace. Webster was right in revamping the bureau toward fraud, white collar crime, and political corruption.

The altered direction was a boon for me and my New York-based art squad. We were no longer Fox Mulder-type lone rangers and outcasts, but instead had become the very model of the new upscale FBI. Our trailblazing, however, failed to earn us the big operating budgets showered on the organised crime and fraud divisions.

Webster sent out word that agents should be on the lookout for more savvy informants like Chuckie Carlo, now retired to the Witness Protection Programme. Undercover operations, once detested by Hoover, would be a top priority.

It was in this highly receptive climate that I encountered a man who was, and remains, the king of all front man informants.

Word came that a con man extraordinaire named Mel Weinberg had gotten himself into a deep jam with the law. Weinberg was a slick, husky, fast talking, faux-gold draped Long Island grifter who often sported a neatly trimmed goatee. He was known for tricking people into various loan scams, claiming to be an agent for a host of foreign banks. For a healthy upfront 'processing fee,' Mel would agree to shower his clients with whatever cash infusion they needed.

When that ploy played out, he brought it into the shop for an overhaul and emerged with an even more enticing variation. He hooked up with a tall, elegant, British lady who he promoted around Manhattan and Long Island as the Patty Hearst-like heiress to a European newspaper fortune. If pressed, he'd drop media baron Rupert Murdoch's name. 'Lady Diane' was either Murdoch's daughter, or the daughter of a 'guy like Murdoch,' depending on the perceived intelligence and research abilities of the mark or target he was talking to.

The woman, of course, was neither, but she did have a really beautiful British accent. That was enough of a hook for Weinberg to hang his magic on. Regal as his girlfriend was, Weinberg nonetheless had to dirty her up a bit to make his con work. He took this 'baroness' and turned her into a high-class loan shark. Why anybody would believe that a near-royal European media princess would stoop to such behaviour astounds. However, as Weinberg knew, those desperate for money, including upscale businessmen, stock traders, gamblers, mobsters, and fellow hustlers, would swallow virtually anything if they thought it would bail them out of a jam.

Weinberg demanded $50,000 up front to secure the often multi-million dollar loans, and that would be the end of it. Those who bought into the scam emerged $50,000 deeper in debt. They also came away with a rage that could turn the meekest accountant into someone willing to commit murder.

The scams worked so well that Mel was used to earning upward of a half million dollars a year, fast money that he burned just as quickly on wine, women, song, and the ponies. After sucking the life out of too many such desperados, and attracting the attention of too many police bunko squads, Weinberg took a fall in Pittsburgh on various fraud and conspiracy charges, agreeing to plead guilty to keep his lovely accomplice out of prison. Ever nimble, he did what any good con man does when the chips are down. He tried to talk his way out of jail by offering his unique brand of services to the police.

It just so happened that I was in need of such a person. I'd recently had a breakthrough in a cold case involving the theft of a pair of million-dollar paintings more than a decade earlier. In 1966, Detroit businessman Lawrence A. Fleischman decided to move to New York and become a partner in the prestigious Kennedy Galleries at 20 East 56th Street. Fleischman, one of the nation's leading art fanciers, shipped most of his multi-million dollar collection of paintings, sculptures, vases, Egyptian statuettes, and other invaluable relics from Detroit to either the gallery, or his new apartment at United Nations Plaza on Manhattan's East Side. There were more than 300 individual items, and most made it.

Emphasis on the word 'most.' Fleischman was given a quick introduction to New York's web of corrupt union officials, mobsters, and thieves when two of his most valuable possessions never arrived. Missing was a 17-by-17-inch oil on wood entitled *The Judgement at Cambyese,* by 17th century Flemish Baroque master Peter Paul Rubens. *The Judgement* was a stunning, if busy, epic bringing life to a Persian legend about a corrupt judge succeeded by his son.

Also gone was a 28-by-28-inch oil on canvas, *Portrait of Lady Johanna Quadacker Bannier,* by Gerard Ter Borch, a 17th century Dutch painter also known for the Baroque style—an explosion of art, music, and architecture that emphasised a bold, energetic, and theatrical style. In art, that translated to naturalistic slice-of-life scenes, landscapes, still lifes, the universe, and genre imagery that relied upon vivid colours, action, and innovations in movement and lighting.

The New York police believed the two classics made it all the way to the loading dock of Fleischman's East Side home before they vanished within sight of the walls they were set to adorn. The pair were worth about $200,000 each at the time of their theft, and up to five times that by 1978. (In 1980, Rubens' *Samson and Delilah* sold at auction in London for $5.3 million. 22 years later, in 2002, Rubens' *The Massacre of the Innocents* sold for $76.7 million.)

After decades without a word about the paintings, one of my informants brought the news that a hefty mob associate named Dominic Caserele was making noise about having two 'million dollar squares' for sale. I marvelled once again how these hoods were prone to inflating the value of art long before the 'legitimate crooks' in the art world showed them how it was done by sending prices soaring.

My informant set up a meeting. To show I meant business, I arranged for the FBI to rent a suite at the Plaza Hotel at Central Park South, the ultra-ritzy joint with the horses and carriages out front seen in all the movies. My cover had yet to be blown by NBC/CBS/ABC in the Rembrandt case (See Chapter 2), so I was able to slip into my role as shady art dealer Thomas Bishop without worry.

Dominic arrived on time, and was duly impressed by the $250-a-night suite. Frankly, I was surprised they let him through the door. Another in a long line of, men like Caserele live their lives on the fringes of the mob, never showing enough 'cojones' to become a bona fide 'made man,' a ceremonially inducted Mafia soldier. An obese hanger-on in his late 40s, Caserele had black hair and the wrinkly, ill-fitting, ripping at-the-seams suit that is the bane of every grossly overweight man's existence.

He hailed from Brooklyn by way of Glens Falls upstate.

I was intensely curious to know how, after all these years, this slob had come into possession of two such historic masterpieces. There's no way he was acting as a front for a more sophisticated thief or collector, because such a person wouldn't be hanging with a goon like Dom. I suspected Dom had stolen the masterpieces from an equally low-life character. How many times the Rubens and Ter Borch had changed hands over the past decade was anybody's guess, but it appeared that the pair had remained within 50 square miles of the Kennedy Gallery the entire time.

My curiosity would remain unsatisfied. Dom was wary, elusive, and tight-lipped. He volunteered nothing, and I wasn't able to probe too deeply. Most thieves on either end of a deal couldn't care less about how someone got their hands on such a prize. Anybody asking too many questions would be suspect. All that mattered was what the goods were worth, and how the deal would go down.

Dom needed to develop a level of trust with me before he would go any further. The Plaza Hotel was nice and fancy and all, but that meant nothing to Dom. In gangster street parlance, he needed someone in his world to 'vouch' for me.

That's where Mel Weinberg came into the picture. Special Agent Myron Fuller in the Bureau's Long Island office had already met with Mel in Pittsburgh, and gave him a glowing reference. Fuller referred him to me and we set up a meeting. I agreed with Fuller's assessment and signed Mel up.

Mel's debut assignment in his new career as an undercover snitch was to vouch me to Dominic Caserele. 'Piece of cake,' Weinberg said, taking the information. 'I'll get back to you.'

Turns out Mel Weinberg was one vouching machine. He could vouch the devil's way into heaven. He had Dom's head spinning with personal tales of hanging with high-level gangsters like Colombo underboss Sonny Franzese and his ultra-slick son Michael, 'The Yuppie Don.' He knew this guy and that guy, and he and the area mob bosses were so tight they were practically at his bar mitzvah.

It wasn't all a scam. Mel was such a talented and colourful character he indeed had friends and associates throughout the New York Mafia families. He even had a sandwich named after him at Orlando's, a Huntington, Long Island restaurant frequented by Anthony 'Tony Ducks' Corallo, the boss of the Lucchese Family, and other top echelon members of the bent nose set. That sealed it for Dom. Anybody with a sandwich named after him in a mob joint had to be okay.

True to his word, Mel smoothly slid me into his boasting to the point where it was nearly overkill. Dom came away thinking Thomas Bishop might be too dangerous to deal with. Picking up on that, Mel, puffing on a thick stogie, assured him I was only interested in the paintings and wouldn't try to muscle him.

Mel returned with the news that Dom was ready to deal. I was impressed. Even more impressive, Mel brought photos of the pieces in question. There was little doubt that they were the right paintings, or at least, they were masterful forgeries of the right paintings. The ancient masterpieces, propped on the dirty linoleum floor of somebody's run-down kitchen, were dead on the mark.

Dom, Mel, and I soon became the best of friends. Since we were such buds, and I was playing the money-is-no-object Thomas Bishop, we didn't even try to beat him down on the price—at least not in fencing terms. We agreed to pay Dom a cool $100,000 for both paintings—the typical 10% fencing fee for the million-dollar goods.

Actually, this wasn't because we were buddies, it was because the money wasn't going to walk as it did in the Rembrandt case. Dom would be taken down the moment the paintings were in sight, so it really didn't matter how much we offered. Dom wouldn't get to pocket a dime.

That said, the bureaucratic pencil-pushers at the FBI weren't about to loan out $100,000 in flash cash, only to have us walk into a rip-off. The best they would do was give us $10,000 in mostly ones to make the stacks look impressive. We were forced to put $100s on the top of each stack of a thousand, and then rely upon our acting skills to make sure Dom didn't notice.

Mel and I both said a lot of prayers for our acting skills because that was the deadliest of gambles. A quick riffle through one of the stacks would reveal the pending double-cross and would lead to immediate bloodshed. That the FBI would put their agents through such risky situations to avoid losing a few extra bucks was forever baffling. Regardless, one must play the hand one is dealt, and Mel and I agreed to work through the handicap.

The last wrinkle was figuring out how precisely the deal would go down. Mel was wary of carrying that kind of alleged cash around and sensed that Dom was expecting something dramatic that gave everyone layers of protection. Mel came up with the wild idea of popping in and out of various small airports upstate. The FBI was tight with cash, but they had a lot of neat equipment they were eager to put to use. That included a fleet of planes they either owned or leased. As I predicted, the brass didn't whine too much before green-lighting our Hollywood-like scheme.

And what a scheme it was. We headed out from LaGuardia to the Stewart airport in the upstate Newburgh/Peekskill/Fishkill Hudson River Valley area on a cold winter day in February 1978. I was familiar with the location because the FBI had a firearms training camp in Peekskill.

Inside the four-seat, twin-prop plane was FBI pilot Eddie Woods, Mel, and myself. The remaining seat, next to the pilot, was reserved for Big Dom. I was holding a briefcase full of ones disguised as hundreds in my left hand. In case that lame deception didn't fly, there was a snub-nosed .38 strapped to my right shin.

1,000 feet above us were two additional twin props filled with FBI agents, eight in all, to act as our backup. They would remain airborne as we made the 'Pickup near Peekskill,' and then would fall back into line as we continued on to the mystery drop location.

Stewart Air Base was years away from being upgraded to the big city–sounding Stewart International Airport, as it's known today. We touched down on a barren strip of asphalt, hopped out, and had no trouble finding Big Dom in the deserted mini-terminal. He was in good spirits, but appeared to have put on another layer of winter fat since we last saw him. I guessed that he was pushing 300 pounds on his 5-foot-9-inch frame. He must have already started living large, dining out on the expected score.

Mel and I traded concerned looks, and we knew exactly what the other was thinking. 'Are we going to be able to get the puddle jumper off the friggin' ground with this big hog riding shotgun?'

Eddie Woods shot back a similar dismayed glare when Dom rolled up and splatted down in the seat beside him. Hang on boys, I thought, stealing a line from Bette Davis, it's gonna be a bumpy ride.

The little-plane-that-could huffed and puffed and struggled mightily to lift off without a deadly right hand dip. It was touch-and-go for a few seconds before we finally became airborne.

I hadn't patted Dom down in the terminal because that wouldn't have been kosher among us buddies. If he was carrying, we were just going to have to deal with it at the appropriate time.

The 'appropriate time' came sooner than expected. Before we had even levelled off, Dom turned toward us in the back and asked to see the cash.

Good, I thought. Whatever the consequence, we weren't going to have to sit there and sweat the moment for an hour. Might as well get this over with. If there was shooting to be done, at least we'd be closer to the ground than we would be in 10 more minutes. I lifted the briefcase off the floor, flattened it on my knees, flicked the snaps and popped the tops, revealing the neatly stacked rows of crisp 'hundreds.'

'Give it here, I want to count it,' Dom said, reaching over. I yanked it from his stubby reach. Suddenly, the small aircraft felt as constricting as a matchbox. I glanced at Mel as we had arranged. It was time for him to take the stage.

'What are you talking about, counting it?' Mel groused. 'There's no room on the plane. What's the matter with you? You don't trust us after all this? We don't even know where the hell we're going. You got us by the balls, and you want to play accountant? If you go flopping around in the seat with your weight, trying to count out a hundred grand down to the penny, you're going to flip us over! We'll all end up in the Hudson!'

'Okay, all right,' Dom said. 'Calm down. It's okay. I'll count it on the ground.'

Mel and I suppressed our huge relief. Dom, of course, had failed 'Contraband Buy 101.' He should have counted the money. Anytime the purchasing party in a deal objects to a seller counting the cash, one should immediately smell a rat. Fortunately, we were all such good pals, and Mel had that sandwich named for him in the mob bar and all. Dom could trust us!

'So where are we going?' I asked.' We can't stay up here all day.'

'Wallkill,' Dom responded. 'Kobelt Airport.'

'Got it,' Mel said. 'That's near Poughkeepsie. Just another 20 miles to the northwest or so.'

We relayed the information to Woods at the controls. He radioed the Kobelt tower for landing information. 'Kobelt come in. Wallkill, come in.'

Only he wasn't talking to the tower. He was signalling our shadows where to go. All that 'Wallkill, come in' stuff should have been a tell to Dom, but he didn't notice or care. He had visions of $100,000 worth of lobster bisque dancing in his head.

'Roger that,' the radio squawked, indicating that our peers read us loud and clear.

The next move was for Eddie to stall and let our team-mates get ahead of us, land, and be in place before we arrived. The pilot angled wide left to lengthen our journey. If Dom noticed, he didn't let on. Whatever his true profession was, it obviously wasn't an aviation navigator.

The rest of the flight went without incident—that is, until we touched down in Pipsqueeky or Pocahontas or wherever the heck we were. That's when the fun started again. Dom reached into his pocket and pulled out a black object. In an instant, my mind flashed a terrible thought.' The fat SOB is going to hit us and take the dough!' I reached for the .38 on my leg as Mel clutched his chest in horror.

'It's a walkie talkie,' Dom explained, noticing our anxiety. 'You guys really need to cool it.' Dom showed us the transmitter, then fired it up. Restarting our hearts, we listened in.

'Foxy One to Foxy Two. Can you read?'

'Roger,' came a voice.

'How is it?'

'All clear here.'

'Foxy One to Foxy Three. How is it on the road?'

'Nobody here,' came another voice.

As these conversations were going on, we taxied by both FBI shadow planes parked on the runway. Agents were all around, pretending to be washing their windshields, kicking their tires, changing the oil, gassing up. The tiny airport was crawling with Feds. Mel and I looked at each other and had to bite our tongues to keep from laughing. The tension of the flight had wrung us out to the point where we nearly had a deadly case of the school-girl giggles. Thankfully, neither of us broke.

I changed the subject in my mind by making a note of how lucky we were to have developed the grandiose flight plan rather than having the backups drive to the airport. If we had, Foxy Three was certain to have spotted them and ruined the deal.

After we stopped and exited the cramped plane, I was struck by what a magnificent winter wonderland surrounded us. It had snowed heavily the night before, and the place looked like one of those quaint ski towns in Colorado. How fitting, I thought. This was, when it came right down to it, all about the beauty and magnificence of great art, about freeing two kidnapped masterpieces from their dark cellars and allowing them to wow the public with their majesty again. I was certain that masters Rubens and Ter Borch, wherever they were, had to approve of the exchange playing out in this breathtaking landscape.

In a flash, the Hallmark moment was replaced by a more chilling thought. Was I seeing things in such surrealistically beautiful hues because I was about to die? Were these the last images I would ever see? Did Foxy Two and Foxy Three have me in their crosshairs, a little red laser dot dancing between my eyes at that very moment? Was I going to get shot by some lowlife in stinkin' Wallkill?

I felt myself shiver. I didn't know whether it was from the cold or the dread. Such is the world of an undercover agent.

Dom's voice rocked me back to my senses. 'There's a big white van in the parking lot. The paintings are in the back.'

As I strolled over to find the specified vehicle, I again took in the beauty of the area. It was like a Christmas card. The only thing that didn't fit was this beat-up old van in the parking lot. It looked like it had been through a war.

It took me a few beats to realise that the blight on the snowy horizon was the van I was searching for. I opened the creaky rear door. Two thin rectangular objects wrapped in a tatty green blanket were sitting on their sides among the other greasy junk. I pulled off the rag and there they were, the Rubens and Ter Borch, found after 12 long years. Rubens' Persian court scene was bold, brash, and emotional. The faces of the powerless and oppressed gathering at the feet of the new crooked judge vividly revealed their downtrodden status. Ter Borch's canvas reflected the mostly stark black and white portrait style of the era. His thin, dark-haired, very young, very elegant *Lady Johanna Quadacker Bannier* was standing with her hair pulled back with the adorned bottoms hanging down in twirling spit curls. She was draped in a long, flowing, heavy fabric gown with wide, three-quarter sleeves.

They were both breathtaking. If only *Lady J-Q* could talk, what a tale she could tell.

'Muy bien,' I announced to myself. No, the awe-inspiring art didn't prompt me to start speaking in tongues. The Spanish words for what I thought meant very good (it's technically very well) was the signal for the surrounding window-washers and tire-kickers to jump into a phone booth, transform like Superman into special agents of the FBI, and do their thing.

As I waited for my backup to swarm me—Mel and I were set to be arrested along with Dom to protect our cover—I had a few minutes to further scope the masterpieces. I whipped out my lighted magnifying glass and flipped them over. They both had the proper 'provenance', the auction house markings that revealed the history of their travels from creator to museum to gallery. Correction, the history of their legitimate travels was recorded by these indicia.

Back at the plane, Dom was taken without incident. It turned out he wasn't armed. Mel, was giving an Academy Award performance as a dupe caught in an FBI trap. Before Dom could put two and two together, Mel naturally turned it all on him, accusing Big Dom of setting us up. Dom was not only under arrest, but he had to face the wrath of all Mel's mob pals down at the sandwich shop.

Not a good day for Big D.

The two young agents sent to arrest me were quietly efficient as they turned me around and snapped on the handcuffs. 'Nice job,' one whispered as they took me to a waiting vehicle that arrived after the trap was sprung. Mel, Dom, and I were placed in separate vehicles and taken to the Poughkeepsie FBI field station.

Foxy Two, a guy in his thirties named Edward Palmer, was rounded up nearby. He was loitering near the van when we grabbed him, and later claimed to be an innocent bystander walking his dog. Foxy Three poughkeepsied it out of there, never to be identified.

Dom and Foxy Two clammed up and refused to reveal how they acquired the paintings–whether they were in on the original theft, or came by them through another route. Nobody else stepped forward with the story either. The mystery of where the Judge and the Lady had been all those years would never be solved.

In contrast, there was no mystery about what happened to Mel Weinberg. Truly thankful for his help, I arranged for him to collect the $30,000 reward offered by the insurance company. It wasn't quite what he was used to earning for pimping out Lady Diane as a bogus loan shark, but it was a nice score nonetheless. In typical fashion, Mel told people, including his own biographer Robert W.

Green (*The Sting Man*), that it was only $10,000. That was done to dupe the IRS.

Shadiness aside, I was so impressed with Mel's unique skills that I offered him a chance to team up on a regular basis. We developed a partnership complete with a well-crafted cover. Mel took on the guise of the right hand man of a Saudi Arabian oil sheik who was an avid art collector. I was the sheik's art expert. The loosely operated sting was so elaborate that we had a company name—Abdul Enterprises—an office at the Plaza Hotel, an employee at Chase Manhattan Bank who would vouch for the sheik's 'multi-million dollar bank account,' and nifty business cards. Mel used his wealth of contacts to put out the word that we were interested in every piece of stolen art existing anywhere in the world.

Within weeks, we had our first fish. Mel had a guy on the line, Ron Sabloski, who claimed to have a number of hot paintings. After a preliminary meeting, he asked to meet the sheik. I scrambled around the New York headquarters trying to find an Arab employee, eventually locating a young translator. However, at the last minute he pulled out, angry that he was still a lowly language transcriber and had not been promoted to special agent. I wanted to wring the guy's neck, but he was adamant.

Desperate, I spotted Special Agent Mike Dennehy, the burly, bearded brother of well-known Hollywood character actor Brian Dennehy, the blond, beefy sheriff who hunted Sylvester Stallone in the first *Rambo* film, among myriad other roles. I figured maybe some of that acting skill had rubbed off on Mike.

Mike Dennehy was our division's jewellery expert. In the same way I trained in great art, he knew all there was to know about jewellery, especially antiques. I had first choice to do either, and picked art because the paintings and artefacts remained intact even when stolen. Jewellery was often melted down and transformed into something else. That was a whole new quagmire.

We dressed Mike in Lawrence of Arabia gear rented at a local costume shop for $37, and brought him to the Plaza. He did surprisingly well for a white boy playing an Arab, but we had to think fast numerous times. Turned out Sabloski had some vague knowledge of Arab culture, which was more than any of us, especially Dennehy. He recognised Dennehy's Halloween headgear as designating the rank of Emir, which was pretty heady.

Every time Dennehy stood up for any reason, Sabloski stood in respect. Soon we were all bobbing up and down like a jack-in-the-box, trying our best to keep from laughing.

I told Sabloski that the Emir could understand English but couldn't speak it very well, which enabled me to keep Dennehy from talking and revealing his New York accent. He communicated with grunts.

Weary of all the sitting and standing, and knowing my fellow agents were about to lose it any second, I signalled Dennehy to withdraw to the adjoining bedroom with an attractive, red-haired agent posing as his personal secretary. Mel explained that redheads were a rare treat for the horny Emir, and he needed a 'nookie break.'

During the discussions, a loud clunk was heard behind us. The preparations crew had used the high-tech technique of duct taping a tape recorder to the underside of the table. It had come loose and plonked to the floor. One of the agents nearby kicked it out of sight before Sabloski saw it.

Fortunately, it wasn't a major screw-up because it turned out to be a Keystone FBI Agents affair from the start. Quick on his feet, Mel fast-talked his way through every flaw. The giggling agents were brushed off as staffers who were forced to drink with the party boy Emir and couldn't hold their booze. Similarly, a spread of Kosher deli treats Mel bought raised Sabloski's eyebrows. He wondered why a rich Arab would be ordering lowbrow Jewish food like corned beef, pastrami, potato salad, and coleslaw. Mel explained that aside from redheads, the guy secretly loved Jewish delights. He craved both when he was out of his strict, repressive country. It was a clever ruse. Mel had to improvise the lunch because the FBI brass refused to go for the expensive imported delicacies the Plaza could have provided. Naturally, he selected what he liked.

Along those same frugal lines, the attending backup agents had to stock the bar with half-empty booze bottles taken from our own homes. The suite ended up looking more like the domain of a bunch of high school kids on prom night rather than the lair of an Arab oil sheik. In keeping with that crazy image, the messy food had to be eaten by hand because Mel forgot to provide plastic forks and spoons. He passed it off as digging in authentic 'Arab style.'

As for Sabloski's art offerings, as far as I could tell, it was all junk. He might as well have brought a copy of Cassius Coolidge's dogs playing poker. (Although the original would have been a score.) I couldn't determine if the scattered landscapes and Revolutionary War scenes, all from unknown artists, had even been stolen. Sabloski may have purchased them from the guy standing on the street corner below.

I advised Sabloski that the esteemed Emir was only interested in the great classics, and called the absurd meeting to an end. Putting aside the glaring errors, we did learn a great deal from the dry run. In the future, we needed a real Arab to play the Sheik, although that was almost a 'duh!' The food and atmosphere should be authentic, and the number of agents in the room should be kept to a minimum to cut down on the giggles. Additionally, the suite had been arranged with chairs placed in a semi-circle with a lone one, for Sabloski, apart from the rest. Mel pointed out that it was a typical cop interrogation set-up, and advised us to make the décor more natural.

Before we could regroup and try again, Abdul Enterprises was taken in an entirely different direction. Because Mel lived out in the Hamptons on Long Island, and I lived closer to the city near Kennedy Airport, I sent him back to Myron Fuller and Jack McCarthy, special agents based closer to Mel's house. (McCarthy later became head of security for Texaco Worldwide.) We were in a planning meeting one afternoon with a supervising agent from their division, John Good, when somebody mentioned that FBI Director William Webster was interested in fighting political corruption.

'I can do that,' Mel piped up. 'I know a lot of crooked politicians.' He began rattling off the names of various elected officials he claimed were dirty, starting with Angelo Errichetti, the mayor of Camden, New Jersey. Good, who had been ambivalent at best to our masterpiece-hunting efforts up to then, instantly perked up. With the few minor tweaks, he figured our operation could switch gears from art to politics.

And so began ABSCAM, the 'Arab Scam' effort that would become the biggest and most famous political corruption sting in American history. The set-up was virtually the same one Mel and I developed. Mel was the front man for a wealthy Arab sheik, only now the sheik was interested in buying political influence, not stolen art. The operation started in New York and eventually expanded up and down the East Coast, focusing on Washington, DC.

I was asked to go for the ride, but begged off. I was addicted to the art sleuth game, and had studied and trained for it during the previous decade. I had a pile of active cases with many live leads. I didn't want to change horses and leave all the loose ends.

Mel went on to play his role famously, ultimately bringing down a United States senator, seven congressmen, Mayor Errichetti, and a score of local politicians and lesser lights. The unprecedented sting's two-year life ended in 1981.

As for the Rubens and the Ter Borch, they had one last adventure before retiring to their new home at the Kennedy Gallery. During the criminal trials, I was called upon to take the paintings from the evidence vault on the west side of Manhattan to the courthouse in the Southern District of New York at 1 Saint Andrew Plaza. Thanks to the notoriety, coupled with the surge in art values, the panel and canvas were now worth close to $5 million. I tossed them in the back of a government issued two-door Chevy and made my way across town. On the way, I decided to make a short stop at the FBI office two blocks from the courthouse to take care of some unrelated business. I parked on a side street, adorned the car with the proper FBI markings, and slapped a bubble gum machine on the dashboard. I was upstairs about 15 minutes.

You can see where this is going. When I returned, not only were the paintings gone, the whole freakin' car was gone! It was one of the most horrible moments of my life. Don Mason and I had tracked those painting for 14 years, and here I had lost them again. What could I say? What could I tell my bosses? The judge? The prosecutor? William Webster? This was an FBI disaster of Biblical proportions!

I began frantically asking the people on the street if they saw what happened.

'Oh that car,' one shopkeeper explained. 'It was towed five minutes ago.'

Mother of. . ., I thought. A stinkin' New York tow truck? These were the same lugs who regularly tow police blue and whites. They once towed the limousine of a presidential cabinet member who was bringing the budget of the United States to a meeting.

I found out where the holding yard was for that area, went back upstairs, recruited another agent, and swore him to silence to the grave. We rushed to the pier compound a couple of miles away where the cars were stashed and busted in like Teddy Roosevelt taking San Juan Hill. I was screaming and yelling like a total maniac, flashing my badge and gun, making it crystal clear I was eager to use the power of both. 'You towed an FBI car, you morons! What's wrong with you?'

'Calm down man,' the lot supervisor said. 'You're going to have a heart attack. It's just a car.'

Little did he know—thankfully. He led me to a corner of the lot where the vehicle had been dumped. Somewhere in the process somebody with half a brain noticed the markings and realised what they had. The car was covered in yellow police tape.

'See? We took good care of it,' the super said, as if he wanted a medal.

'Hey, it's not like that limousine we took with the budget in it.
That was wild!'

I ripped the tape off and anxiously checked the back. Thank the
Good Lord the paintings were still there.

'What's the fuss all about, boss?' the super asked.

'None of your business,' I spat, still furious. 'The next time you
tow an FBI car we're going to nuke this whole lot!'

The nerve-shattering ordeal cost me an hour and a half.
Fortunately, the trial was proceeding slowly and the 17th century
evidence wasn't needed until later. Caserele and Palmer were
subsequently convicted of possession of stolen property and were
given the usual short sentences.

On the positive side, sensational art cases are extremely likely
to be prosecuted to the full extent by career-minded state, county,
and Federal attorneys. In fact, Caserele and Palmer originally had
their charges dropped to protect the ongoing ABSCAM sting. In an
extremely rare move, the charges were reinstated after ABSCAM
was shut down. Savvy prosecutors eager to get in on the subsequent
media frenzy knew a good thing when they saw it.

We were able to suppress the ABSCAM connection enough in
the spring of 1979 to return the paintings to Lawrence Fleischman's
insurance company. An elated Fleischman was able to make a deal
with his insurers that enabled him to return the $135,000 settlement
with interest and reacquire the paintings—which were now worth
20 times that much. He displayed them in his gallery, much to the
delight of the record crowds intrigued by the news stories.

I was comforted to know that in the right circles of people who
truly love art, including a cutthroat insurance company, it remained
all about beauty, history, and the sharing of great treasures.

Yeah, right, I thought, looking at the tall stack of open cases
on my desk. I wondered if any of the money-hungry characters
populating those files felt the same way—particularly, the man,
woman, or child currently in possession of a giant Picasso stolen in
Texas months before.

.4.

PICASSO'S $100 MILLION PURPLE REIGN

*I*NFUSED WITH DARK comedy, mythical curses, and maddening futility, the previous chapters detail what usually occurs when a run-of-the-mill thief stumbles upon the theft of a lifetime. Overwhelmed by the nuances of the snobby art world, these sad-sack crooks have no clue how to turn their big score into cash. As with the Rembrandt, Rubens, and Ter Borch stolen from France, Michigan, and New York, the paintings can often become a suffocating albatross squeezing tighter and tighter around the necks of their unworthy new owners.

The great irony of the $100 billion annual international art trade is the vast divide that exists between the thieves and the potential buyers, a chasm that is rarely bridged. Although art theft is rampant—a bullish $5 billion a-year business, according to Interpol and the FBI—the thieves are most often 'sub-commoners' who are scraping the bottom rungs of society. In turn, the big money buyers are a closed fraternity of mansion and penthouse–dwelling modern-day noblemen. Never the twain shall meet.

If 'the rich aren't like you and I,' no truer example exists than the art world. It's an exclusive club unlike any other.

Beauty can be a drug, but beautiful art is nothing like the drug business. Rich yuppie kids and young professionals on the fast track think nothing of cruising their BMWs into the mean street ghettoes to score some coke, meth, or pot. Gamblers come in all colours and stripes, with Arab sheiks and Japanese auto tycoons sharing the same bookies with bus drivers and dishwashers. Prostitutes service doctors and lawyers as well as construction workers. Loan sharks break the legs of both commodities dealers and junkies. Mob guys squeeze trucking moguls in the morning, have lunch, then extort the guy selling hot CDs on the street corner in the afternoon.

Yet these same tycoons, sheiks, moguls and CEOs never have to worry about trying to outbid a bus driver, dishwasher, junkie, or homeless guy for a van Gogh at Christie's.

The exception to this ironclad rule is something known as a 'commissioned theft.' In this instance, the twain meet, although the lower end of the connection is frequently a whole different breed of upscale criminal. Filthy rich giants of industry have been known to hire a crack band of Ocean's Eleven-type professionals to target one specific painting, then bring it to the buyer almost immediately. The trail is short and sweet, and nothing is ever heard afterward but, to steal a line from Simon & Garfunkel, 'The Sounds of Silence.'

These thefts, as one might expect, are the hardest of all to solve. Some in law enforcement, echoing back to the early days of *La Cosa Nostra*, have become so frustrated by it, they deny the crimes even exist.

'There's no mastermind, no international art Mafia,' French government art expert Gilbert Raguideau sniffed to *Time* magazine at the end of the 1970s, when art prices, and theft, began to rocket. 'We all have heard the legend of the mad, rich connoisseur who buys stolen masterworks. He does not exist.'

Au contraire, Monsieur Raguideau. He, and she, exist all right. From Riyadh to Beverly Hills, they're out there gazing up at their special prizes each and every day, proving once again that 'stolen apples taste the sweetest.' They're just extremely difficult to catch.

At any given time, if you check the worldwide stolen art registries kept by Interpol, the FBI, and numerous private concerns, you'll find that there are hundreds, sometimes thousands, of paintings and other works of art worth a quarter of a million dollars or more each that are listed as missing. There are individual paintings valued at $10 million and up that have been ghosts for decades. They are not hanging in the washroom of 'Joe's Garage' somewhere. Somebody saw them, wanted them, and got them. And it wasn't good ol' Joe. It was somebody with serious juice.

In 1976, the owners and curators of Houston's Jasper Museum decided to pull up stakes and move their operation to Manhattan. It wasn't an unusual move. Manhattan is the fine art capital of the world. Houston, by contrast, is thought to be more of a two-fisted, oil industry, roughneck Texas cow town. As the joke goes, art in Texas is the latest revamp of the Budweiser can. (Andy Warhol would agree!)

However, as so many have learned over the years—especially in politics where the Bush family has long reigned over America—you can never underestimate the understated intelligence of those clever Texans.

To make their jump to a deluxe gallery in the Big Apple, the Jasper Museum hired a specialised moving van company to expertly pack and crate hundreds of paintings, relics, and historical artefacts worth tens of millions of dollars. Included among the bounty was The Jasper's prized possession, a massive 6-foot-by-4-foot Picasso with a James Bond-ish name: *The Man with the Purple Hat* aka *L'Homme a la Casquette*.

Even before the rampant art value inflation of the 1980s and 1990s, Picassos were red-hot. The prolific 20th century Spanish master, who lived most of his life in France, was and remains the king of the abstract artists. His works are known publicly for their wild disembodied faces and bodies, and are respected privately for their brilliance in 'cubism,' colour, and design.

After Picasso's death in 1973, the value of his vast body of work began to skyrocket. In 1980, his *Saltimbanque Seated with Arms Crossed* sold for $3 million at Sotheby's, the famous auction house in New York and London. A shocker at the time, the Picasso craze was merely warming up. Nine years later, Picasso's *Les Noces de Pierrette* sold for an astounding $49 million. Eleven years after that, in 2000, *Femme aux Bras Croisés* brought frenzied bidders at Christie's in New York to a blood fever. When the gavel slammed, the price stood at a cool $50 million.

Currently, Picasso is credited with the highest sale of all time. The quirky master topped the watershed $100 million mark in 2004 as *Garçon a la Pipe* rocked the world by fetching $104.1 million at Sotheby's.

It should be noted that this doesn't mean that *Garçon a la Pipe* is viewed as the most valuable painting on the planet. It's impossible to quantify art that way. A great number of the most well-known classics are owned by countries and museums and have never been offered for sale. Leonardo da Vinci's *Mona Lisa*, widely regarded as the most famous and valuable painting in existence, was insured for $100 million in 1962. It would be worth upward of a half billion dollars if auctioned today. Because virtually all of da Vinci's masterpieces are held tightly by museums and nations, his name doesn't even appear in the top ten of the highest priced paintings ever sold.

That said, $100 million for some paint on canvas is still nothing to sneeze at. Which brings us back to *The Man with the Purple Hat*. Picasso is known for going through periods distinguished by colours. He had his 'Blue Period,' then shifted to his 'Rose Period.' The $104 million *Garçon a la Pipe (Boy with a Pipe)* was done during his unofficially recognised 'Purple Period,' where the purples began leaping out from the rosy backgrounds.

The Jasper Museum, knowingly or unknowingly, was sitting on a gold mine. *The Man with the Purple Hat* was even more gloriously purple than the Boy with a Pipe. Somebody down there in Texas was either very astute, very prophetic, or very lucky, because when the specially ordered, expertly packed, 18-wheeler rolled into New York, the Purple Picasso was gone.

It was some trick, too, because the trailer of the truck had been sealed with metal when it left Houston with the Picasso aboard. The seal was unbroken when it arrived in New York minus the massive painting.

I was paid to think less fancifully. The case fell to me when the Jasper owner appeared in my office one afternoon and told me the sad tale. He was a tall, lanky fellow with 1970s-style long hair surrounding his oval face. I studied him carefully as he spoke, because a 'miraculous' theft of this nature reeks of an inside job. A man moving his collection halfway across the country to set up shop in an environment that has the most expensive real estate in the world raises a sea of red flags. Was he 'double dipping' to finance his operation in New York—i.e., did he sell the painting twice, once to a secret big wallet collector, and a second time to the insurance company? It wouldn't have been the first time someone did that.

I did a background check on the guy and nothing raised suspicions. He was spick and span. I contacted my sources in the art world, including Picasso restorers and experts, and they all said that as far as they knew, he was a straight shooter. No gambling problems, women problems, drug problems: Nothing that would turn him into a desperado. From personal observation, he appeared genuinely broken over the loss. As with Detroit businessman Lawrence A. Fleischman and his similarly trucked Rubens and Ter Borch, this man's introduction to New York wasn't a pleasant one.

Next on the list of 'usual suspects' was the truck driver. If something fishy had gone on during the three-day trip, he had to be in on it. The trucker was a heavy-set Latino, about 5-foot-9, 220 pounds, black hair, probably of Mexican descent. He professed his innocence with a terrified passion that made a strong impression on me. A family man with no criminal record and lots of children, he didn't seem to be the type to get involved in what was already starting to smell like a professional job. In addition, the driver had no contacts in the art world and would have had a difficult time trying to move the immense painting. He didn't balk at taking a lie detector test, and the polygraph came out truthful.

There is indeed a bustling market for stolen American goods across the Texas border in Mexico, but that generally translates to more practical merchandise—cars, cash, electronic equipment, movie and music DVDs and CDs, items like that. In turn, Mexico has a wealth of extremely talented artists who can duplicate practically anything. You can buy a dead ringer *Mona Lisa* on the beach for $20. Heck, you can buy a dead ringer *Mona Lisa* with a rabbit for a hand, a squirrel hidden in her face, and a donkey obscured in the background for $20, a quizzical style of abstract Mexican art that is wonderfully creative. It was therefore highly doubtful that this theft had a Mexican connection. If anybody in Mexico wanted *The Man with the Purple Hat*, all they had to do was give their neighbourhood artist a picture of it and voilá, they'd have their Picasso.

Eager to help, the driver insisted that nothing unusual happened during the trip, and reiterated that the metal seal had not been broken at any step along the way.

Stymied, I contacted John Good, the future FBI ABSCAM supervisor who was in charge of the agency's Truck Hijacking Squad along with being the Organised Crime chief. He sat in on a follow-up interrogation of the driver, and he agreed with me that the man appeared clean.

Good helped me understand and analyze the sealing process of the truck trailer's sliding door. Highly valuable cargo is usually shipped with the truck's rear and only door secured in the same manner as dripping wax on a letter flap. Specifically, the trucking industry uses a metal bar or flat ruler-like slab that's slipped through a channel that straddles a door and the outer walls. Once it's set in place, the only way to open the door is to break the bar. The trucking company keeps precise logs of when the door is sealed and when the seal is broken. Everything came up normal—the bar was locked with the Picasso inside, and unlocked in New York with the Picasso gone.

Good explained that truck hijackers usually dispense with that nonsense by simply pulling a gun on the driver and ordering him to open the door by doing whatever it takes. A knowledgeable, do-it-yourself hijacker might know the procedure for snapping the bar, but he wouldn't give a damn about trying to reseal it afterward. The horse was already out of the barn.

If the Picasso was indeed taken en route, it would have to be the work of an ultra-savvy thief with highly specialised talents, one who came prepared with the right tools and identical sealing materials. He or she not only wanted to take the painting, but schemed to shroud the theft in mystery while buying two to three days of lead time.

A person with those skills would have to be something like a truck cat burglar, a species so rare Good said he was unfamiliar with such a creature. That left me back at square one.

Going further down the list of suspects, I checked out the loaders on both ends. As mentioned, the Houston firm was known for shipping precious artefacts, and banked on their honest reputation to do business. Had someone among them been dirty, there was a wealth of smaller, easier-to-steal, much easier-to-sell items in the truck that would have resulted in a similar or even better cash-out, so it was unlikely any of them would have picked such a cumbersome item to take. Interviewed individually, they all recalled the odd Picasso hoisted on the truck.

At the New York end, anything was possible. The mob has long infiltrated the trucking business and the loading/unloading unions, and thefts are routine. This one, however, didn't have mob fingerprints on it. For one, the gangsters would have cleaned out the entire truck, not picked out the single item that was the most difficult to handle and hardest to fence. From an aesthetic standpoint, the goombah crowd would have no doubt blanched at a disembodied Picasso with the nose going one way, the mouth going the other, and three toes on the right foot. They would have deemed it junk and picked something more traditional to steal. (The image of this one in particular was in such disarray anatomically speaking, it was hard to make out where the so called 'purple hat' sat, or even the location of the man's out-of-kilter head.)

Another factor was the timing. This theft occurred a few years before the Picasso explosion, and the eccentric artist had indeed been extremely prolific. Picassos were everywhere, especially in New York. To the uninitiated, they were a dime a dozen.

Some reports speculated that the painting somehow made it to the trucking company's storage facility in East Harlem, and was taken from there. I wasn't buying it. If there was a six-foot Picasso roaming around New York City, my alter egos Robert Steele or Thomas Bishop would have been the first to hear about it. Yet nobody, from one end of the world-renowned Manhattan art spectrum to the other, knew a thing about this painting. And these were the precise people who'd have advance knowledge of what such a painting would soon be worth.

Further, the unsealing had taken place in the presence of the owner and other gallery officials. The purple-hatted one obviously was gone before that truck rolled into town. Even the always-suspect New York loaders insisted as much with genuine emotion.

No, my instincts told me that this baby was taken in Houston, and remained in Texas. One of those bored, egomaniac Texas oilmen, or an Enron/WorldCom/Tyco-type corporate embezzler had gotten wind of the Jasper's closing and hired some top professionals to make sure the Picasso never left town.

Certain as I was, I couldn't prove it and therefore had to work the case by the book. I put the word out on the street that Thomas Bishop was in the market for a big purple Picasso and waited for my phone to ring. Nothing. Dead silence. I sent out memos to all 50-

plus FBI field offices around America and the world. *Nada*. I wired Interpol and told them the Purple Picasso might be heading home to France or Spain. Zipola. I reached out to virtually every Picasso expert, dealer, and collector on the planet. Nobody knew anything.

All of which solidified my belief that this one was 'stolen to order.' Somebody wanted it. Somebody got it. And that somebody's still got it. It's probably hanging in a crusty rich guy's house down in Texas, and has been all this time. Thousands of his friends, acquaintances, and party attendees have gazed at it, and either didn't know it was stolen, or wouldn't think to rat the powerful old goat out.

Such a scenario is more common than one might think. A doctor in Florida proudly displays Robert Henri's *Portrait of Anne* on his living room wall. I know it's stolen. He knows it's stolen. His pals at the country club know it. But I was unable to grab it back because it would have compromised the life of a valued informant. We had to let it slide. (Henri was a 19th and 20th century American realist best known for city scenes and landscapes. His paintings can sell for as much as $4 million.)

In another instance, FBI agents raiding the modest Mount Vernon, New York home of an Italian loan shark were shocked to discover a half dozen $250,000 to $1 million paintings on his walls. They had all been stolen from Madison Avenue galleries, and were used to pay business and gambling debts. The guy had a Renoir, a Monet, a Cassatt, and a Georges Rouault among them. Incredible.

Dead as the Picasso trail was, there were a few blips on the radar over the years. While working another case, I came across some unrelated information that caught my eye. Irish mobster Danny Kohl, a vicious cokehead who terrorised the area around Third Avenue and 70th Street, was known to have an affinity for art and antiques. An informant told me that Kohl had a warehouse in Houston where he stashed the goods he stole in New York to let them cool off. His partner in Houston was a man whose son had freaked out on a New York subway and made headlines for brawling with transit cops. That was an interesting connection. A New York gangster with an eye for art who had an associate in Houston? Unfortunately, all I had was circumstantial evidence and putting two and two together, which wasn't enough to bring Kohl in.

Kohl did, however, have a pet parrot. I briefly considered kidnapping the bird to see if it would talk. Probably not such a good idea, I concluded.

As mentioned in Chapter 2, Rembrandt thief Johnny Rio said on an undercover tape that he knew about a stolen Picasso, but clammed up after his arrest.

Other than these drips and drabs, there was nothing. The Purple Picasso has been a thorn in my side ever since. In magazine and newspaper stories about my career, I'm often compared to Inspector Javert of *Les Misérables*, doggedly hunting the painting like the obsessive Javert tracked poor Jean Valjean. I relish the comparison and eventually hope I have the same luck Javert did.

Another sticking point is that I've kept track over the years of the increasing values of all the art I recovered in my career. The figure has recently exceeded $300 million. Nice number, but it doesn't have the same ring as a half billion. The Picasso alone could push me within reach.

Although I'm now retired from the FBI and labouring as a criminal defence attorney and art theft consultant, I continue to beat the bushes and work my informants regarding the Picasso and other cold cases. (If anybody has a lead, feel free to call my co-author Dary Matera at 602-351-8684. You can also e-mail him at dary@darymatera.com.)

That 'Purple Picasso', now worth as much as $25–$100 million, is somewhere out there. People have most assuredly seen it. It'll turn up eventually. Paintings have vanished for centuries, only to suddenly reappear and continue their dramatic lives.

For example, there was this Tintoretto stolen by Russian soldiers during World War II.

. 5 .

THE RUSSIANS ARE COMING FOR TINTORETTO

*D*ATING BACK TO when the first cavemen drew pictures on their rock walls, art has always been one of the main spoils of war. Vast artistic treasures of various civilisations throughout history have either been destroyed, ruined through neglect and improper handling, or carted off to points unknown by opportunistic soldiers, officers, and looters.

The few that survive can show up anywhere, anytime, often travelling great distances and resurfacing centuries later.

Recovering *Raiders of the Lost Ark*–style ancient treasures can be one of the most satisfying aspects of the art detective trade.

In January 1945, the Germans were being squeezed by the Americans from the west and the Russians from the east. World War II was coming to a close, and the looting of Hitler's nation had already begun. The Russians alone are believed to have taken more than 100,000 works of art (a good measure of which the Germans had stolen themselves), and had specific regiments designed to do just that.

After Dresden, Germany was virtually incinerated by a massive air raid that killed some 130,000, the Russian army poured into the smoking ruins and began helping themselves to whatever valuables they could find. Despite its historical stature, the damaged Dresden Museum was not spared the indignity of being treated like a Wal-Mart abandoned in a Louisiana hurricane. Among the hundreds of items snatched from its shelves, walls, and display cases was a 3-by-5-foot religious painting created by 16th century Venetian Renaissance master Jacopo Robusti Tintoretto entitled *The Holy Family with St Catherine and Honoured Donor*.

St Catherine was a 14th century nun and nurse from Siena and Rome who tended to the sick and who was believed to have had many celestial visitations. She is known for her channelled visions of Hell, Purgatory, and Heaven, and experienced 'familiar conversations with Christ' before becoming his 'bride'. She is the patron saint of fire-fighters and nurses, among others.

The fact that the bearded 'honoured donor' had actually commissioned the work, altering the time-space continuum by plugging himself in historically with Jesus and the two saints like the Academy Awards host Billy Crystal used to do with Oscar-nominated movies, has not detracted from the painting's popularity.

Tintoretto's mostly Biblical and mythological scenes, like those of his upper level 16th century peers in France, Spain, and Holland, have seen their value soar into the millions. Part of that is due to the Italian artist having been a student of the esteemed Venetian grand master Vecellio Titian, whose *Venus with a Mirror* was sold in the Depression year of 1931 for an astounding $12 million.

The Holy Family, worth a few hundred thousand at the time of its inglorious theft, would increase in value tenfold during its long sojourn underground.

As with so many other stolen paintings throughout history, the religious implications didn't dissuade the thieves one iota. Yet in this instance, those same implications played a major role in the painting's history from that point on. It's not known whether the Russian officer who took it in Dresden was Jewish, or if he sold it to a Jew, but Tintoretto's *Holy Family* joined the exodus to the new nation of Israel in 1948. It kicked around there, off the radar, as its owners found it difficult to sell a painting glorifying the birth of Jesus in an embryonic Jewish nation where everybody was starting from scratch, and there wasn't a great deal of disposable income to be spent on something as frivolous as Catholic-inspired art.

The painting nevertheless remained in Israel for most of the next 30 years. However many hands it passed through during that period, if any, is a mystery. What's known is that its then owner decided to try his luck overseas in a wealthy capitalistic nation filled with Catholics, Protestants, and other Christians. He contracted with a 42-year-old Russian Jewish antique broker named Rajmond Vinokur to market it in the United States.

Shortly after arriving in New York, Vinokur began spreading the word that he had a million-dollar painting to sell. Among those who got wind was an informant of Special Agent Jerry Lang, a fellow St Francis College alumnus who had followed the same career path as I had. Agent Lang immediately contacted me. I checked my art guides and manuals and was thrilled to match the Russian's story of a Tintoretto stolen during World War II with historic records confirming such a theft. Could this be the real thing?

Two days later, I shed the conservative FBI uniform and crawled into the far hipper threads of Thomas Bishop, complete with a vest, silk tie, and faux diamond pinky ring that was as phoney as Bishop himself. I gathered up my lighted magnifying glass, black light wand, and borrowed a portable X-ray machine from the bomb squad.

The introduction was set for 13 December 1976, which happened to be my 36th birthday. I was to rendezvous with the Russian at 8pm inside a specified room at the Westbury Hotel on Madison

Avenue and 69th Street, across from the more famous Carlyle Hotel. A second agent, posing as a fence and carrying whatever we were fabricating as cash, would already be in position when I arrived. Downstairs waiting in cars, or strolling around the lobby trying to blend in, was a crew of special agents that would be called in to make the arrests.

The Russian self-appraised the painting at $1.5 million. He was willing to let go of it for the special rate of $250,000, which was actually $100,000 more than the normal 10% fencing fee for stolen property. We didn't quibble with the inflated price because this was going to be a 'bait and grab,' meaning as soon as the goods were verified, we'd signal for the 'cavalry' to take us all down. We could do it this way because once the painting was in the room with us, we were in control.

I went in with the standard Nagra body wrap wire, the Swiss recording device seen in all the movies. My secondary assignment was to get the Russian to incriminate himself by admitting the painting was stolen. That was critical because of the decades that had passed, and the multitude of international borders it had crossed. I was also going to try to get Rajmond to talk about the painting's history to make absolutely certain this was the Tintoretto in question.

A slender man with a heavy Russian/Jewish accent met me at the door. He was about 5-foot-7, with modish brown hair hanging over an animated face. Totally unthreatening, he looked like any number of non-Orthodox Jewish merchants who populated New York's diamond district, many of whom also hailed from Russia, Germany, Israel, or other parts of Europe. I noted that his clothing was a bit off in the humorous Eastern European style of a man trying to be hip, but not quite getting it right. His tie was too wide, and his chequered jacket was a shade or two overly bright.

I nodded to my fellow agent and walked inside. After exchanging greetings, we got down to business. The Tintoretto was propped on the couch covered by a brown sheet. I wasn't expecting much because the photographs in the book made the painting seem rather bland and uninspired. In person, however, it proved to be one of the most magnificent works of art I'd ever seen. *The Holy Family* was glowing to a degree that made this former Irish Catholic altar boy well up with unexpected emotion. I nearly lost it, which would have been bad form since the rule is you never rave over something you're trying to get for a lower price from a thief.

Regaining my composure, I began a preliminary review. The wide, rectangular painting was in remarkable shape for its age and turbulent history, a condition that would bear out under more intensive inspection. Tintoretto is noted for muted cranberry reds, and there it was, right in front of my naked eye: St Catherine herself was draped in a robe of precisely that hue. I felt like an ornithologist seeing a rare serpent-eagle in the wild for the first time.

Reaching into my bag, I withdrew the black light wand, searched for a plug, then took a deep breath. A chilling sidelight to clandestine art exchanges is that much of the preliminary scrutiny has to be performed in the dark. No other undercover operation forces its operatives to work under such dangerous conditions. Killing the lights in a room with a potentially armed international thief sniffing at what he thinks is an attaché case packed with $250,000 is as dangerous a high wire act as the undercover profession can offer. Not only that, I'm completely vulnerable while going about my intricate inspections. A lamp could be seconds away from splintering shards of glass into the back of my head, and I wouldn't notice. That's why it was vital to have a second agent in the room covering my back. It's a luxury that can't always be arranged, but it's sure comforting when it's there.

After locating an electrical outlet, I proceeded to go through the actions of searching for evidence of the fluorescing cadmium greens, azurite blues, and other elements used in the paints of that era.

The unsigned Tintoretto revealed everything I expected of a 600-year-old masterpiece. There was evidence of multiple repairs and restorations over the centuries done with increasingly modern paints and styles—something that is nearly impossible to fake because of the chemical time stamping involved. A talented artist can duplicate the imagery, but it's nearly impossible to fake the ancient paint composition, the canvas preparation, and half a millennium of restoration work. It's not like rubbing your blue jeans in the dirt and putting them through the washer a half dozen times to give them that stylish worn look. Some forgers attempt to cook authenticity into a fake by sticking it in a pizza oven for a while, but those schemes are both literally and figuratively half-baked.

Equally hard to duplicate are the myriad tiny scratches and rips, the standard craquelure (a fancy way of saying spider web cracks), a skilful pattern of chiaroscuro (diversified light shading and use of shadows), the appropriate age specific undercoating, water stains, and blistering, which were few in this instance.

The thickness of the paint was also a consideration. Tintoretto preferred thin, smooth coats, unlike Rembrandt's lavish cake icing style. Individual brushstrokes can be akin to a master's fingerprints. Some artists, like Raphael, Michelangelo, and Leonardo da Vinci, were left-handed and the difference is dramatically noticeable. An expert additionally looks for embedded brush hairs. The old masters used mostly stiff badger hair as opposed to the synthetic fibres of today.

If the wood in the panels, original backing materials, or framing came from Home Depot last week, that's not a good indication. The wood has to have aged in conjunction with the paint and canvas. Amateur inspectors often overlook things like the nails in the joints as well. One wouldn't expect to see, say, a coloured thumbtack back there. You'd be surprised how many otherwise brilliant forgers make the mistake of securing a canvas by hammering in a tiny nail from the local Ace Hardware.

For most of my career, I relied upon an expert restorer with a state-of-the-art lab in New York to school me on these subtleties. The guy, who wasn't opposed to shady dealings himself, was the most knowledgeable, hands-on expert I'd ever met.

Moving along, I took out an official appraisal form modelled after the ones used by the Metropolitan Museum of Art, and filled in the standard information: artist; title; description; media; signature; origin; date of origin; size (height, width, depth, diameter); frame; source; notes; location; accession number (if applicable); negative number (if applicable); and appraisal value.

Everything was copacetic. The painting came up sevens on so many levels I decided to bag the X-ray machine. They're a pain in the butt to set up and operate, and we were going to confiscate the work anyway, so it wasn't critical to dig that deep below the surface. Instead, I did a final scope with a jeweller's loupe—a strong, half-dollar-sized magnifying glass that pops out of a protective leather sheath like a switchblade knife. Following that, I closed the curtain on the show. It was now 8.45pm.

Turning back to the patient Rajmond, I informed him that things were looking good, but I needed to confirm the background and history. This was designed to set the legal hook, but it's not uncommon for a legitimate buyer to request this information.

Unfortunately, it's not uncommon for a savvy seller to be spooked by such questions. I kept casually pounding away until he finally warmed and cautioned that the painting could be sold, 'but not very publicly.' It was best to keep a low profile, he added, because it had been taken during the war, and although the statutes of limitations had long expired, 'there are different laws pertaining to different artists.'

That was news to me. I'd never heard of a Renoir Law, a Rembrandt Law, a Vermeer Law, or anything remotely similar. I suspected he was referring the varying art-theft laws established by different countries, and the fact that some nations were especially protective of their native artists.

Peppering him with questions, I was eventually able to get him to confirm the historical account of well-known Russian General Georgy Zhukov ordering his men to loot the Dresden Museum. Bingo. Rajmond was toast. (Or so I thought.)

Just as I was ready to summon the troops, Rajmond mentioned that he had some other paintings taken from the Dresden as well. That stopped me cold for a moment as I considered if we should hold off and work this new angle, or grab the bird in hand. I asked him who and what, but he wouldn't elaborate, indicating that they were still in Russia and might be difficult to get out of the country. No surprise there. There were thousands still in Russia.

Instead, he expanded on the history of the Tintoretto, saying it had spent some time in Vienna, and had even been in New York in 1974 while in possession of a diplomat assigned to the United Nations. In between, it was almost sold to a famous musician in Israel who he wouldn't identify despite my natural curiosity.

I glanced at the other agent to see if he felt it was a wrap. He nodded ever so slightly. The arrangement was that when we were ready, he'd call room service for some snacks. Before I could give the okay, Rajmond dropped another bomb. A bit perturbed that I questioned the care and condition of some aspects of the Tintoretto, he mentioned that he had an etching of Jesus by Albrecht Dürer taken from the Bremen Museum that contained the same natural age flaws. That really caught my attention. In a book I'd read about the looting of Germany after World War II, it mentioned that a soldier had traded Dürer's *Christ Child Enthroned* for a pair of boots. Could this be the same work? (Dürer was a 16th century German craftsman whose etchings, engravings, and woodcuttings sell for up to $300,000 today.)

My head was spinning. Should I let Rajmond walk with the Tintoretto and go for the whole enchilada, or stick to the plan? Reason prevailed and I decided to proceed with the bust. Since the other paintings were overseas, it would be too elaborate and time-consuming a process to wait. Plus, it might be possible to squeeze Rajmond for more information after the arrest.

'Let's order something to eat,' I said. The specific food requested in the call to the waiting agents was the signal that it was yeah or nay. Since most hotels are set up so that punching a single number connects guests to the kitchen, I had to distract Rajmond a bit so my partner could beep seven times to drop the dime.

Ten minutes later, there was a knock at the door. 'Must be room service,' the other agent said, walking over to let the waiter in. Instead of an assortment of hors d'oeuvres, in came Jerry Lang and the Feds, guns drawn, IDs dangling from their necks. They pushed us against the wall, spread us out, and did the pat down. When my fondler discovered my weapon, he loudly announced it to the others. 'This guy has a gun!' That raised the intensity level. My partner's .38 was withdrawn as well. Rajmond, the only true bad guy in the room, wasn't holding.

The budding actor tossing me ignored my Nagra set-up. I was glad he didn't lose himself in the performance and shout 'Hey, this guy's wired!'

We were cuffed and marched through the hotel like a bunch of Mafia goons. Oddly enough, I was never embarrassed when playing these scenes. I guess I've lived in New York too long, but it's almost a badge of honour to parade around in the silver bracelets while hauled in by the Feds.

The Tintoretto was carefully placed inside a protective cardboard crate designed specifically for fine art captures, and was taken to the evidence facility at 26th and Federal Plaza. The supervisor, Lynn Shorski, was especially adept at taking care of the immensely valuable contraband I was known to bring in. We often joked about sneaking one out and running off to the Bahamas together. If only it wasn't an idle dream.

Back at the hotel, we were shoved into separate cars and driven off. Everyone stayed in character until the cars had long left the scene. Rajmond may have had somebody watching the lobby and entrance, and we didn't want to tip our hand. Many an undercover bust has been compromised by the law enforcement agents showing their cards too soon by releasing their man and glad-handing in public view.

I was eventually unchained down the street, and the appropriate high fives and 'attaboys' commenced. It appeared to be an open and shut case. We had the painting, and we had Rajmond on tape admitting it was stolen.

It turned out that the tense takedown was the easy part. Once the case was sent to the prosecutors, there was one snag after another. Rajmond's heavy accent fuzzed his confession. The tape was sent to the lab in DC, where sound technicians were able to pull it out more clearly.

The next hurdle was trying to penetrate the Iron Curtain and get the East Germans to confirm that the painting was theirs, and that it was indeed stolen. Trouble was, this was in the midst of the Cold War, and the East Germans weren't cooperating. America had been banging on them for juicing up their Olympic athletes, turning their women into man-beasts among other travesties, and they were indignant.

We were also mad at the Russians for invading Afghanistan and turning 'freedom fighters' like Osama bin Laden into sainted Muslim heroes. (As if that wouldn't have any future consequences.) We boycotted the Moscow Olympics, and they boycotted the Los Angeles Olympics, and everybody pretty much hated each other's guts and wouldn't cooperate for love, money, or Tintorettos.

Adding ice to the cooler was the fact that the East Germans were under the oppressive thumb of the Russians, so nobody could express rage or feel violated over the callousness of the original theft. The Russians were violating the rights and possessions of the East Germans on a daily basis. The Tintoretto theft was no big deal.

That left us with an alleged criminal and the evidence, but no victim. The adroit prosecutors said not to worry, that there was more than one way to skin a wild and crazy Israeli cat. They'd nail him on a United States Customs violation of bringing in a stolen painting without declaring it.

Except Rajmond had declared it! The little goofball had waltzed right up and announced he was 'coming on through' with a rare

Tintoretto. All the papers were in order and nobody at customs raised an eyebrow.

With things starting to go his way, Rajmond wisely zipped it. So tight, in fact, he suddenly lost all ability to speak or understand English, Russian, Hebrew, or Yiddish. The parade of translators we brought in somehow spoke the wrong language or vernacular. Apparently, Rajmond hailed from a Jewish corner of the Soviet Union populated by 12 people, and only four of them knew his specific dialect. Oy vey! Regrouping, Assistant US Attorney Susan Campbell noticed that Rajmond grossly undervalued the painting when he declared it, designating it as 'household goods'. That left us with the weak, but still applicable charge of making a false statement to a US Customs agent. Rajmond pleaded guilty and was told to beat it back to Israel.

It got worse. After stalling, wringing our hands, and wrangling with the unpleasant Russians and East Germans, the FBI eventually had to give *The Holy Family* back to Rajmond's partner, the Israeli who claimed ownership. He appeared in New York and snatched that thing quick as a flash.

Only in the art world.

As an interesting aside, the Russians weren't the only allied forces helping themselves to German artefacts at the end of World War II. American army officer Joe Tom Meador grabbed The Quedlinburg Treasures, a bevy of gold, silver, and bejewelled medieval artworks owned by a Christian cathedral in the storybook Harz Mountain community. Stubbornly clinging to the international law of 'finders keepers,' Meador, a gay Texan, used the 20-plus items, worth up to $200 million, for little more than a lure to seduce curious young boy-toy lovers. His heirs eventually sold some of them back to Germany for a cool $2.75 million in 1990, a transaction that had many in government, law enforcement, and legal circles gnashing their teeth over the implications. The church sued for the rest, and most were subsequently returned in a civil settlement.

.6.

PICASSO CHECKS INTO THE MOTEL MONET

*S*TUFFY AS THE high-end fine art business can be, art itself is something that reaches out to everybody. Whether one lords over a mansion, or gets by in a worn-out trailer, the odds are that there will be something hanging on the walls. It doesn't matter if it's a priceless da Vinci, or a bowl of fruit painted by numbers, it still qualifies as art.

Check into the most expensive hotel in town, or crash at the cheapest motel available, and the situation is invariably the same. Something's on the wall.

In the previous chapters, the criminals, both skilled and unskilled, hit galleries or museums. The loss hurts, but as the prophet Nathan told King David regarding his adultery with Bathsheba, a sheep snatched from a flock of a thousand isn't the same as a lamb taken from a family that has only one and treats it like a pet.

Thieves, of course, rarely share such sentimentality. They'll steal from anybody, anytime, without regard to the pain they cause or the consequences of their actions. To them, a sheep's a sheep, beloved pet or one of a million. All they care about is devouring it—i.e., turning it into cash.

In any given year, there are likely to be more thefts of valuable art from private homes than from galleries and museums. These can be the most painful cases of all.

Granted, in some instances, wealthy private collectors have turned their homes into virtual museums, filling every spot on the wall with astounding collections. Even so, these obsessive collectors usually have an emotional connection to every work of art they've purchased. They bleed just as crimson red when one or more are taken.

Considering the above, it's not surprising that the largest art theft in Long Island, New York, history was not from a gallery or museum, but from a private home. On 13 April 1982, three masked men armed with guns and knives charged into the Sands Point estate of garment manufacturer James Howley and his wife, Coty Award–winning fashion designer, Tina Leser, an innovator of tropical coloured playsuits for women that came into vogue in the 1940s. The power couple weren't home at the time of the break-in, leaving their pretty Ecuadorian maid to experience the horror of being accosted at gunpoint, bound and gagged.

The crooks knew exactly what they wanted, and where to go to get it. They proceeded to ignore the offerings in the museum-like mansion and ventured up into to the attic where the overflow was stored. They made away with 24 paintings and other works of art worth nearly $4 million then, and 10 to 20 times that today.

The two prize catches in the score were Picasso's *La Dame a la Toilette*, and Monet's *Chateau Villa*. As outlined in Chapter 4, Picassos were on the verge of exploding in value, selling for as much as $50 million just seven years later in 1989. In 2004, one topped $100 million.

This doesn't mean *La Dame a la Toilette* is remotely that valuable. Paintings, to a lesser degree, are like songs. Some are hits worth millions, while others are just album fillers that can be purchased for thousands instead of millions. Still, unlike songs, a once-forgotten painting can suddenly bring in $20 million at auction without any seeming rhyme or reason. It's often more about the artist than the image.

In this instance, Picasso's dame wasn't even what one might expect from the odd painter. It was a conventional portrait, meaning the lady's eyes, nose, and lips were all in the right proportion.

At the time, it was actually Howley's Monet that was considered to be the more valuable. Harder to come by, and held tightly by museums and governments, the works of the 19th and early 20th century French master were already selling for as much as $2 million in the late 1960s, and have surpassed $10 million in the new millenium.

Claude Monet was a trailblazer of the 19th century Impressionist movement that used splashes of colour rather than distinct lines to create images. In layman's terms, it's kind of a dabbed-on style that isn't as sharply focused as other techniques. Monet is best known for vivid landscapes, and for the occasional portrait. He explored how nature's hues and tones changed over the course of the day, and how they are further altered by weather and atmospheric conditions. For example, slate-tinged overcast skies tend to bring out grey streaks in peoples' hair that aren't noticeable in the bright yellow sun or under soft evening lights. Along this same vein, eyes rimmed or flecked with gold look especially sparkling at dusk.

Monet's vision faded badly over the years, but the once-suicidal Frenchman refused to allow the handicap to still his brushes. The resulting paintings are even more 'misty' as he termed it, than those of the Impressionist style he helped pioneer.

Also in the stolen batch were some paintings by Maurice Utrillo, a 20th century French artist noted for capturing everyday scenes in and around Paris. His best works go for the mid six figures, and are notorious for being widely faked.

The Howley / Leser theft concerned the Nassau County police and the FBI on many levels. The violent nature of the crime spoke of a dangerous gang that probably wasn't specific to art theft. These were no stealthy cat burglars. They were armed robbers who were just as likely to rob a bank the following week—and shoot a cop in the process. They needed to be hunted down, tagged, and caged, ASAP.

As I expected, the trio of thugs weren't wired into the art world, nor were they working for a rich Machiavellian collector or a business rival of Howley or Leser. Those folks wouldn't be associated with a knife-wielding gang. Word soon flooded the streets that they were ready to wrangle. This told me what I had already suspected— we were dealing with yet another band of low-life cretins with no clue how to fence their tremendous score.

At least one of them, however, had known what they were after, and now knew what he or she wanted for it. Relying upon the newspaper accounts of the total $4 million value, they were looking for a fencing rate of 12.5%, about $480,000. Since there was no way the local police were going to give us that kind of flash money, this had the makings of a long and drawn out battle.

The Nassau County cops brought me into the case when they were contacted, strangely enough, by a New Orleans police detective with a wild story. He had an informant who had been contacted by the thieves. Apparently, the impatient gang thought there was too much publicity and heat to try and cash out quickly in New York, so they started going through their criminal Rolodexes looking for contacts in other states. Somebody knew somebody down in 'Nawlins', and the next thing we knew, a Cajun-flavoured Crocodile Dundee–type was flying to New York.

The ambitious Louisiana cop insisted on handling the case himself, and set it up so that the boys in Nassau had no option but to play along and let him call the shots. The thieves were expecting a rich, good ol' boy art collector from bayou country, and those types are in short supply on Long Island. Regardless, the detective's source was controlling the flow of information, which meant Nassau was cornered.

The determined detective was smart enough to realise that he needed an art expert with him to set the hook. I was the natural choice not only because of my expertise, but because my brother Frank was a Nassau County police officer and I'd previously worked with the department on a number of cases, including a kidnapping. They reached out to me and I quickly signed on, figuring at the very least, this would be an adventure.

I met the New Orleans detective at Kennedy Airport because my office was closer than the Nassau Police headquarters, and I wanted to size him up before the others got involved. He and I would be on the front lines, and I needed to know what he was made of. As far as I could tell, it was Cajun spiced snails and puppy dog tails because this was one tough, gnarly, and extremely interesting fellow. Decked in a brown suit the shade of a river after a hard night's rain, he reached out his hand and offered a greeting in a language I strained to comprehend.

Of all the diverse cultures in America, Louisiana Cajuns are some of the most distinctive people you'll ever come across. Heavily influenced by the French who populated the area, they are equally born and bred of the Deep South. Think of a shrewd, cultured Frenchman mixed with a wily Mississippi redneck, then give him an English dialect that sounds like some kind of foreign tongue, and you have a Cajun. Tarzan would not have been more out-of-place in New York than this guy.

An avid outdoorsman (is there any other type of Cajun?) the wiry, curly haired detective had a fit, muscular body honed by hauling bass and catfish, into his skiff, hunting bullfrogs, and bashing gators to keep them from stealing the bass, catfish and frogs. His legs were strong and nimble, no doubt from chasing quail and pheasant over hill and swampy dale. The guy was a hoot and I liked him right off. Within minutes, he was inviting me down South to go huntin' and fishin' with him.

My new partner was also a damn good cop who was no stranger to undercover work. He didn't appear to be the type to be rattled by the unexpected twists and turns that invariably pop up in such dangerous activities.

We formulated a basic plan on how we'd play the bad boys, and discovered that we were on the same page. The Nassau cops suggested that we hold the sit-downs inside the John Peel Room of the Island Inn, Carle Place, Long Island. The restaurant was one of the most popular places in the area, and was the kind of place frequented by everybody from police chiefs to mob bosses. Whatever you were, whichever side of the fence you were on, you'd feel at home in the John Peel Room.

The Cajun's informant relayed our preferences, and the crooks readily agreed. We booked a room there, then had a war meeting the night before with the Nassau cops at their headquarters to work out the details. I paid close attention to each speaker because I was the only FBI agent in the bunch, and therefore needed to reach a quick comfort level with my new team-mates.

I was thoroughly impressed with Nassau's initiative and operation. The squad, headed by Detective Inspector John McGowan and Detective Sergeant John Rinaldi, were set to replace many of the Island Inn's staff with their own officers. The front desk man, waiters, maids, bellhops, even some of the guests wandering about would be moonlighting members of Nassau's finest. Our room was being wired at that very moment in case we withdrew to do some business there. Monitoring vans were to be stationed on the premises.

On the downside, the Nassau cops insisted there would be no flash money. Not a dime. They either had a regulation about it, had been burned in a deal, or were suffering from the ABSCAM fallout. Having worked the initial stages of ABSCAM (see Chapter 3), I knew well the congressional heat that was coming down on police departments nationwide. The FBI's ABSCAM sting had embarrassed the US Senate and House of Representatives, and they were wasting no time making new laws ham-stringing such operations. Congress' biggest weapon was to crack down on the use of cash to lure otherwise 'honest citizens' like themselves into committing crimes. Both the Cajun and I felt this was a crock, but we agreed to fish with the bait on hand.

The preliminary meet was scheduled for the next morning at breakfast. The Peel Room set out a nice buffet spread, and was known to attract a solid crowd of morning people. Some wolfed down their bacon, eggs, and hash browns, then rushed off to work, while others dined at a slower, more leisurely pace. The hustle and bustle was just the atmosphere we needed to mask any tension that might arise in a first encounter.

The Cajun and I made for an interesting contrast. He was looking the Bourbon Street Dandy part in another brown suit over a sports shirt that actually had a fish pattern on it. I was in my hip New York art scene threads. Neither of us came across remotely like a cop. We both, however, were packing very unfashionable government-issued firearms.

After waiting a few minutes, we decided to hit the buffet. Often, a mark won't even show, having been spooked by clumsy surveillance officers. If that had happened, we might as well enjoy the food.

We had just returned to the table when we were approached by two men, George Haag and Lester Williams. Haag was a heavy-set dockworker type in his late 50s, about 5-foot-8, wearing a cheap, wrinkled suit with no tie. He spoke with a thick Brooklyn accent, the consequences of which already had my synapses spinning. I was about to do a deadly, cloak and dagger deal with the Ragin' Cajun and Archie Bunker.

Haag's associate, Williams, was totally nondescript. A blank slate, he barely said a word the entire time.

The odd couple, Haag and the Cajun, did most of the talking early on. They got along surprisingly well for such diverse characters. Haag was soon invited to go fishin' and huntin' down in the bayou with us. Somehow, the conversation turned to a hit song of a decade earlier called Amos Moses. Sung by Jerry Reed, the truck driver from the *Smokey and the Bandit* movies, the Creole-influenced tune chronicled the life and times of a one-armed alligator poacher in the Louisiana swamps. We all agreed that we liked the song, liked Jerry Reed, liked Burt Reynolds, liked black 1978 Trans Ams with honeycomb wheels and gold birds on the hood, and liked *Smokey and the Bandit*. We were bonding over the damnedest things.

Our future fishing vacation began to hit a snag when we dropped all the small talk and got down to business. Haag reiterated his 12.5% price and wanted us to show him the money so he could go out and buy a Trans Am with a gold bird on the hood. I countered that we couldn't talk money until I inspected the merchandise. Haag brushed that off and promised that the art had been 'babied'. Neither side brought up the theft. It was too early in the game, and I suspected from experience that the tape in my briefcase was picking up more restaurant noise than conversation. It's a frustrating phenomenon with clandestine recordings that every fork clinking on a plate across the room is captured in vivid clarity, but the guy across from you screaming, 'Okay I admit it. I was the guy on the grassy knoll who shot Kennedy,' comes out slurred.

The breakfast conversation, taped or otherwise, grew increasingly heated. Neither side was budging. I tried to shame Haag and Williams by pointing out that this was an art sale, not a drug deal, and we didn't need to flash no stinkin' cash. He turned it around and said we didn't need to test the potency of the merchandise; that he was vouching for it.

The Cajun jumped in and said, 'I ain't gonna be buyin' no pig in a poke,' a familiar expression now reduced to its original roots. I could tell Archie had no clue what it meant, and explained that a pig in a bag bought unseen might turn out to be skinny or sick, or maybe even a skunk or a rattler. When Haag remained lost, I translated it to a wrapped painting that might be a fake. Haag finally got it, but still refused to show us his pigs. He just kept poking, claiming: 'Dees paintings are da real thing, forgetaboutit.'

After a few more dizzying rounds, Haag threw down his napkin. 'Dat's it. I'm getting' outta here. Forgetaboutdisshit.'

Signalling his lifeless associate, they both stood to leave. The Cajun calmly said he'd have their mutual friend, i.e., his informant, verify the money. Haag groused some more and stormed out.

At that point, I figured the deal was done, but the Cajun insisted the hook was set deep and the fish were still secure on the line. They had merely gotten a glimpse of the boat and had taken out the drag line. A fisherman myself, I knew exactly what he was saying. The lure of a half-million-dollar score was too strong to walk away from.

'They're floppin' onda river bottom,' the Cajun observed. 'My informant, he's a clever critter. He'cn talk the giblets outta a boilin' kettle a jambalaya. Let 'im weave 'is magic and we'cn go attit again.'

Sounded good to me, whatever he said. I knew well that such operations were often wholly dependent upon the skills and connections of the unseen informant. If the Cajun felt his man could repair the damage, it was certainly worth hanging around another day.

Trouble was, much to the chagrin of the Nassau force, I meant that literally. Everything had to be frozen in place. The cops pretending to work at the Inn had to finish their shifts. The guys in the van had to stay in the vans. There couldn't be a sudden massive pullout of vehicles or personnel. We couldn't have a parade of cops cruising in to pick up other cops. The crooks could be watching us as well. We had to stay in character.

I understood the subsequent uproar. Nobody wants to hang around inside a cramped van all day and night with nothing to do, missing dinner with their families, the Little League game their son's pitching, or the dance recital their daughter's performing that evening. That bites. A college educated policewoman with eyes on being a detective didn't want to spend the rest of the day scrubbing toilets and making beds either. It was a lot to ask.

Yet, my instincts told me we were being watched. If we wanted a second chance at busting the biggest art robbery in Long Island history, we were going to have to go stir-crazy in the vans and scrub those toilets.

Arguing our case with a passion, the Cajun and I convinced the Nassau brass to keep everyone in place for another 24 hours.

It wasn't long before some news arrived that pumped life back into the deflated troops. The Cajun's informant had indeed convinced his contacts that he himself had seen the stacks of money brought from New Orleans for the buy. Haag and gang agreed to meet again at the same place the next morning. I complimented the Cajun on his confidence, and the quality of his snitches. It dawned on me that I didn't even know if the mystery man or woman keeping the deal afloat was in New York, or doing all the arranging via long distance calls from New Orleans.

The next morning, I decided we needed to get down to business and not mess around with another breakfast showdown. We arranged to meet the thieves in the lobby. Unless we wanted to stand around like putzes, something had to give.

Archie Bunker and the mute were in quizzically good spirits when they met us. 'All right,' Haag opened. 'I'm convinced youse guys ain't coppers. We're gonna to show you da goods.'

I was too curious to leave well enough alone and let that revelation slide without explanation. Undercover operations are a learn-as-you-go process, so anything I derive from one that might help in another is beneficial. 'What convinced you?' I asked.

'We had da joint under surveillance all day and night. Nuttin' moved in or out. Nuttin' suspicious.'

I knew there was a reason I played hardball with the Nassau squad. I hoped they heard Haag's comments loud and clear. The pullout and restaging they were pushing for would have instantly exposed the sting. One cop shows up in a police cruiser to pick up his buddy or girlfriend, and the whole operation is blown. One maid yanks a walkie talkie out of her white gown and starts whining about picking up her kids, and the jig is up.

Instead, we were now in like Flynn with the skittish crooks. Haag and the mute lumbered to the parking lot, jumped into a beat-up Chevy, and told us to fall in line behind them. The separation enabled me to freely broadcast specific directions as to where we were going.

The Chevy led us on a short trek to the Black's Raceway Inn Motel, a rat hole for degenerate gamblers and hooker liaisons near the Roosevelt Raceway, a decaying harness track that would soon give up the ghost. It looked like the perfect place for a double-cross, an especially disquieting thought because the Cajun and I were now unarmed. Since we were playing on their court, there was a chance that we'd be frisked. The transmitter was hidden away in a secret compartment of my briefcase, so we were clear there.

We pulled right up to the room, got out, and followed Haag and the mute into the dingy room. Two more men were waiting inside, which was good news and bad news. Good news because we now probably had the whole gang corralled. Bad news because it smelled even more like a violent rip-off. Thankfully, we weren't carrying a briefcase packed with $480,000, or things would have surely gotten ugly. The new players were Michael McLaughlin, 50, a short Irishman with a ruddy complexion, and Antonio Anfossi, 43, a typical pointy-shoed gangster wannabe. Haag introduced us, and nobody bothered to pat us down.

Also present in the room, much to my relief, was a whole gallery of fine art. It was everywhere, stacked in piles on the bed, propped up against the walls, on the floor, in the chairs, you name it. The Picasso and Monet were prominently displayed right up front, so I focused my attention on them. Neither were particularly inspiring, in my humble opinion. The Picasso was a portrait, as mentioned, of a pretty lady combing her long dark hair. The Monet was a typical suburban landscape that was a blur of colour splashed behind the small figure of a man ambling along a path. Nice work, but nothing to die over.

McLaughlin began talking up the art and mentioned various characteristics he felt were important. I made a mental note that he was no doubt the gang member with the semblance of art knowledge, and had probably set up the theft. He had to be the one who knew the paintings were in the attic.

That level of sifting would come later. Of immediate concern was performing my light show, signalling the troops, and getting out of that mildew-infested box with all my blood still in my body.

Both the Picasso and the Monet looked legit from my preliminary inspection. I knew enough about those two giants of the trade to tell right off they were on the mark. The Monet included clear signs of the melancholy artist's obsession with authentic time-of-day stamping via the use of light shading.

I fired up the black light wand, but didn't snap the room switch. No way was I wandering around in the dark with these knife-happy thugs. A precision inspection wasn't critical anyway because we were going to round up this motley gang in a matter of minutes.

Addressing McLaughlin, I explained that there were a rash of fake Picassos going around, and that Monets were especially easy to copy because of the artist's dabbing style. He nodded, pretending to be in the know. Truth was, I sensed I could tell him that Monet actually painted with his nose and he'd nod as if he already knew.

The Cajun misread my idle chatter with McLaughlin as giving the final verification. The plan was that I would express my pleasure with a particular painting by exclaiming 'Whoo weeee, a huntin' we will go!' I hadn't remotely come close to uttering that. Nonetheless, the Cajun went out to have a smoke, and promptly signalled the troops. I nearly jumped out of my skin when they suddenly broke down the door and exploded into the cramped place. It was totally unexpected, and I wasn't near ready. We had yet to even count the goods to make sure there were 24. They could have been holding back the Utrillo.

The premature signal reiterated the pitfalls of working with new partners, even if you seem to have gotten along famously during the planning phase. On the other hand, the gang sure couldn't accuse me of setting them up, not by the way I reacted to the dramatic take down.

The frontline SWAT cops threw us against the wall, patted us down, and slapped on the cuffs. I was treated especially harshly and figured the raiding party wasn't given specific instructions as to who was who. Many times, the arresting officers are not briefed on the identities of the undercover agents so they won't cut them any slack and blow their cover. They just sweep everybody into the net and sort the crabs from the tuna down at the station. Having been arrested scores of times, I've been manhandled pretty good over the years. Once, an unknowing officer brutishly ripped my pistol from a concealed strap holster under my beltline and nearly sliced open my stomach.

My Irish art connoisseur buddy Michael McLaughlin was not having much fun either. He was slammed so hard in the early seconds of the fray that the cops knocked him right out of his shoe. He was screaming for them to let him retrieve it. They refused. The hobbling lug was marched through the parking lot, taken to the station, booked, tossed into a cell, then escorted to arraignment—all with one shoe!

Somebody knew enough to stick me with the Cajun in the same paddy wagon, which is always a plus. The rides to the police station can be hairy if the crooks get wise and figure things out. The Cajun and I were eventually set free at the station. Not long afterward, he was back on a jet to his beloved bayou, no doubt eager to start catching crawfish and knocking alligators on the head with a stump, just like Amos Moses.

The gang turned out to be an assortment of wannabe crooks and burned-out blue collar types looking to catch the American Dream via the American Scheme. None were able to even make bail. Archie Bunker Haag claimed to be a law clerk by trade. McLaughlin said he was a computer broker. Anfossi gave his occupation as a freight elevator operator, which sounded like one of those Soprano-ish

Mafia no-show jobs. Williams, ever the silent one, didn't even bother to invent an occupation. They all either took a plea or were convicted at trial, and were given the usual short sentences.

As I suspected, McLaughlin had done some electrical or plumbing work at the Howley house, and spotted the paintings in the attic. Had he quietly burglarised the place instead of blasting in like Jessie James and manhandling the Latin maid—who movingly testified against them—Howley and Leser might not have missed the stash for months or years. That would have enabled McLaughlin's gang to sell them one by one without police interference, maximizing their profits and avoiding nosey Cajun detectives.

During the trials, I was assigned to babysit the Howley maid and ease her into her critical testimony. I was struck by how much she looked like another famous maid, Gloria Olarte, the diminutive Colombian housecleaner-turned-lover of Gambino family mob boss Paulie Castellano.

We had squeezed Olarte and eventually got her to cooperate with us. Among the things we learned was that the macho, killer gangster needed a penile implant so he could have sex with his hot-blooded South American import. The information Olarte provided became moot in 1986 when John Gotti, 'The Dapper Don', blew Castellano away outside Sparks Steak House in Manhattan so Gotti could begin his legendary reign.

After the court proceedings, the Howley/Leser paintings were returned to their delighted owners. It's not known whether the Picasso and Monet were finally put on display, or went right back to the attic.

As for me, I never made it down to Louisiana for that promised fishing trip. Wonder if the offer is still good? I did, however, travel to another alligator hotbed later that same year. Seems there were two Rubens missing in South Florida.

. 7 .

RUBENS' SPRING BREAKOUT IN FLORIDA

I'D BARELY RETURNED from the roundup in Long Island when the news arrived that my G-men counterparts in South Florida had hooked a hot one. They had a plant inside a bizarre cadre of mostly Jewish businessmen in South Florida who were about to launch an elaborate plot to steal $25 million worth of paintings from a sitting duck museum in Farmington, Connecticut.

The gang—Oceanberg's Seven—was preparing to stage a dramatic daylight raid they had been developing for more than three years. The plan was to have a duo of armed robbers burst into the Hill-Stead Museum, hold the curator and elderly tour guides at gunpoint, snatch a load of Monets, Manets, Degases, and Whistlers off the walls, then ransom them to New York's Metropolitan Museum of Art for $7 million. If the museum balked, the cutthroat gang would feed the irreplaceable masterpieces one by one into a shredder, and send the strips to the *New York Times* art critic, until somebody relented.

It was a wild plot, almost too preposterous to believe. Nonetheless, these suntanned Sons of Solomon and their Italian cohorts, no doubt dressed in white shoes and matching belts, were as serious as the Florida humidity.

I had to admit, the scheme did have a strong measure of Hollywood intrigue to it. The chop suey act would certainly be a powerful counter to the standard 'We don't negotiate with kidnappers' stance most governments and museums take. Art aficionados from New York to Peking would die a thousand deaths each time another Manet was shoved into the hungry blades. The rest of the world would be enthralled by the sheer sensationalism.

The special agent handling the case, John Hanlon, was no stranger to sensational events himself. He was busy cleaning up mess after mess in South Florida during the bloody days of the Cocaine Cowboys from Colombia. That was coupled with the very sudden invasion of thousands of *Scarface*-like psychos and hoodlums flushed out of Cuban prisons by Fidel Castro and sent to Florida on thousands of small boats during the botched Mariel Freedom Flotilla.

In the midst of all this, Hanlon was monitoring the progress of Oceanberg's Seven, waiting for the ambitious thieves to put their long-awaited plan into motion. The group of investment brokers, finance counsellors, and motel owners had done their homework, acquiring detailed schematics of the turn of the century neo-colonial museum and its surrounding 150 acres of forest and grasslands. They mapped out the precise locations of the 10 targeted paintings, outlined an escape route, and developed an elaborate method of phoning in their ransom demands from the perceived safety of a foreign country. Yet, despite all this brainpower, none had the courage to participate in the robbery itself. For that, they subcontracted out, hiring a pair of snarling armed robbers to do their dirty work.

For numerous reasons, this kind of risk-management strategy rarely pays dividends in the criminal world. If something goes wrong, the hired guns have no personal allegiance to the rest of the gang and will deal them up to the cops in a heartbeat. If all goes according to plan, the tough guys will think twice about their smaller cut and will invariably turn on their less macho employers.

Add the prospect of being blackmailed by the gunmen years later, robbed by them, or used as a 'Get out of jail free' card the next time any of front men takes a fall, and one begins to understand how the oft-repeated warnings against going 'outside the circle' are well advised.

In this instance, the gang fell into an even more biting trap. They unknowingly included Special Agent Hanlon in the job interviews for the leader and chief recruiter of the outsourced gunmen.

Not very astute.

Tipped that they were seeking gunslingers, Hanlon had an informant set up a meeting in a hotel so he could audition for the role. One of the Jewish recruiters sensed something wrong, pulled a gun, and accused Hanlon of being a cop. Staying calm, Hanlon denied that he was a good guy, went to a drawer, removed a Mac-10 submachine gun pistol he'd confiscated from a drug dealer, and told the recruiters that this was the weapon he would use to take down the museum. They were so impressed with the 1,100-rounds-per-minute, 30 shot clip .45ACP, and Hanlon's grandiose plans, that they forgot about their earlier suspicions and signed him up.

The Florida and Connecticut Feds now had things completely under control, alerting the museum that the hit was scheduled for 4 August. The tour guides and other staffers were going to be replaced by special agents. Everything was set. The rabbits would be snared in progress.

Then, without warning, the gang threw a last-minute wrench into the mix. To help finance the operation, they wanted to sell a pair of ancient paintings a few of their members had already stolen in an unspecified prior heist. The pair of 'million-dollar babies' were just that, two elaborate religious scenes containing the baby Jesus alleged to have been painted by Flemish master Peter Paul Rubens.

I was told to get Thomas Bishop ready. The inspection and exchange would be in Hartford, Connecticut, the staging area for the pending raid on the Hill-Stead Museum.

Just as I was about to head for the airport, the plan changed course yet again. One of the Italians controlling the paintings had agoraphobia and was afraid to fly. The meet would have to be on his home turf in Fort Lauderdale.

Have black light, will travel. I changed into Thomas Bishop's tropical summer wear, a nifty blue suit with half-inch chalk-white stripes, accented by a fake Rolex, a fake diamond pinky ring, a real $200 Mont Blanc pen, a gold-plated, engraved business card holder, and a buttery soft pair of genuine $500 Gucci loafers. I bought the shoes at a steep discount while working an international murder case in which the suspect wore a special brand of Gucci shoes sold only in Italy. It was an O. J. Simpson kind of thing.

The employee who rang up the transaction had been transferred to New York. He didn't remember the buyer, but offered to assist my undercover career by selling me a similar pair for a mere $100.

Decked out, I caught a flight to the famed Spring Break capital of the world. On the way, I re-familiarised myself with the works of one Peter Paul Rubens, my 17th century pal from the ABSCAM case. Rubens was proving to be a favourite among thieves. So many of his works appeared on the worldwide stolen painting registries that I couldn't get a bead on which ones these might be. The frenzy had been kicked off two years earlier when another Biblically inspired Rubens, *Samson and Delilah*, broke the bank in London for $5.3 million. The Rubens hysteria was destined to continue unabated into the new millennium. *The Massacre of the Innocents* rang up $76.7 million in 2002.

Operating under a twisted version of the old adage that a Rubens in hand was more valuable to recover than a museum full of Degases in a bush, the operation naturally shifted gears to what had been stolen rather than what might be.

Hanlon's team met me at the airport and briefed me on the way to the nearby Marriott hotel. In typical fashion, I'd be hitting the ground running. Skimpy information was doled out on a 'need to know' basis. From what I could gather, I'd be meeting the gang's representatives in the lobby of the hotel, and then we'd go to my room to inspect the paintings. The place was wired and waiting. A squad of agents would be in the adjacent room monitoring the proceedings.

The hotel featured those inside connecting doors designed to give bigger families or groups easy access to each other in separate quarters. My particular passageway would be locked on the agent's side as if there was no connection between me and the neighbouring guests. Additional agents would be scattered inside and outside the buildings.

It sounded workable to me. What none of us caught at the time was that we'd totally overlooked one of the most critical aspects of an undercover operation—one that nearly proved to be our undoing.

Blissfully unaware that there was a giant chink in my armour, I was dropped off out front and proceeded to loiter around the lobby until I was contacted by the gang. They had been given a description of my dapper self by other undercover agents, and noted that I would be carrying an art book.

I was perusing the pages when a short, paunchy man in a Hawaiian shirt, blue slacks, and light suit jacket approached. He introduced himself as Philip Shapiro of nearby Lauderhill. Right off, he began apologizing: 'My people have not yet arrived.'

In previous conversations with the undercover agents, Shapiro had indicated that 'his people' were the guys who had originally 'boosted' the paintings.

His people, whomever they were, had led me on a wild goose chase from Hartford to Fort Lauderdale, and I was worn out. He apologised again and blamed it on the 'Big Guy', the fear-of-flying Italian. I complained that the August heat and relentless Florida humidity had clobbered me like a steam bath, and I'd use the extra time to freshen up in my room.

Doing exactly that, I showered, shaved, changed into a dry shirt, then put the damp striped suit back on. I didn't have a choice. It was all I'd had time to pack.

Not knowing what to expect, I was unarmed, and I wasn't wearing a wire. The Miami techs had taken care of that with the room. I wasn't carrying any money either. It's never smart to walk into a first encounter with a load of cash begging to be stolen. That's a good way to get yourself killed.

While waiting, I arranged my gear on the table. I'd brought the ever-present black light wand, the lighted magnifying glass, a jeweller's loupe, a tape measure, a stack of appraisal forms, and various *objets d'art* catalogues. I'd be doing the inspection show for real this time because, as mentioned, we had no clue what to expect. Were these guys really going to show up with two masterpieces that might soon be worth as much as $10–15 million? If so, the boys in the next room wanted to know before they came blasting in.

About an hour after I'd left him downstairs, Phil Shapiro came knocking at my door. Opening it, I was shocked to see him standing there dwarfed by the biggest Jewish man I'd ever seen in my life, a 6-foot-5-inch, 335 pound, matzo-ball-eating monster named John Michael Tiedeberg. Dressed in a nylon jogging suit, Tiedeberg proceeded to clank into the room like one of those Transformers from the comic books.

'We've got to search you, and search the room,' Shapiro announced. Boy was I glad I wasn't taped or armed.

'Go ahead. I'm clean as a whistle. I just showered,' I joked. The giant didn't so much as crack a smile. He came over and starting patting me down like a pro, checking inside my legs, waistband, ankles: the guy knew his stuff. I took the opportunity to check him out a bit myself. He was solidly packed and had a lot of muscle underneath the fat. He was not someone I wanted to tussle with.

After he finish feeling me up, Tiedeberg began tossing the room with equal precision, going so far as to take the drawers out of the desk and bureaus, and whipping the mattress off the bed like a flapjack. I sensed by his thoroughness that the man had a law enforcement background. The Miami agents hadn't said a word about a massive cop or ex-cop moonlighting as an art thief, so I didn't know if they even knew about this gorilla.

Seems if they had, they would have given me some warning.

As is normally the case, I had no idea where and how the Miami agents had wired the room. The tech crews always keep that secret to prevent agents from being forced to disclose favourite locations and techniques under oath during trials. This meant I had no clue if the roaming mastodon was warm, hot, or cold, and if he was about to turn around, wave a bug with a wire tail in my face, then pound me into the floor with sledgehammer blows from his meaty fist.

While he was busy destroying the place, I tried to engage him in some small talk. I wanted the listening agents to know there were two men with me now, and that one was Kosher King Kong. No matter what I did, said or asked, Kong just grunted and remained silent.

After nearly a half hour, Kong signalled to Shapiro that the room was clean. I whispered a silent prayer of thanks for the skills of my FBI techno-geek brethren. It's no wonder they're so protective of their prime hiding places.

Shapiro told us to wait, and he promptly left. I was now sitting there alone with the Kosher Kong, trying to engage him in some kind of conversation to get him on tape. He wasn't having any of it. He just stood there as if he was in a trance, radiating tension at 100,000 watts. By the time Shapiro returned, I was ready to jump out the window.

Shapiro had brought another guest to the party, the 'Big Guy', introduced as Robert Sarro. He was carrying a brown shopping bag that apparently contained the paintings.

The 'Big Guy' was actually about the size of one of Kosher Kong's legs. He stood 5-foot-9 with a solid build that appeared dangerously slim next to the Really Big Guy. Sarro was mob-ish looking in his blue suit, white shirt open at the collar, shiny shoes, pinky ring, and gold chains. He appeared to be in his 50s, and looked like he'd been around the block a few times. He had an air of confidence about him and a bit of a gangster swagger. I suspected he wasn't going to apologise like Shapiro for what I'd been put through, and he didn't.

Shapiro alerted Sarro that the place was clean, and that they could talk freely. Unlike Tiedeberg, Sarro began chatting without restraint, telling me he was from Chicago, and adding that if this transaction went well, he had more things to sell. I told him I'd certainly be interested.

Sarro withdrew the objects from the bag, set them on the desk, and began to gently remove the brown paper that covered them. While doing so, he talked some more, mentioning that he didn't like to fly, that it was too hot and humid in Florida, and that he didn't want to go up north to do the deal.

I was only half-listening, too distracted by what was being revealed in front of me. They weren't big ones, only about 10-by-12 or -14 inches, but they were stunners. I immediately recognised them from the books, but couldn't put a finger on their titles. They were definitely Rubens, or at least, brilliant copies of Rubens. I could tell from the characters, designs, and brushstrokes that these were probably legitimate.

The first, which turned out to be a work called *Presentation in the Temple*, depicted the Virgin Mary offering baby Jesus to a priest for some ceremonial blessing or baptism. Despite its small size, it was crammed with people in the usual Rubens style. Saint Joseph was kneeling, two elderly women were lending their support, and bystanders observed. The background was ornate and detailed.

The second one, *Adoration of the Shepherd*, again starred the Christ child, this time shortly after his birth in the manger. He was being, as the title implies, adored by a shepherd, among a host of others, drawn by the birth of the world's saviour. Other versions of *Adoration of the Shepherd* or *Shepherds* by Rubens are hanging in The Louvre in Paris, considered the world's most prestigious museum.

As a lifelong Irish Catholic, these images choked me up. As an undercover agent trying to talk the sellers down, I couldn't let on how much.

Since I had virtually no background on these two magnificent masterpieces, I peppered Sarro and Shapiro with questions as I began my inspection. I told them I kept my finger on the art world pulse, and wasn't able to anticipate what I'd find here.

'They're hot,' Sarro said.

'Yeah, I know they're hot. That's why I'm here. But where did they come from?'

Shapiro avoided answering, changing the subject to price. He wanted the full $1.4 million value, a figure that raised my eyebrows. Normally, a hot painting goes for 10 cents on the dollar. These Jewish horse traders, however, wanted full retail! I contemplated educating them on the ways of the underworld, but decided it wasn't necessary to raise such a contentious spectre at that juncture. Instead, I dangled the bait of the wealthy South American buyer I was scouting for, a man who was currently in Texas eager to drop some serious cash for high-quality art. That wasn't just idle chatter. Getting the sellers to agree to such a deal brought in the interstate transportation of stolen property statutes that enabled the FBI to actually work the case. If the paintings had been pinched in Florida, they weren't in our jurisdiction. But once I introduced the buyer in Texas, and the sellers agreed, it was our baby.

Shapiro and Sarro took the bait, saying they were pleased it was going to Texas and then out of the country because there would be a lot less heat. That tipped me off that they probably had been stolen right there in Florida.

As I continued, Shapiro and Sarro began to take a serious interest in what I was doing. To keep their attention, I began my checklist out loud. Neither painting was signed, but that was in keeping with Rubens.

The medium was oil on canvas, and there was a water stain on the upper left corner of the *Presentation* along with a small tear. Easy to fix, but I wasn't going to tell them that. I frowned and mumbled, 'This is a problem.'

Adoration had paint missing in some spots, and had a small tear. That was also deemed to be a problem. Sensing that they were hanging on my every word, I spoke of the craquelure, chiaroscuro (light and shadow) and whispered the fancy artsy names for pigments like bitumen (brown), azurite (blue), and alizarin (reddish purple).

Rubens, I explained, worked with chalk grounds bound with animal glue infused with oil. An innovator in priming a canvas, he applied a brownish lean oil with long, streaked strokes to produce a translucency that made for a less-monotonous background. A virtuoso with a brush, Rubens frequently diluted his paint with turpentine to lighten the shades and speed the stroking, enabling him to go on creative tears. Either linseed, or preferably walnut oil was used in the paint to combat yellowing, and he preferred to cap it off with a resin-oil varnish to better endure the cold northern weather. Sometimes, especially when Rubens painted on wood, the edges were left bare because he had the unusual habit of framing a work before he finished it. All of the above was apparent in the two paintings.

Since the guys were so into watching what I was doing, I decided to take the painting into the bathroom and really wow them with the black light show. As expected, they readily followed me in, first Sarro and then Shapiro. The Really Big Guy was too Really Big to squeeze into the bathroom, so he remained on guard outside. I didn't think he cared for such nuances anyway.

I schooled the others on the sparkling minerals, ancient pigments, restorations over the years, signs of the age: the works. After a half hour or so, I was convinced the paintings were either real, or real enough ancient fakes to take the guys down.

After bringing the paintings back into the main room, I was ready to signal the troops. The proposed buy, worked out by the ever-cautious, strategy-happy gang, was a complicated process of having different teams of sellers and buyers in different hotels. One team would have the money, the other the paintings. When the cash was exchanged in one place, the paintings would be turned over in the other. Apparently, when it came to handling money, there was no plan too cumbersome or elaborate for these 'investment brokers'.

Since nobody among the contingent of good guys wanted to go through that headache, we were going to take these guys down right there at the Marriott. All I had to do was give the signal.

The signal? What the hell was the signal? Suddenly, I was rocked by the gut twisting realisation that there wasn't any signal! We had failed to devise one during the ride over. I began to sweat, and felt the first signs of panic. How could a group of veteran agents have overlooked such a critical detail?

I tried to improvise, making up things that sounded like it could be a signal. 'Well, I'm finished. I've done my job,' I said.

Nothing happened.

'Uh, these paintings definitely look good. I don't know what more I can do.' The doors remained firmly on their hinges. There wasn't even so much as a rustle in the next room. 'I'm ready to talk money.' Silence. Now I was really sweating. Shapiro and Sarro were waiting for me to direct them to the mountain of cash, and all I could do was stand there making stupid, almost comical statements to the ceiling.

Feeling the room closing in, I told the guys that I had an X-ray machine downstairs and needed their help bringing it up. Of course, I could have called the front desk and asked for a bellhop to do it, but thankfully the others didn't think of that. The ruse seemed reasonable considering the show I was giving, so they swallowed it without question. Even the big matzo ball didn't raise an objection. Shapiro told him to wait with the paintings while we fetched the magic box.

The trouble with this move was that there was no X-ray machine downstairs. I was hoping to spot an agent lurking in the shadows somewhere along the journey and signal him to pounce. Since I didn't know all the agents, I could very well be frantically waving to a confused tourist from Milwaukee.

This was rapidly turning into a surrealistic Salvador Dalí nightmare. Fortunately, I passed a recognisable agent in the hallway. I nodded to him, he nodded back, and before we could get to the elevator, we were swarmed. The agents pushed us up against the wall, patted us down, and slapped on the cuffs.

'You know, I was trying to signal you guys from the room, but we didn't have a stinkin' signal,' I said after the others were taken downstairs. The agent just shook his head and laughed.

A second group of Feds blasted through the connecting doors to grab Tiedeberg and the paintings. They emerged from the room with some disturbing news. The paintings were gone!

'What?' I said. 'They were just there. What do you mean?'

'No paintings. Nothing.'

We rushed back inside and sure enough, the twin Rubens were missing.

We searched around and found nothing. A couple of us noticed the sliding glass doors leading to a balcony and dashed outside.

'Is that them?' an agent said pointing to a pair of square objects on the grass three stories below.

'Yeah,' I said, recognising the frames. 'I can't believe the bastards tossed them off the porch like Frisbees. Million-dollar paintings, whoosh, over the porch.'

The arrest team signalled for the ground crew to vacuum them up before the Cuban landscaper went home with the find of a lifetime. Incredibly, they were virtually undamaged, having hit the soft, soggy grass.

Back inside, the Florida agents complimented me on my work and mentioned that the two other guys were on their way to the clink.

Two other guys? I couldn't believe my ears. Two guys?

'There were three guys. Three guys!' I insisted.

'Nope, only two in the hallway, aside from you.'

'What about the big guy in the room? The big ape? What happened to him?'

'There was nobody else. Nobody in the room.'

'There was a Goliath! A big gorilla. Didn't you seem him?' They were all looking at me like I was crazy. I was now Inspector Clouseau again, this time on crack.

'How did you miss him? He was a monster.'

'There was nobody else on the tape. We didn't hear any other voices.'

Oh man, I thought. This was really looking bad. No Kosher Kong. Nothing on the tape. The big matzo ball had vanished into thin air, leaving me to look like I was ready for a straitjacket.

When things calmed down, I started describing the guy. Finally, one of the agents perked up and said, 'I think I know who that is. He's a local bodyguard. John Michael Tittyberg or something. Big goon. He's the son of a local deputy sheriff.'

Next thing I knew, somebody was flashing a picture in front of my face. 'Yeah, that's him!' I said excitedly. 'That's the guy. He was right here in the room! He frisked me.'

'He was here? How did he get out?' one of the agents wondered.

'He's a black belt or something. Ninja-type guy,' the agent who knew him answered. 'He can move around for a big man.'

Convinced that I wasn't insane, we determined that the giant had climbed down the balcony to the one below, then repeated the step two more times until he was close enough to hop to the ground and scamper off.

'Don't worry. We know where he lives. We can pick him up anytime,' the Florida agent assured.

'Wonder why he didn't scoop up the paintings?' I asked no one in particular.

'He must have run right by them.'

'He was too busy saving his skin. They weren't his paintings. He wasn't going to get stuck with the evidence. Shrewd guy,' the second agent speculated.

As we were talking, the phone in the room rang. Special Agent Eugene Flynn answered, then relayed to me that it was someone asking for Sarro. We all looked at each other like 'What's this?' I motioned for Flynn to hand me the phone. I told the caller I was the appraiser and asked him who he was. He readily responded that he was one of the gang, and was downstairs waiting in the bar. He'd be handling the money exchange, he informed me, because the paintings were his. 'Oh good,' I said. 'Everything is going well and we're about to get to that.'

He asked about his associates Sarro and Shapiro. I told him they were 'tied up at the moment,' a groaner joke I'd always wanted to use. I'd be happy to come downstairs and update him, I offered. He agreed, then volunteered that he was Sarro's son-in-law from Chicago, 'I've got good news for you,' I lied. 'I'll be right down.'

After hanging up, we just shrugged at each other in total bewilderment. Could it be that this knuckleheaded lookout missed all the action? The arrests? The flood of government cars? FBI agents swarming the place like bees? Million-dollar paintings flying off the balcony? A giant Jew climbing down the side of the building like King Kong? This I had to see.

I told Special Agent Flynn, whom the others called 'The Riddler' because of his complicated, convoluted, yet brilliant investigative deductions, that I'd go in first, check it out, then they were to come in and arrest us—me for the second time in 20 minutes.

Down the elevator and into the lobby I ventured, searching for the lounge. It wasn't hard to spot the son-in-law because he was the only person in the bar, sitting there sipping on a cognac. He greeted me all smiling and handshaking, explaining again that he was Sarro's daughter's husband, James Tortoriello Jr. I countered that the paintings were primo stuff and that we were ready to deal. If he indeed had a cut, he'd soon be in the money. As I spoke, I glanced around and noticed that the tavern was in a secluded part of the hotel and didn't have many, or any, windows. That explained why this clown had remained oblivious to all that had happened.

The Riddler and his partner strolled in and made a beeline for us with guns drawn and badges dangling. They slammed us against the bar, slapped on the cuffs, and escorted us out in front of everybody. It was the first time I was ever arrested twice in such a short period. They bounced me around pretty good each time. I'd be leaving the Sunshine State with scattered purple bruises instead of a smooth bronze tan.

While I was at the field station taking care of loose ends, the South Florida and Connecticut agents swept up the rest of the gang, including the Kregelstein brothers, Walter and Francis. Francis was snatched at the airport in Miami, while Walter was pounced on in a Sears parking lot in Farmington, where he was monitoring the activities of the 'armed robbers,' who were actually Special Agents John Hanlon and Bobby Brown.

Another gang member, Israel David Glassman, was at Miami International Airport in the Pan Am Clipper Club lounge with Francis Kregelstein. The pair were on their way to Paris where they were to make the ransom demand calls and shredding threats following the robbery in Connecticut. The two must have pulled the long straws to get that peachy assignment.

Tiedeberg, the balcony-hopping mastodon, was eventually hunted down, as was Tortoriello's brother Mark, who was suspected of being part of the original burglary team. (Mark Tortoriello had met with undercover agents earlier in the case.)

When everybody regrouped to compare notes, we learned that Walter Kregelstein's greenlighting of the robbers' plan in Hartford showed the same lack of imagination as his recruiting them had. The special agents masquerading as hired guns were going to simply bust in, wave their nasty Mac-10 around, shove the weakling curator and senior citizen tour guides off to the side somewhere, then grab the specified paintings. The paper-thin scheme made no concession for the fact that the art was secured with sophisticated alarms designed to instantly alert a Farmington, Connecticut, police squad that had been trained to swarm the museum in minutes. The game would have been over before the robbers snatched the second Monet.

Possibly even earlier: the robbers had not been briefed that instead of shrinking violets, the new curator and some of the guides were retired military veterans who might not faint in fear at the sight of a gun.

I found it amazing how this all-brain, no-muscle gang had totally reversed the normal process of art theft. Nine times out of ten, you have robbers who devise clever ways of stealing valuable art, then don't know what to do with it afterward. Oceanberg's Seven had a pretty ingenious way of handling it afterward with their transatlantic blackmail calls, but had put little thought into the theft itself.

With a stack of files on my desk in New York, I didn't have the luxury of hanging around to put the last pieces of the puzzle together—where did the Rubens paintings come from? The Florida agents later relayed the story.

Shortly after the great Flemish master created them, the two works vanished for 300 years. In 1931—the same year John Dillinger went on a bank-robbing spree that resulted in the creation of the modern FBI—a woman waltzed into a Chicago antique shop, was struck by the beauty of a pair of religious paintings, and purchased them for $150 each. She had no idea who the artist was.

The woman had a son, Jason Whitney, who grew up to become a wealthy yacht broker in Fort Lauderdale. In 1967, Whitney's mother gave the paintings to his wife Martha as a birthday present. They were hung on a hook above their marble staircase.

On 2 July 1980—Martha Whitney's birthday again—they were stolen by burglars who simply lifted them off the hooks. Shattered, Martha kept the attachments up as sort of a burning-lamp-in-the-window, hoping the twin baby Jesuses would one day find their way home.

They did, two years later, after being scooped from the grass behind the Marriott. The happy Whitneys put them back on their original hooks, and all was well in South Florida.

Meanwhile, Tiedeberg appealed his subsequent conviction with the others on the grounds that he was just an innocent bodyguard who wasn't responsible for his employers' criminal activities. It was an interesting argument, one that was watched closely in legal circles. In the end, a majority of the appellate judges bought it. The black-robed gang in United States Court of Appeals, 11th Circuit, ruled that silent bodyguards hired to provide muscle in the early stages of a criminal scheme are not necessarily along for the whole ride, and thus cannot be convicted of conspiracy without evidence that they were full partners in the entire plot.

Say what?

The prevailing judges weren't swayed by the fact that Tiedeberg tossed the goods to the ground, fled down three balconies like Spider-Man on steroids, and skittered off into the humid day like a thundering buffalo.

We have consistently and strongly emphasised that presence, followed by flight, is inadequate proof of actual and knowing participation in a conspiracy. Tiedeberg may be guilty of some offence, but not conspiracy to transport stolen paintings interstate.

A dissenting judge thought that was hogwash, and felt that a Neanderthal standing there watching and listening to the negotiations over price, background, and quality, and hearing about plans to transport the stolen goods out of the country, is equally guilty. 'The jury was not bound to believe any of Tiedeberg's testimony that he was simply a partially deaf bodyguard naively obeying his employer's orders.'

Whatever, as the kids today say. My job was to get the paintings back, and that was accomplished. Put a bow on it and move to the next case.

Update.

Four years later, Special Agent John Hanlon barely survived one of the deadliest FBI shootouts in history. In April 1986, a bloody street war broke out between a squad of eight South Florida agents and two heavily armed bank robbers they surrounded in the suburbs south of Miami. The incident, which resulted in the deaths of two FBI agents, Jerry Dove and Benjamin Grogan, and injuries to five others, was made into a gripping television movie, *In the Line of Duty*, that starred *Family Ties*' Michael Gross and David Soul of *Starsky and Hutch* as sociopathic bad guys William Matix and Michael Platt. Both Matix and Platt were killed in the violent exchange. Hanlon was shot in the hand and groin.

Afterward, FBI supervisors were issued Heckler & Koch MP-5 40-mm submachine gun pistols to make sure Hoover's boys would never be outgunned like that again. I was given one because I was a Special Ops Team Leader at the time.

It was a neat weapon, no denying that, and it could certainly do some serious damage. Still, I much preferred fighting crime with a black light wand.

. 8 .

A Big Dog, Grandma Moses, and van Gogh

NEW YORK-BASED Lloyd's of London adjuster Harold Smith was on the line one cold January morning with some disturbing news. Smith, an American who was one of the world's foremost art recovery experts, relayed that there were rumblings on the snow-covered streets that a gang of brutish mob associates was trying to fence five valuable paintings from a recent heist. Among them was a van Gogh.

'Are you working a case like that?' Smith probed.

I glanced at my two-foot-high stack of art theft files and let out a deep sigh. I didn't have to search through the pile to know the answer.

'That's news to me,' I said, rifling through my drawer for a blank folder. 'If somebody snatched a van Gogh, I'd usually know about it.'

'Not before me,' Smith volleyed with a laugh. 'When I find out more information, I'll call you back.'

Despite my initial scepticism, I had a nagging suspicion that my long-time art world cohort was on to something. It wasn't unusual that an insurance adjuster would be the first to get wind of a big-time burglary, nor was it odd that an informant would immediately seek him out. Unlike the FBI or other government agencies, the adjusters are known to pay good money for information, with no strings attached. And they don't have to go through the stifling layers of institutional approval that often drag police and FBI investigations down.

'Vinnie van Gogh,' I said to myself as I scribbled the troubled, ear-slashing artist's name on a crisp new file tab. 'Even in death they won't let you rest.'

I slipped the empty sleeve into the ever-growing stack, right in front of Whistler and Wyeth, and leaned back in my chair to take it in. The art-theft business was definitely on the upswing.

Smith, a tall, thin, balding former merchant marine who loved playing golf and hosting parties at the best area country clubs, caught me at the FBI's New York headquarters a few days later just as I was leaving the building for lunch. His update riveted my attention because it was now dead-on specific. I quickly grabbed a pen and pad to jot it down. Smith's informant had named the artists and titles of all five paintings, including van Gogh's Paris bridge landscape *Le Petit Pont* worth untold millions today. (Another van Gogh, *Sunflowers*, would sell for $40 million in 1987. Three years later, *Portrait of Doctor Gachet* was auctioned for $82.5 million.)

There was also a cityscape, *La Seine au quai St Bernard 1885* from 19th century French neo-impressionist Albert Dubois-Pillet that was nearly as valuable, and a contemporary nature piece from the famed American artist Anna Mary Robertson Moses, better known as Grandma Moses. (Dubois-Pillet's and Moses' best oils and temperas sell for the low to mid-six figures today.)

Smith's information had to be legit. The nagging mystery that remained, of course, was who had been hit, and why wasn't the theft reported? If mobsters were involved as rumoured, that narrowed things down considerably. This wasn't going to be another maddening, continent-hopping international fox hunt. The New York Mafia is far too provincial. No, the starting point had to be in Manhattan somewhere right under my nose.

For the thieves, the silence surrounding the heist should have been working to their advantage. In the art world, the so called 'perfect crime' is one that goes undetected or unreported. If a theft hits the media, the painting can be awfully hard to sell. Potential buyers are scared off by the prospect of one day having me and my G-men associates paying them a surprise visit.

In contrast, if nobody knows the paintings are 'hot', they can be transported and sold without interference.

Even with the bare-bones information Smith provided, I could start profiling the suspects. If the word was on the street, it was obvious that despite pulling off their quiet 'perfect crime', the wise guys were having trouble unloading the goods. This was also indicative of the highly territorial New York gangsters. While the Mafia is unmatched at compromising insiders and pulling off sensational heists, they're lost when it comes to moving valuables through high-class niche markets like the art world.

Due to the intrigue involved, I gave this unconfirmed van Gogh theft my time and attention even though it wasn't officially on the books. I could only do so for a limited time, with no help or resources, before the brass came down on me. Smith was keenly aware that the clock was ticking, which explains why he was riding his informant hard.

As Smith knew, the key to getting an official FBI investigation rolling was locating the victim. Without a victim coming forward to report the theft, I wasn't at liberty to bring in the FBI and its vast resources. With 60 to 80 case files spilling out of my in-box, I couldn't afford to go on another wild goose chase.

Complicating matters was a recent fiasco that was still fresh on everybody's minds. I'd tracked a hot Rembrandt halfway around the world, located it in California, authenticated it, nabbed the culprits, then couldn't do a thing because we were never able to trace it back to a legitimate owner. Some of these centuries-old masterpieces are bought, sold, stolen, and hidden so many times it can be frustrating trying to trace their lineage. If one thief steals from another, who stole it from a collector who bought it illegally from someone now dead, nobody is going to appear in my office with a raised hand.

Smith, anticipating that the ultimate responsibility to make good was going to fall on his unhappy bosses in London, promised to have a starting point soon. Sure enough, he called later that day with a hush-hush tip. 'My informant thinks they may have been taken from the Hammer Galleries.'

That made perfect sense. The Hammer Galleries near Trump Plaza in Manhattan has long boasted one of the finest collections of artwork on the planet. It's also a peculiar place tinged with no small amount of irony when it comes to high-class crime.

Its founder and chief benefactor, famed industrialist Dr Armand Hammer, was a controversial figure who made his early 20th century fortune, in part, by exporting pharmaceuticals and business supplies, sometimes illegally, to communist nations. These shady dealings included extensive relations with Russia. Hammer, born in New York in 1898, was the son of wealthy Soviet Jewish immigrants who fled the racist pogroms in Odessa, but still pined for the old country and longed to return home.

Using his father's connections, young Armand began building his fortune by flooding America's long-time Cold War enemy with, among other capitalistic products, an ocean of cheap pencils.

A licensed physician, the high-flying Dr Hammer never practiced medicine beyond selling tons of legalised drugs, but loved clinging to the title of 'Doctor'. As CEO of Occidental Petroleum Company, Hammer created and managed a Depression-era fortune of staggering dimensions. His legendary company remains a leading player in the oil and natural gas exploration and production business to this day.

Despite common belief, he was not involved with the naming and original production of the popular Arm and Hammer baking soda brand. Displaying his whimsical side, however, he did eventually buy an interest in the company that manufactured the cooking ingredient, and sat on its board of directors.

Personally, Hammer wasn't beyond living by his own rules in America as he had during his nefarious overseas ventures. No stranger to the concept of buying power and influence, he was convicted in the late 1960s of funnelling illegal campaign contributions into Republican Party coffers to help elect President Richard Nixon. Hammer's Texas oil buddy, President George H.W. Bush, later granted him a pardon.

When he wasn't wheeling and dealing on an international level, or meddling in American politics, Hammer spent his leisure time searching the globe for valuable art. He founded his namesake gallery in 1928 essentially to display his private collection, and those of his robber baron friends William Randolph Hearst and J.P. Morgan. Hearst, the renowned newspaper tycoon, was believed to have the largest and most valuable private art collection in the world. Morgan, a banker and financier who provided the capital to create the world's first billion-dollar corporation, US Steel, had a respectable collection as well.

Over the years, the still-thriving Hammer Galleries has owned or displayed billions of dollars worth of paintings, specialising in European masters Bouguereau, Corot, Monet, Renoir, Picasso, van Gogh, Matisse, Miró, Rembrandt, and Chagall, among others. It has also made room for the best of American artists like Chase, Wyeth, Cassatt, Hassam, Sargent, and Thomas Hart Benton.

Hammer's favourites, oddly enough, were a series of nudes from a lesser known 19th century French painter named Jean Jacques Henner. The Frenchman had a penchant for painting tall, fleshy, naked redheads, usually in subtly erotic positions. Hammer had a penchant for seducing tall, fleshy, flamboyant redheads he ached to see naked in similar erotic positions, especially any woman who reminded him of one of Henner's models.

The ironic aspect of this particular gallery being hit by thieves is that ruthless businessmen like Hammer, Hearst, and Morgan would have been suspects one, two, and three on my list of egotistical collectors most likely to purchase—for any price—the precise pieces of art taken from the Hammer Galleries. And they'd do so for no other reason than to privately outdo each other.

Going further, I wouldn't have put it past any of them in their heyday to actually finance and orchestrate such a theft—even from each other. Actually, especially from each other.

Considering the players involved, I couldn't help feeling a bit of poetic justice was at work. Morgan and Hearst were long dead at the time of this mysterious 1980 theft, so I ruled them out. Additionally, their heirs didn't seem to have the motivation to find amusement in stealing prized works of art from one of their father's or grandfather's old cronies.

Hammer, on the other hand, was very much alive. While collectors have been known to steal from themselves to initiate insurance scams, that didn't appear to be Dr Hammer's modus operandi. He was far too wealthy to sink to that. In fact, in the midst of the investigation, Dr Hammer made the news when he bid a record $5,126,000 to purchase a Leonardo da Vinci treatise entitled *Of the Nature, Weight and Movement of Water*. That wasn't a work of art, mind you, just an old manuscript.

I picked up the phone and dialled Richard Lynch, the Hammer Galleries curator. Lynch wasn't your typical rail-thin, Gucci-suited, snobby art connoisseur. The stocky, moustachioed manager proved to be refreshingly down-to-earth, especially when discussing his constant battle to quit smoking. Nonetheless, he lived and breathed the oil-on-canvas business, and presided over an immaculately kept gallery. Lynch's eyes literally twinkled with excitement when he discussed anything to do with classic paintings. Shrewd and knowledgeable, he could be a formidable adversary in art purchase negotiations, and, as I speculated, a nimble antagonist in FBI investigations.

Personable and appealing as he was, I couldn't rule Lynch out. At that juncture, I couldn't rule out anyone working at the Hammer Galleries, or any of their contractors. In the early stages of a case, everybody is a suspect. That includes the alarm company, the electricians, the painters, the pesticide sprayers, the security guards, the cleaning ladies, the truckers, the caterers, the cop on the beat out front, and the guy who runs the place.

When a 10-by-10 inch painting on a wall can buy a person an oceanfront mansion on a tropical island paradise, and fill it with all the friends and lovers they'll ever need, I have to look at everybody.

'Did you, uh, happen to get burglarised recently?' I opened with Lynch, too busy to beat around the bush.

'No. Why do you ask?' Lynch responded, cool and completely unruffled.

'We've been hearing things. Street talk at the moment, but very specific. A van Gogh among them. Here, take this list down and double check for me.'

'Certainly,' Lynch said, figuring he might be of assistance in determining what other museum, gallery, or private collector had been hit. As I rattled off the list, I sensed a discernible change in Lynch's mood. His confidence and gregarious nature were eroding so rapidly I thought he was going to faint. 'I'll get right on it,' he promised.

Although my instincts told me I was already on the right track—and that Smith's informant knew far more than he was letting on—I still went through the standard motions of working the phones and files. I wanted to be prepared in case Lynch tried to pull a fast one. Since I was in the process of developing the FBI's highly regarded worldwide stolen painting registry, that was my first step. None of the five specified paintings were on the list.

I then called Allan Gore, an American working for Interpol in France. Gore—not to be confused with the former vice president—

didn't have any of the paintings on his 'hot' list either. (Gore later wrote the book *King of the Pickpockets* and became the security director for New York's Metropolitan Museum of Art.)

My second call was to Donna Carlson and Gil Elderman at the Art Dealer's Association of America (ADAA), another organisation that keeps a diligent worldwide account of missing paintings—a list that can number in the thousands at any given time. There were no matches on ADAA's records.

Finally, I checked in with Bonnie Burnham and Connie Lowenthal at the International Foundation for Art Research (IFAR), which was then located at 70 East 70th Street in New York's famed Explorer Building. IFAR was assisting me in upgrading the FBI's 'Most Wanted' art list. Van Gogh's little bridge theft was news to Bonnie and Connie as well.

The next morning, I'd barely taken my first sip of coffee and dusted the snow off my coat when the phone rang. It was Richard Lynch. I'd never heard him so crestfallen.

'That matter we discussed yesterday,' he said, almost whispering. 'They are indeed ours.'

'No kidding,' I said. 'How?'

'We don't know. Can you please come over, Special Agent McShane?'

When he suddenly addressed me formally like that, I knew something very strange was in the wind. I also knew this was finally going to be an official FBI 'A-File' (Art File) investigation. And unless Lynch was an actor of Oscar calibre, he wasn't involved. What I didn't know was that it was going to be one of the wildest, deadliest, and most bizarre cases of my entire career.

Before heading over to the Hammer Galleries, I called Harold Smith to give him the news he probably already knew. The Hammer Galleries happened to be one of Smith's major Lloyd's of London clients, so I surmised he would be especially interested.

'Lynch just confirmed it,' I opened.

'Now why doesn't that surprise me?' Smith said with a chuckle. 'You heading over there?'

'I'm on my way with the microscope team. Not sure what we're going to find. The way Lynch tells it, the paintings walked out on their own legs.'

Smith howled with knowing laughter. 'I *hate* when that happens. Here we go again, old friend.'

We both knew the score. The Hammer Galleries, while staggering in wealth and historical value, were in fact little more than a rich man's semi-pornographic playpen. If the financial hit, or personal insult to his artistic legacy, fazed Armand Hammer, he wasn't letting on. He left it to Lynch and his other underlings, along with Smith and Lloyd's of London, to handle the investigation and recovery.

To put it another way, only a 1930s robber baron could lose a van Gogh without even knowing it was missing.

Fuelling Dr Hammer's apparent ambivalence, no doubt, was the fact that the thief or thieves obviously didn't share his devotion to fleshy redheads. All the kitschy, schoolboy-enticing Henners in the gallery remained untouched.

'If they'd taken one of those,' I commented to Smith, 'the old coot would be on the next plane chewing out everybody from the police commissioner to J. Edgar Hoover's ghost.'

'Yeah, and he'd have the entire Lloyd's of London board of directors on the first Concorde so they could be in his office by noon.'

Kidding aside, the coy Dr Hammer may very well have been expecting to have the last laugh. A stolen masterpiece recovered, thanks to months of sensationalised publicity, can triple in value overnight. That's because a large part of great art's highly volatile and speculative worth lies in its vivid capturing of history. If the painting itself has its own titillating adventure to add to the mix, the price can go through the roof.

Regardless of Dr Hammer's real or imagined lack of alarm—or lack of an effective alarm system—it was my job to track down those responsible and help Harold Smith and Richard Lynch recover the missing paintings. I was duty-bound to give them my best effort.

On a personal level, I was even more duty-bound to give the FBI bosses in Washington my best effort. Following in the longstanding tradition of its media-savvy founder, the post-Hoover FBI continued to keep a close watch on cases that garnered widespread press attention.

I had a leg up on this investigation because I knew the Hammer Galleries district inside out. As with other world-renowned galleries and museums in and around New York, I'd taken courses at the Museum of Modern Art, The Kennedy Galleries, and Sotheby's, all within walking distance of the Hammer Galleries. Absorbing this fascinating world like a sponge, I learned the secrets of how to verify artist signatures, identify an artist through his/her fingerprint-like brushstrokes, determine the age of canvas to see if it matched the time period, and pinpoint the era and blends of paint to separate fakes from originals. I also learned how to estimate the age of wood used in frames and backing materials (a science known as dendrochronology), and how ultraviolet light is used to 'X-ray' paintings to see if one picture is covering another—a common criminal technique designed to the move hot art through customs searches, countries, and airports.

Combining that hands-on education with pestering the technicians at the FBI's state-of-the-art criminal investigation labs, I came away knowing nearly as much about art as some of the world's top curators.

While the technical, forensic, and CSI (crime scene investigation) knowledge was helpful, all the painstaking study paid even bigger dividends in another area. Once I could 'talk the talk,' I could effortlessly transform into various undercover alter egos ranging from a curator, to an appraiser, to a broker, to a gallery owner, to a rich collector.

That said, I predicted that none of the technical innovations would make an ounce of difference in this theft. To start off, there was no indication of when the heist had occurred. It might have been months earlier. Thus, the crime scene was sure to be thoroughly corrupted.

At the gallery, the twinkle was noticeably gone from Lynch's eyes as he led me through room after room of breathtaking imagery captured in spectacular fashion by the world's greatest artists. The meticulously groomed curator's incessant smoking and nervous manner seemed terribly at odds with the awe and splendour of his beautifully arranged gallery. Quizzically, we kept walking until a sheepish Lynch led me down a back stairway to the crime scene.

I was fascinated, but not surprised, to discover that the burglary had occurred far from the majestic showrooms the public enjoyed. The stolen paintings were lifted from the musty basement of the turn of the century townhouse now serving as a world-class art emporium. They were among 50 or more that were unceremoniously languishing in inventory. That explained why the theft had gone unnoticed.

This might seem shocking to a layperson, and I'm sure Mr van Gogh was in his grave twisting at his remaining ear over the indignity, yet it was indeed in keeping with the 'iceberg' quality of most of the world's finest museums and galleries. On any given day, the paintings on display represent only a small fraction of a museum's or gallery's holdings. Vast stores of art—often worth hundreds of millions of dollars—collect dust in basements and storerooms waiting for their turn on the limited wall space.

Talk about a thieves' paradise.

This is done, in part, so that museums and galleries can keep their displays fresh and newsworthy, and bring in their crucial base of repeat customers. The stolen Grandma Moses, for example, had just recently been on prominent display at the Hammer Galleries. It was part of an Anna Mary Robertson Moses retrospective that kicked off the Hammer Galleries' grand re-opening just months before celebrating the move to their current site at 33 West 57th

Street. The thief or thieves may have spotted it while casing the place, and then had to go searching for it during the actual theft.

As expected, the technical aspect of the crime scene investigation—so popular today on the various CSI television shows—came up totally empty. Not one fingerprint, clothing thread, hair, fingernail scratch, or footprint pointed me in the direction of the culprits. There was no sign of a break-in, no clue how the theft was accomplished, and no indication of how the elaborate state-of-the-art security alarm system was defeated. I could only conclude that it was an inside job. One of the gallery's employees, working with or without an outsider, simply lifted the paintings from the basement and walked them out through a rear service exit.

Sad to say, no amount of high-tech security in the world, then or now, can stand against an inside job.

Among the sea of unanswered questions this puzzling burglary presented was the fact that it was proving impossible to get a fix on the mindset, rationale, and expertise of the insider and his or her accomplices, a group that was probably separate from the middlemen gangsters currently in possession of the art. While the small van Gogh was a solid score, the gallery had far more valuable masterpieces, both on display and in the basement. If the culprits had really wanted to hit the jackpot, a crew that included at least one knowledgeable art expert could have chosen among a wide selection of larger, more valuable paintings. Why they singled out this particular handful of disconnected artists and works was bewildering. In fact, one of the works was a quirky 19th century drawing of a man beating a dog with a stick by French caricaturist and social satirist Honoré Daumier. With hundreds of options at their disposal, why would anyone pick such an unpleasant image worth only a few thousand dollars at best?

For the next few months, Smith and I couldn't make any headway in the investigation. His informant went mute, and my sources remained at a loss. Then suddenly, as winter eased into spring, things heated up again. Smith's source resurfaced with tales of a man named

'Phil' who was interested in selling the entire collection back to the Hammer Galleries. At the same time, I fielded a lead that a man named 'Sal' was attempting to sell a hot van Gogh in Brooklyn. Sal was said to be an associate of notorious mobster Lewis D'Avanzo. We didn't know if Phil and Sal were working together, or were the same person, but both leads appeared to be hot. I focused on Sal, while Smith tried to flush out Phil and arrange a buy.

Without a full name, I couldn't get a handle on Sal, but I sure knew all about Lewis Vincent D'Avanzo. I'd received a tip three years before that the ominous-looking Italian was trying to move paintings taken from another undetermined burglary. It was an odd sidelight for D'Avanzo because he was better known as the cold-blooded ringleader of a lucrative, mob-connected auto-theft ring that was estimated to have stolen $300 million worth of luxury cars.

D'Avanzo, 36, was also the first cousin of future New York Mayor Rudy Giuliani, a popular Republican politician destined to be selected as *Time* magazine's 'Person of the Year' in 2001 for the way he handled the aftermath of the 9/11 Twin Towers terrorist attack. At the time of the art theft, Giuliani, ironically enough, was gaining fame as a mob-busting New York City prosecutor. His cousin Louie, in contrast, took an altogether different path. The 'bad sheep' in the Giuliani clan was busy rising up the ranks in the Gambino Family, the mob empire soon to be ruled via assassination by John Gotti, the famed 'Teflon Don'.

Burly and lumbering, the 250-pound D'Avanzo was additionally a deeply closeted homosexual who decades later would serve as a model for a hefty gay mobster living in fear of exposure in the acclaimed HBO original series *The Sopranos*. The macho Mafia doesn't tolerate homosexuals, and to be caught was an instant death sentence. Louie was definitely living life on the edge.

These dicey revelations, however, were a quarter century away from being made public. Louie had more immediate problems to deal with in 1977. Unbeknownst to him, he was already under surveillance by another team of FBI agents seeking to put a dent into the spiralling automotive crime wave.

Back then, FBI agents and teams had to do their own surveillance. Today, thanks to the efforts of forward-thinking bosses like Jimmy Kallstrom, the agency has developed specialised surveillance units that assist investigative teams with that time-consuming aspect of a case. This frees the lead agents to pound the streets for accomplices, trail stolen goods, and chase additional leads. (While Kallstrom is a hero among the Special Agent fraternity for the surveillance squads, he's better known publicly as the lead investigator of the 1996 TWA Flight 800 crash on Long Island, and as New York's Director of Homeland Security.)

With staffing at a premium, Bob Gilmore and Horst Drewnoik, the special agents in charge of the Brooklyn/Queens Organised Crime Squad, welcomed my presence on their team. During one of my shifts, I shadowed D'Avanzo from Staten Island to LaGuardia Airport, then observed with only passing interest as he made a quick stop at a service station on Hicks Street in the Carroll Gardens section of Brooklyn. If not for the fact that the pumps were around the corner from the boyhood home of famed 1930s mobster Al Capone, I wouldn't have noted the stop at all.

A few days later, it was decided that it would serve both Gilmore and my FBI team's mutual interests to pop D'Avanzo and squeeze him for information on cars, mobsters, and paintings. Gilmore, naturally, wanted his squad to make the arrest, which I totally understood. Lucky for me, I don't have an ego about such things because the capture did not go smoothly.

On Halloween Day, Special Agent Gilmore and his men tracked D'Avanzo through Brooklyn to the Bay Ridge/Bensonhurst section, then watched as he was dropped off by some associates at the corner of 65th Street and 12th Avenue near the Verrazano Narrows Bridge. That particular bridge, once the longest suspension spans in the world, was widely known in those pre–politically correct days as the 'Guinea Gangplank' because of all the bodies dumped into the murky Upper New York Bay below.

D'Avanzo climbed inside an empty 1975 Ford Maverick that was parked near the stately Regina Pacis Church and Elementary School. His location so close to hundreds of small, Roman Catholic children was disconcerting. After some serious hand-wringing, Gilmore decided that since the team was in place, and the kids were tucked inside the fortress-like, Renaissance-style building, he'd okay the arrest.

Upon Gilmore's signal, an agent quietly pulled his vehicle into the space behind the green Maverick to block D'Avanzo in and cover him from the rear. The arrest team, six strong in full FBI SWAT gear, surrounded the mobster with guns drawn. A bullhorn announcement set the stage.

'Lewis D'Avanzo, you are under arrest. Exit your vehicle and put your hands on your head.' D'Avanzo refused to budge. The command was repeated as the wary agents edged closer.

Instead of complying, D'Avanzo foolishly cranked his engine, threw the Ford into reverse, and smashed into the government vehicle behind him. He then slammed the transmission into drive, floored the accelerator, and rocketed forward, his smoking tires squealing so loudly they startled the children in their classrooms. The frantic mobster steered straight for a pair of special agents in his path, Richie Mika and John Kuhn, both good friends of mine. D'Avanzo was planning to flatten them where they stood.

Fearing for their fellow agents' lives, the marksmen on the SWAT team simultaneously fired their weapons, a massive .357 Magnum and 12-gauge shotgun, blowing out the gangster's windshield and turning his pudgy face into hamburger. He was dead on the spot. Shattered glass was everywhere, and blood streamed down D'Avanzo's limp body.

Kuhn and Mika quickly sidestepped the Maverick as it continued to lurch forward. They escaped unharmed.

Although it was a good shot, and I couldn't blame the SWAT guys for using deadly force, they certainly put an instant end to that lead. With D'Avanzo sprawled on a slab at the morgue, what remained of his lips permanently sealed, I was never able to get a bead on what paintings he was trying to sell.

Now, however, not only did I have a lead on the van Gogh, I had a suspect, D'Avanzo's associate 'Sal', who might know something about the previous art theft. Better yet, Sal might be able to explain why future potential presidential candidate Rudy Giuliani's gay, wise-guy cousin chose to die fighting an FBI posse rather than submit to a routine arrest.

Smith's skittish informant came through first. After months of dealing with voices on the phone, rumours, ghosts, and shadows, Smith called and said a buy was finally on. Phil, oddly enough, was willing to meet with the Lloyd's of London agents and Hammer Galleries' officials right at the gallery itself. With memories still fresh of Louie D'Avanzo's messy death, Smith and Lynch were reluctant to sit down with the mystery man alone. It was time for me to transform into art expert and Hammer Galleries employee Thomas Bishop, a man who was also quite adept at using a snub-nosed .38, a small handgun with a short barrel that's easy to conceal.

Just in case things indeed got a little sticky, I decided to recruit FBI Special Agent Barry Mawn to cover my back. Mawn, an ambitious, no-nonsense type, would one day become the director of two of the FBI's largest field offices, the Boston and New York branches.

The agreement between Phil and Smith was that Phil would sell a single painting for a paltry $4,600. If that went well, he'd open negotiations for the rest of the batch. This was a common practice for art ransoms. The 'kidnapper' would dole out the goods a little at a time to get the best price, to keep from being robbed himself, or to avoid getting busted by the cops. Naturally, he'd hold back the prize—in this case the van Gogh—until last.

The painting selected for the initial transaction was predictable. Choosing the second most valuable one, Dubois-Pillet's river scene

La Seine au quai St Bernard 1885, showed that the kidnapper was legit, was operating in good faith, and was eager to whet the appetites of the buyers. The only aspect that signalled the seller wasn't a slick art pro was the price. He easily could have gotten ten times that for a historical masterpiece soon to be worth considerably more.

On the day in question, Smith, Lynch, Special Agent Mawn and I waited patiently for the 1pm meeting. The plan was to play it straight, let the buy happen, and allow the kidnapper to stroll out of the gallery with Lloyd's of London's $4,600 in his pocket. If he never came back, that was the risk we were willing to take to get the rest of the paintings and break up the theft ring. More accurately, it was a risk Lloyd's of London was willing to take. Had it been the FBI's $4,600, we'd have had a lot harder time convincing the higher ups to 'let the money walk'—to risk losing even that relatively small amount.

The morning of the meeting, I dressed in a colourful, disco-era suit to avoid coming across as one of Hoover's starched automatons and spooking Phil. My long black hair, Burt Reynolds sideburns, and Tom Selleck moustache—tolerated by the ultra-conservative agency because of my frequent undercover activities—helped complete the picture.

'You look like a high class pimp,' my wife sneered disapprovingly as I left the house.

'Good,' I shot back. 'That's the image I'm going for.'

I advised the more G-Manish Mawn to dress similarly. We wanted to come across as art world hepcats straight from Andy Warhol's famous 'Factory'. The results were mixed. Mawn arrived looking pretty much the same as always. He protested that he normally didn't wear a tie that red.

When 1pm rolled around, in walked Phil with the Dubois-Pillet under one arm, and the biggest canine beast I'd ever seen attached to a leash on the other. Mawn and I looked at each other with wide eyes, expressing the universal unspoken signal for, 'Uh oh!' The monster dog, a tawny Great Dane mix as big as a horse, posed innumerable problems—not the least of which was the prospect of getting our heads bitten off to the nub. I glanced at Richard Lynch and he was nearly apoplectic for an entirely different reason. If that beast squatted to take a giant dump somewhere in his spick and span gallery, I figured the fastidious curator was going to have a heart attack on the spot.

Another obstacle the dog presented in that literal bull-in-a-china-shop setting was the high potential for collateral damage. To ease Phil's mind, we had purposely arranged for the transaction to occur during business hours when the gallery was open and peppered with art lovers. The midday crowd was already recoiling at the unnerving sight of a massive animal in such elegant surroundings, and the fun hadn't even started yet.

Surveying the scene, I whispered a prayer of thanks that we weren't planning to arrest the guy then. If that monster dog went berserk in the process, there was no telling how many innocent bystanders he would dismember. I noticed Mawn wipe his brow in relief as well, obviously thinking the same thought. He had a big future ahead of him, and a dinosaur dog chewing the limbs off a bunch of Monet fans during an undercover operation wouldn't look so good in his personnel file.

I tried to take my eyes off the beast long enough to get a read on Phil. He was a white male, about six feet tall, who appeared to be in his late 20s. Casually dressed with shaggy brown hair, he was overweight and unrefined, probably blue collar.

We speeded things up to end this encounter quickly and get the surly guard dog that was watching my every move the hell out of the gallery. I studied the painting, did the usual ultraviolet light show to verify its pedigree, then received a signal from Lynch confirming that it was authentic. This was important because sophisticated art thieves like to commission copies of paintings they steal so they can ransom and sell the fakes numerous times before finally coughing up the original.

Thankfully, Mawn's un-Warholish attire and stiff manner failed to tip Phil about our true identities. Lynch and Smith did an adequate acting job as well. I fully expected as much, considering that they were playing themselves and shouldn't have encountered problems slipping into their roles. With everyone keeping it together and doing their part, Phil appeared at ease with how the transaction was going. So much so, that he promised to return within the hour with additional paintings. He agreed to bring three more—all but the van Gogh—and turn them over for $25,000. Since we were planning to arrest him, the price didn't matter.

Due to a lack of manpower, we weren't able to shadow Phil to locate his stash or identify any possible accomplices. We were flying on blind faith.

After Phil left, I huddled with Mawn to formulate a new plan. We both agreed that we had to get Phil and the dog out of the gallery and arrest him on the street. We decided to tell him that the money was around the corner at a nearby bank, and then escort him there. Two additional agents would be called in to assist outside.

While waiting for Phil's return, it suddenly occurred to me that if he was in on the actual theft, Phil might have chosen the strange French drawing of the abused dog because he was an animal lover. Stealing that one might have served as some form of reverse karma. Art, after all, is designed to appeal to one's emotions.

Less than a half-hour later, Phil and his canine pal returned with the three diverse works of art: Grandma Moses' tranquil marshland scene; a vividly coloured oil painting of a Native American warrior sitting by a river from Eanger Irving Couse, a 19th and 20th century American artist who was a founding member of the Taos Society of Artists in Taos, New Mexico; and the Daumier sketch of the poor beaten hound. (Couse's oils sell for up to a half million dollars today.)

I gave them a quick going-over with a black light—used to reveal age, repairs, and alterations—studied the signatures, measured the size and dimensions, scoped the brushstrokes, then dramatically dubbed them authentic.

Lynch, with one eye on the big dog's potentially offending rear, signalled that he was in agreement. I then explained to Phil that the money was waiting at the nearby bank. The unplanned wrinkle and location change should have been clues that something was amiss, but Phil agreed without protest.

Outside, Mawn and I escorted Phil and the dog around the bend, hooking east on 57th Street. We stalled a bit to wait for a break in the heavy Manhattan foot traffic. The sidewalk finally cleared. I pulled the snub-nosed .38 from my body holster and calmly stuck it into Phil's well insulated ribs. 'If that dog moves you're a goner,' I barked. Phil nearly fainted, a situation which may have unintentionally ignited the situation. 'Stand straight and stay cool,' I ordered, adding that we were FBI agents, not robbers, and that everything would be okay if he stayed calm.

So far, so good. The big dog just stood there looking at us with its head turned wearing a perplexed expression, no doubt waiting for his master's 'kill' command.

As we gingerly and unobtrusively put the cuffs on Phil, a street hustler saddled up to Mawn, opened his jacket, and tried to sell the future New York FBI boss a counterfeit watch. Ever the diligent G-Man, Mawn arrested him on the spot and pushed him into the car with Phil. We now had in custody a man who might prove to be the key to solving one of the biggest thefts of the decade, and a guy selling fake Rolexes.

We also still had a very large, very confused dog separated from his master to deal with, an unpredictable animal that might go nuclear any moment. Sensing our discomfort, and fearing for the health and welfare of his beloved pet and protector, Phil confessed that his girlfriend was right down the street. She'd be happy to take the beast off of our hands, he offered. Normally, it's dangerously irresponsible for a law enforcement officer to allow an unknown accomplice to stroll into the picture during a tense arrest. Mawn and I shrugged, tossed the cadet manual aside, and readily agreed to expand our growing circus.

After exiting the car, Phil turned and waved his arm. Within seconds, a brown Chevy pulled up and a plump blonde in a white blouse and black pants materialised. Quickly brought up to speed, she agreed to take custody of the canine. Technically, she was a criminal partner, but as outlined, we were more than happy to let her solve our biggest logistical problem. Besides, as long as we had Phil, I was certain we'd be able to locate his mate.

Phil and his new friend, the watch salesman, were driven to FBI Headquarters at 26 Federal Plaza. There, the timepiece hawker was immediately cut loose by our baffled superiors, allowing us to focus our energies on interrogating Phil. Eager to make a deal and save his skin, he quickly agreed to roll on his connection. I couldn't help shaking my head in quiet exasperation when he gave me the name and location—Salvatore Pisano, the owner of the gas station on Hicks Street near Al Capone's home. That was the same place Louie D'Avanzo had made a pit stop when I was tailing him three years earlier.

Funny how things tie together.

To complete the picture, every Italian 'Salvatore' I'd ever known, arrested, or followed went by the name 'Sal.' Smith's source had closed the circle and led us to the prime suspect I'd been searching for.

Phil further explained that he was only a small-fry middleman. Pisano, he claimed, had the van Gogh, and might know the identity of the major players, including the original thieves. I did a background check and Pisano came up clean. Not even an unpaid parking ticket smudged the retired longshoreman's sheet. He was an older man in his sixties who wore horn-rimmed glasses, had thick, wavy, salt-and-pepper hair combed straight back, and was usually dressed in the typical grease-stained service station uniform. Sal was neither a top echelon mobster nor a refined art aficionado. Even so, his business was deep within the Colombo Mafia Family's territory, so we suspected Sal was at the least some kind of low-level associate.

In return for a full walk, Phil agreed to wear a wire and set up Pisano. His girlfriend, standing by her man, offered her services as well. It only took them a day or so to arrange the deal. We gave Phil $10,000 cash to flash in front of Pisano, and instructed him to promise that another $40,000 would be coming when the van Gogh was sold. In case Phil and the blonde had any ideas about taking the ten grand and running, we made sure all roads leaving the gas station were covered.

Phil and his lady played their roles perfectly, digging the hooks into Pisano with little effort. As we listened in utter shock, Pisano got up from his squeaky chair in the grimy gas station office, walked into the cluttered service bay, reached out with greasy hands, and lifted up a flat, rectangular object covered in brown paper that was straddling the tops of two mucky, 50-gallon oil drums. He turned around and unceremoniously handed the object to Phil, leaving black fingerprint smudges on the flimsy wrapper that appeared to have been constructed from a used grocery bag. It was the van Gogh!

Ripping off part of the soiled covering, Phil nodded as he recognised the now-familiar Paris bridge, and promised Sal he'd be back with the full $50,000 later that day. Phil cradled the historic painting under his arm, returned to the vehicle, tossed the multi-million-dollar van Gogh into the back seat like it was a $6 picture frame, hopped inside, and sped off, rendezvousing with my agents down the street. He dutifully turned over the recovered relic, giving no indication that he and his lady were even tempted to take the money and the masterpiece and run.

Moments later, Mawn and I paid Mr Pisano a visit. With guns drawn, we marched inside and informed him he was under arrest for possession of stolen property. Pisano immediately began to wail that he didn't know what we were taking about, that we were crazy, that he didn't know van Gogh from Van Halen, and that he was just an honest citizen trying to operate a small business. He even had the gall to ask us to leave so he could return to work.

We told Sal to turn off the violins and informed him that we'd just busted his buddy Phil down the street with a van Gogh decorating the worn interior of his girlfriend's Chevy—a story designed to maintain Phil's cover—and added that everything had been recorded.

'We've got you dead to rights, Sal,' I said. 'We have your place bugged. It's all on tape, and it's as good as a confession.'

As we drove our latest prisoner across the Brooklyn Bridge, the legendary expanse that the proverbial conman is always trying to sell, Sal started doing a sales job of his own.

'Come on guys, it's almost Mother's Day,' he whined.

'My mother's gonna to be bent outta shape if I'm not there for dinner. She's getting up in years, ya know. Almost 90. Her health's not so good. My wife's gonna go nuts as well. Wait till they find out I'm in jail! I don't know what they'll do. It could kill them both! You gotta give me a break. I don't know nuttin' about this art stuff! I didn't know what was in the package. I swear! I was just doing a friend a favour. I didn't think nuttin' of it. I hardly even know the guy. Come on, you gotta help me out here. What's my momma gonna think?'

'I'll make you a deal, Sal,' I said. 'Tell us where you got the paintings, how the theft went down, who the insider at the gallery is, and what artwork your dead buddy D'Avanzo was trying to sell a few years back, and I promise you'll be having pasta fazool with momma on Sunday as scheduled.'

At that, Sal zipped it. And he kept it zipped all the way through the yearlong prosecution. Sal was the mob-approved fall guy, and he was savvy enough to know better than to point the finger at a cutthroat Colombo or Gambino Mafia soldier.

As I feared, the whole Louie/Phil/Sal daisy chain was typical, tried-and-true Mafia-style insulation. Even if Sal coughed somebody up, it would just be another sacrificial lamb with limited information. No matter how many arrests we made, we'd eventually nab a person who was too close to the gangland fire, and he'd clam up. In this case, Sal was the designated clam.

I couldn't really blame the guy. If he talked, he'd be killed. That's the way things work in Al Capone's old neighbourhood.

Despite a sewing basket overflowing with loose ends, everybody pronounced themselves happy and the case was closed. The Hammer Galleries had their masterpieces back. Lloyd's of London didn't have to fork over millions in insurance. Phil and his Rubenesque girlfriend were into the wind, no doubt planning their next hapless scheme. And the Brooklyn DA had a stooge to throw the book at and grab some artsy headlines. Everything was tied up in a nice little bow.

Even Sal made out okay. With his clean record, the judge figured he was just a Mafia pawn and gave him five years probation. It turned out Sal pulled another fast one. He had allegedly been making a killing selling cut-rate gasoline, minus all the bothersome government taxes, for Colombo Capo, Michael Franzese, the fabulously rich 'Yuppie Don' who later wrote the trailblazing exposé *Quitting the Mob*.

The only person who wasn't doing cartwheels over the ending was me. This wasn't my idea of a job well done. We never determined how the paintings were stolen, who the inside turncoat was, and which mob soldier was pulling the strings.

We had hoped that the organised crime bosses would be so turned off by D'Avanzo's and Pisano's futile attempts to introduce the Mafia into the art business that they would decide to get out of the game altogether. Unfortunately, as the price of paintings soared into the tens of millions, that was decidedly not the case. The mobsters would be back, and with them would come every imaginable breed of thief, burglar, con man, hustler, and opportunist.

Until then, it was off to Boston for me. A skilled team of international thieves had the audacity to hit the esteemed Fogg Museum at Harvard University. The cunning gang made off with an astounding 7,000 irreplaceable historical artefacts, including 800 ancient Greek and Roman coins that could be sold for thousands of dollars each.

It was time for Thomas Bishop to mothball the New York disco suit and slip into a navy blue, pinstriped number more befitting a globetrotting numismatist willing to stop at nothing to add some prized antique currency to his private coin collection.

.9.

THE BOSTON MUSEUM MASSACRE

OIL PAINTINGS ARE without question the top dogs in the multifaceted art world. Putting aside the occasional Michelangelo sculpture, brushstrokes on canvas have the greatest monetary value, garner the most attention, and generate the highest level of emotion and awe.

From a thief's perspective, however, this form of art can be cumbersome, difficult to transport, and hard to sell.

If there's an easier way, a crook will find it. Paintings aren't the only museum-class historical artefacts that can be fenced to collectors. Often, while the medium might be different, the same big-name artists are involved. Some of the great masters dabbled in multiple fields, producing sketches, engravings, jewellery, frescoes, furniture, silverware, sculpture, and even literature.

In one particular area, art and money merge into a single entity. Talk to a coin collector and they'll tell you that some of the finest art the world has known can be found on a small piece of tin once worth no more than a penny. Thieves frequently agree, most notably the ones that hit Harvard University's esteemed Fogg Museum on a cold December day in 1973.

Ignoring walls overflowing with paintings spanning the Middle Ages to the present, incorporating everything from Italian Renaissance to French Impressionists, the Fogg robbers went right for the money—literally. The beautiful imagery of Rembrandt, Titian, Renoir, Picasso, Rubens, Cézanne, Matisse, and hundreds of others were completely ignored, cast aside for a collection of 7,000 crudely hammered Greek and Roman coins dating back as much as 2,500 years.

Whatever rocks a crook's boat. While the sea of change might not have been anything to look at by comparison, it was far from worthless. The 6,500 plus coins the thieves made off with were valued at $2.5 to $6 million. That is, if they were sold as a group. In 1973 dollars. Stored for a decade or two, and then sold individually, the value might be 25 times that.

The theft itself was intriguing in its simplicity. *Harvard Magazine* executive editor Christopher Reed revisited the incident in a series of well researched articles that appeared in 2000. Reed was able to fill in details that few, outside the thieves themselves, were aware of at the time.

According to Reed and various police reports, a young man came to the museum on 1 December 1973, and left a shopping bag containing a package of undetermined contents at the security guard station. The practice was not uncommon. Many people combine shopping with sightseeing, and prefer to submerge themselves in ancient history without the burden of having to lug weighty purchases through extensive corridors. Some museums require it. It's like leaving a winter jacket with the coat check girl.

In this instance, the man left without his 'coat'. Five minutes before closing, a 'Mr Ryan' called and said the package contained a birthday present for his young daughter. He needed to pick it up that day, or the tears would flow. A sympathetic security guard arranged for him to retrieve it at the watch station after hours, figuring the man would be right over. Instead, the caller appeared at the north entrance at 12.45am on 2 December. He pointed at the package through the window of the locked door, and mouthed to the night watchman that he was there to retrieve it. The watchman, briefed about the visitor's possible appearance during the shift change, thought nothing of unlocking the door and letting him in. Once inside, Ryan produced a chrome-plated handgun and announced a hold-up.

The security officer was tied with blue plastic tape. A wool cap was pulled down over his eyes so he couldn't identify the four accomplices who slipped into the building to assist Ryan. The quintet marched directly to the coin room, a study and storage area that wasn't part of the public portion of the gallery. Using the watchman's key, they entered the area and began smashing the cases, scooping up approximately 3,000 gold, silver, and bronze coins. They also grabbed a small safe containing another 2,650, worth an estimated $2 million, that were on loan from alumnus Arthur S. Dewing. An undetermined amount of miscellaneous currency was taken as well.

Satisfied with their haul, the thieves exited the building and sped away in two cars. In less than half an hour, they had orchestrated the largest coin theft in United States history.

The gang drove to Ryan's girlfriend's apartment in the suburbs, cracked the safe, and split the booty.

When their pre-arranged fence deals began falling through, probably because of the extensive news coverage of the theft, one of the thieves went back to moonlighting as an armed robber. Anthony Vaglica, 50, was caught trying to rob a credit union and was dispatched to a Rhode Island prison.

Secrets are hard to keep in jail. Nine months later, a California private detective heard about Vaglica's involvement and pressed him for information. The P.I., working on a finder's fee commission he probably dangled in front of the con, learned the true identity of

'Ryan'. He promptly tried to beat the location of the missing coins out of the guy, Martin G. Regan of Attleboro, Massachusetts. Regan didn't break. By then, however, the police and FBI were also on to Regan and closed in. Battered, bloodied, and facing threats of a long prison sentence, he decided to cooperate and give information on the rest of his partners.

FBI agents were soon travelling to a wooded area of Lincoln, Rhode Island, with shovels in hand. They unearthed a bowling ball bag and a metal tool chest packed with a total of 3,036 coins—Regan's and Vaglica's share.

A week later, Boston FBI agents joined with the local police to round up additional members of the gang, two men and Regan's girlfriend. (The young lady was charged as an accessory after the fact for allowing her pad to be used as the divvy location.) The remaining coins, however, weren't immediately recovered as the gang acquired lawyers and refused to talk.

It was later determined that Vaglica had been a prisoner on a work release programme who was employed by Harvard's Widener Library. Vaglica had a considerable interest in ancient coins, mostly in stealing them, and had spent many an hour at the Fogg. He was tagged as the brains of the operation.

I became involved after an informant, probably one of the gang trying to cut a deal, fingered another associate still at large who was said to have 800-plus coins.

Boston wanted both my mentor, Don Mason, and me to be involved because there was a suspicion that this same gang was involved in a Boston to Montréal, Canada, pipeline that was stealing a wide variety of artefacts in both cities. The previous year, the Montréal Museum of Art had been hit by a group that took a Rubens, a Cézanne, a Gainsborough, and a work by 20th century French Salon d'Automne sensation Maurice de Vlaminck, among a dozen other paintings worth nearly $2 million at the time. The thieves entered through a skylight in a section of the roof where the alarms weren't functioning. Once inside, they bound and gagged the guards, and proceeded to take the pick of the litter. Had they not eventually triggered a working alarm, they would have stolen dozens more.

Canadian and Boston authorities thought we might be dealing with the same crew, and needed some undercover specialists to secure the remainder of the Fogg coins, along with anything else that might develop.

I jumped at the chance because Don was talking about retiring, and this might be the last opportunity we had to work together. As it was, Don had essentially mothballed his longstanding alter-ego, Don Raymonds, and was letting my alter egos, Robert Steele and Thomas Bishop, carry the bulk of the undercover load. I chided him about exhuming Raymonds and going back on the streets to get the blood pumping a few more times before he hung up the jeweller's loupe.

Fuelled by the invincibility of youth, I overlooked the danger that's inherently involved in such operations. As it turned out, we both were destined to have a rough time, Don especially, from the most improbable of events.

The plan going in was that I would be the expert, in this case, a numismatist, which is a stuffy way of saying a smart coin collector. Don, letting me do all the heavy research lifting, was going to play the wealthy buyer. I prepared by studying Roman and Greek currency at the Metropolitan Museum of Art, the Frick, and the Museum of National History, along with Sotheby's Auction House. The crash course in the Earth's development of something other than straight horse-for-two-goats trading was absorbing.

The creation of a middle commodity to streamline the bartering process is credited to the Lydians of 640 BC Asia Minor. This enabled the Lydian horse breeder to have something imperishable that enabled him to purchase fresh food for his herd six months down the road. The concept, refined and nationalised by King Croesus, quickly spread, and was critical in fuelling the world's economic development.

Similarly intriguing was the choice of images used on these bold new commerce tools. More often than not, they were either animals, gods, or political leaders. We've certainly progressed beyond those tired ancient concepts, haven't we?

Complicating matters from my perspective was the fact that the brass, copper, bronze, silver, and gold coins were imprecisely made with a handcrafted punch using the rudimentary minting technology of the time. They contained frequent mistakes and were rarely uniform. The punches would wear down, and the punchers would often miss the mark, producing a partial, off-centre image. Not only that, but the owners would shave the edges or cut them in pieces to provide change.

In essence, a genuine 200 BC Roman *aes grave* would have the appearance of a poor fake that wasn't even perfectly round. Talk about a bronze mind fry. The wide assortment of coins usually didn't have specified denominations either. Their value was based upon their size, and upon the weight of the metals they were comprised of, figures that fluctuated with the changing price of the ores. This aspect, interestingly enough, gave us the popular saying 'worth its weight in gold.'

Sufficiently prepared, I was ready to add a new dizzying specialty to Robert Steele's growing résumé —ancient coin expert.

Huddling with the Boston Feds, we were told that the contact was a thuggish felon of indeterminable heritage, some kind of Irish Canadian Bostonian Eastern European knuckle-dragger. In other words, a Hockey Goon.

Don and I, in contrast, would be sophisticated New York art world hipsters. I sensed Don starting to get into it the moment he put on the 'costume.' Mason draped himself in a snazzy blue blazer, black pants, and a powder-blue sweater, and puffed an expensive cigar. I selected a blue suede jacket tailor made on 57th Street at The Custom Shop, along with the usual fake rings, watches, and other flashy accessories. We numismatists were sure one high-fashion vision in blue!

Convincing the bosses that we had to cruise in style to pull it off, we were allowed to rent a limo for the four-hour trip to Boston. We rolled into Beantown that evening and checked into a high-priced hotel near Logan International Airport where the informant arranged the meeting. Because we had been advised that the Hockey Goon was a heavy-hitter, we were both armed.

The suspect, Allen I. Kirchick, came as advertised. He was a big lug, about 6-foot-2, 240 pounds, balding, in his late 40s, wearing a black leather jacket over dark chino pants. It looked like a 50-car freight train had run over his scarred and heavily pockmarked face. I made him for being at least partially Black Irish like me—as legend goes, descendants of sailors from Spanish pirate ships and the Armada that crashed on the Irish coast back before Rembrandt and Titian waved their first brushes. Either that, or they were the original natives of the land prior to the Gaelic invasion. The history is unclear. I considered asking our bulky new friend his theory, but decided he had enough problems with his current muddied heritage, not to mention the dartboard mug. No point in taking him back a couple of thousand years—unless, ironically enough, we were talking about coins.

We mentioned that we were hungry, and he agreed to join us for dinner. Naturally, we Irishmen and Englishmen chose to eat at a Chinese restaurant in Boston, a buffet to be exact, since we were all big guys with big appetites. The buffet aspect also offered me the opportunity to play dutiful manservant to Don, treating him like Mr Big by getting his refills and seconds. I had a blast sucking up to him. Aside from putting on the act—and entertaining the surveillance agents scattered around at other tables—it was my way of showing appreciation for all he had done for me in my career.

In between catering to Don, I tried to get a bead on our mark. The guy wasn't talking much. When he did, I detected traces of a French Canadian accent indicative of a Montréaler. He had also spent a lot of time in America, probably American prisons, as he had the stiff, halting manner of a man who had been institutionalised for a large part of his life and was waiting to be led around by his guards.

It was obvious the man was desperate. The newspapers were full of stories about the Rhode Island recovery, so the remaining 834 coins were red hot. Kirchick needed to get rid of them fast. That knocked the price down from a million to somewhere between $50–$100,000, which was a smokin' deal for us.

With a product that was so easy to transport and conceal, I figured Kirchick would dig in his pocket and show us a coin or two to whet our appetites. He produced nothing. Not a thin, crude, badly punched Greek dime. He was cautious to the point of paranoia, all of which was unnecessary. Even if we were the heat—which we were—we wouldn't have busted him for one coin when we had a chance to get the whole piggy bank. Similarly, if we were rip-off artists, we'd wait for the big score before pulling our weapons.

We limoed our prospective partner back to the hotel. He said he'd be in touch. The following day, we received word from the informant that he was ready to deal. The wrinkle was that the goods were in Montréal. We'd have to wing it there to get them.

That posed numerous problems, not the least of which was that we'd be dealing with a foreign police agency. Since we were out of our jurisdiction, we'd have to solicit the co-operation of the local authorities.

Bonding with our Canadian counterparts proved to be a minor hurdle. Both the Montréal cops and the nationwide Royal Canadian Mounted Police were more than eager to get in on the action. Noting the possible connection to the 1972 Montréal Museum of Art theft, they had their own motivations.

Don and I returned to New York, barely having time to pack a small bag before we were jetting to Canada. Don was fighting a cold, but was too deep into the undercover operation to pull out.

A stereotypical Mountie met us at the airport—in a car, not on horseback—and gave us a quick tour before dropping us off at our hotel. I'd never been to Canada before and found Montréal to be a lovely city. We checked into one of their finest establishments, the St Paul Hotel, then met with the city police, headed by detectives Kenny Abrahams and Pierre Sangillo. Boston FBI agent Peter van Derveer was already in town with a few assistants to help coordinate the operation and to communicate with the informant.

We were pleasantly surprised to learn that the local cops were going all-out. They had already wired our rooms, and would be shadowing us in force. In fact, the Montréal PD had a separate surveillance squad specifically trained in the art of blending into a situation without doing anything to compromise a critical sting. At the time, even the FBI didn't have a squad of this nature, and more cases than I care to remember were blown because of it. All it takes is for one agent or officer to get sloppy and pull his radio, or scratch his arm and reveal his weapon, and a sting months in the planning evaporates in an instant.

After settling in, we had time to go out that evening to look around. Although the French are pegged as being cold and unfriendly to Americans, the French Canadians were anything but. The natives were extremely cordial, and it seemed that all the young women were knockouts, something a single American special agent certainly noticed.

The meeting with The Goon was set for the next morning. He was given our hotel and room number via the snitch, and phoned us after breakfast. He seemed more comfortable and at home in Montréal, and wanted to ask questions much more than before. We were impatient to get the ball rolling, so I essentially told him to 'show us the ancient money.'

He instructed us to meet him at the Royal Bank of Canada, Place Ville-Marie branch, which wasn't far from our hotel. We had enough time to huddle with van Derveer and the Canadian cops before departing. They assured us that we'd be surrounded by a large contingent of surveillance officers, blended in so well we wouldn't notice them. All they'd need was a signal from me and we'd be instantly swarmed.

Since it was cloudy and drizzling off and on, I told them I'd come outside and accidentally drop my umbrella. When they saw the 'brolly' drop, they were to do their thing.

While working this out, I kept hearing radios crackle and cops saying 'des cat' over and over. Curious, I asked what the fuss was over a feline? Had a lion or tiger escaped from the local zoo? I didn't want the beast to come bounding through my undercover operation at a critical time. The amused detectives explained that it was a short way of saying ten-four, i.e., *dix quatre* in French. Glad I cleared that up.

One of van Derveer's agents drove us to the bank, which was located in an audacious stone building with a tremendous open-air courtyard the size of a football field out front. It boasted numerous stone carvings adorning its façade, and was rimmed with flagpoles as if it were some kind of embassy. It reminded me of the Lincoln Centre's grand plaza in front of the Metropolitan Opera House in New York. I looked around the busy plaza and could not make out any of the surveillance team. If these guys were there, they were good.

I did spot The Goon. He was the only person who seemed out-of-place in the surroundings. With his mirror-shattering face and dark green trench coat, he appeared as if he was going to rob the joint. Inside, the bankers didn't seem concerned when he marched up to arrange a safety deposit box retrieval. We all signed in, Don and I using our aliases which we were prepared to back up with layers of phoney IDs acquired off the books. Since Hoover was anti–undercover operations, the FBI had yet to institute an internal process of issuing fake credentials. We were forced to do it on our own, the same way the crooks did, via street contacts who made them for us. We eventually became so good at it we were able to secure workable credit cards under the names of our alter egos.

And once you have one credit card, the other companies start prodding 'Robert Steele' to apply for more. I even had cards for Bob Steele and Thomas Bishop's imaginary wives and girlfriends. The subterfuge can easily snowball into an *X-Files* episode where you lose track of who is real and who isn't. If I was ever tempted to dash to Tahiti with a $25 million Cézanne, I was good to go.

After Congress cracked down on undercover activities following the ABSCAM political sting in the early 1980s, the FBI honchos freaked over the layers of illegal IDs and credit cards its special agents were carrying. They issued a stern, all-points-bulletin to turn them in ASAP. I reluctantly pitched my extensive array into the fire, mourning the demise of my supermodel-quality imaginary wives and mistresses who were really hot, never argued, and hardly ever spent my money!

So credentialed in Canada, we swept through various gates and descended to the vaults without incident. A stunning French Canadian woman greeted us at the entrance to the beehive of safety deposit boxes. She took a key from The Goon, apparently matched it with one on file—or did whatever that particular bank's security feature was—and returned with a rectangular box about three feet long but only five inches wide and three inches deep. Kirchick made no move to open them and just stood there. A minute later, the young woman showed up with a second box, then a third. After she delivered the fourth, Kirchick piled them one on top of the other, tucked them under his arm, and motioned for us to follow him into one of the private viewing cubicles.

The laws are pretty hazy on what people are allowed to keep in their boxes. The intent is for total privacy, so it's hard for banks to police them. Rental contracts usually specify that the renter is forbidden from hiding stolen goods or illegal contraband, but the bad guys don't pay attention to that, and the banks aren't held responsible. This has turned the secured storage boxes into a hotbed of stolen goods, dirty money, drugs, murder weapons, or anything else a criminal can stuff inside.

However, once the cops know an illegal or stolen item is there, they can get a warrant and confiscate it.

In our case, we were looking for 2,500 year old coins, and that's what we got: four boxes full. As expected, they came in all sizes, colours, metals, and shapes, picturing everything from horses to owls, and everybody from the Caesars to Roman and Greek gods. They contained Roman and Greek words and lettering, and varied in quality from dead-on hits with a new punch, to bad misses from worn out stamps. Some were shiny and new, while others appeared to have gone through hundreds of long-dead hands. I only needed to inspect them under a jeweller's loupe for about 20 minutes to determine they were authentic. These were the Fogg's babies all right.

Of particular note was a 10-drachma coin of Akragas from the private Dewing collection, which was the highest denomination made by the Greeks in classical times, along with a Syracusan silver tetradrachm picturing the full face of the nymph Arethusa dating back to 410 BC. The stunning coin, made by the artist Kimon, had dolphins swimming around the woman's braided hair. It looked really cool!

Among the great and not-so-great political leaders portrayed was none other than Nero, the Roman Emperor who was, among other things, a noted counterfeiter of minted money. Nero's stamps pictured him in the act of various feats of physical and military heroism, none of which history says the tyrant ever actually accomplished. They were, nonetheless, fascinating to behold.

Of course, as always, I wasn't raving about them to the seller. Instead, I hemmed and hawed, talked about the bad stamps and worn faces, proclaimed some as fakes, and scolded The Goon for jamming them together like that in the drawers because it scratches their heads and tails and lessens their value.

We haggled for a while over these and other issues, then agreed to buy the whole lot for $50,000. It was the deal of a lifetime; certainly enough to allow Don Raymonds to live like a king in retirement. But we were squeaky clean G-Men, so we banished such thoughts and stuck to the plan.

The coins were returned to their boxes, slid back into their slots, and we exited the catacombs to arrange the exchange. The Goon, buoyed by the expected score, insisted on taking us to lunch. We begged off, but he was adamant that we had to sample the great food at this place nearby. We were going to pop him anyway, but if something went wrong, we didn't want to feel obligated to spend the additional time with the galoot. He was so determined we finally relented.

Outside in the courtyard, I fumbled with my briefcase for a moment and knocked the folded umbrella to the ground. Stevie Wonder could have seen me. We waited, walked a bit, and nothing. Not a leaf rustling in the breeze. There wasn't a Canadian cop in sight.

I pretended to trip over the sidewalk. Down went the umbrella again. 'What's the matter with you?' The Goon asked. 'You drunk or something?'

I just shrugged and collected myself. I couldn't have been more obvious—to everybody except the Montréal police. Nobody swarmed. Suppressing panic, I had the terrible thought that maybe we hadn't noticed the surveillance team because there was nobody out there! Or maybe the Canadians had some Mexican siesta custom and the whole crew had pulled out for a sandwich and a nap.

After another 20 yards, I crossed my briefcase in my hands and dropped the umbrella a third time. Nobody appeared. Not Mountie Dudley Do-Right on a horse, Wayne Gretzky, Shania Twain, Bryan Adams, or Rick Moranis—not a Canadian soul.

The Goon had now given up on me and was confronting Don. 'What's wrong with this guy? He's losing his marbles.'

'Ah, he gets that way sometimes,' Don spat bitterly. 'I've got to smack him around once in a while to snap him out of it. Just ignore him. You know how hard it is to get good help.'

Great. Not only did I feel like a total idiot, and not only had we been abandoned with the bad guy, but we now had to go to lunch with the big lug.

Off we went down the avenue to some slop house eatery. It was on the second story of a building, and there was a long line to get in that wrapped down a narrow tunnel-like staircase to the street. The Goon insisted it was worth the wait, so we fell in queue and inched our way up the steps, wondering what in blazes we were going to do next.

Halfway up the stairs, all hell broke loose. The Canadian cops finally decided to take us down, and picked the absolutely worst possible place and moment to do so. A herd of them came barrelling up the stairway. With guns drawn, they started knocking people left and right, tripping over each other. They ripped Don and I out of the line and dragged us down, nearly knocking people over the railings. The biggest cops stuck their guns in The Goon's ribs, cuffed him behind his back, and left him standing there in the middle of the line for a while before eventually easing him down.

The crowd just gawked in shock, wondering what the heck was going on. Don and I were thinking the same thing. I couldn't have imagined a more dangerous place to make the arrest than on that crowded stairway. They were lucky nobody was seriously hurt.

We were segregated in different vehicles, and the arresting officers gave no indication that they knew we were anything but bad guys. As mentioned in previous chapters, sometimes the front line beat cops aren't told so they don't blow our cover by giving us preferential treatment. This standard law enforcement technique apparently holds especially true in Canada, because these guys were giving us no slack whatsoever.

It turned out that only a select few among the Canadian force knew that we were American FBI agents. We were fingerprinted, photographed, and processed through booking in a long, drawn-out process by French Canadian cops who treated us like the scum of the earth. Don's cold was deepening into a full-fledged flu, and he was getting no sympathy from anybody.

As noted before, I've been arrested dozens of times during undercover operations in every manner possible. I have been dragged through the lobbies of fine hotels, bounced around on the street, thrown up against walls, slammed over bars: you name it. In all those instances, I never felt ashamed. To the contrary, there was usually a New York wise guy sense of macho pride in being important enough to attract so much attention from the vaunted Feds.

Only this time, I wasn't in New York. I wasn't even in the United States. These Canadians were treating me like I was ugly American garbage of the lowest order, and I was feeling the hate.

I kept waiting for Detectives Abrahams and Sangillo to arrive and end the show, but they were nowhere in sight. Nor were my peers van Derveer and his crew. Instead, Don and I were tossed into dingy, rat hole cells with all the junkies, drunks, whores, armed robbers, rapists, and every other breed of Canadian low-life. One guy kept screaming that, 'Jesus is coming. We're all gonna die,' while another kept insisting he was Napoleon and was going to restore France's world respect. How clichéd was that?

We waited amid the stench, squalor, and psychos. We waited and waited and waited. Don was getting sicker and sicker, and still we languished in our little cages. By midnight, we realised everybody had long gone home to their warm beds and sexy French Canadian wives, and nobody was going to come for us at all.

I couldn't believe it. How far were these blasted Canadians going to take this? Here we had rooms in the best hotel in Montréal, which we were still paying for, and we were instead sleeping on a wooden slab in a cold, damp jail cell. Dinner was a wretched bologna sandwich, not Filet Mignon at the St Paul. I angrily ripped the toilet paper roll from the dispenser to use as a pillow and tried to get some sleep.

A scream of undetermined origin woke me at 4am. I spent the next five hours tossing and turning on the slab, trying to fall back to sleep.

At 9am, they came for us—not to set us free, but to take us to arraignment. By then, we both looked like hell, and Don was in seriously bad shape. In one of the hallways, I spotted Detective

Abrahams. I was about to go ballistic when he signalled me to remain quiet. We were taken to the courthouse, where we were finally let go.

I had a million questions, and sought Abrahams out for some answers. He explained that Montréal is not a giant city like New York, and they had to play the arrest out to the end because, 'Everybody knows everybody here,' and nobody could be trusted to keep such a secret. The beat cops, booking staff, and jailers all have friends and relatives on both sides of the law, and once they started telling their wives and pals down at the pub, there was no turning back. The arrest was big news in Montréal, splashed across the front pages of all the papers. The stories reported that three Americans were arrested, so that's the way they had to play it.

That seemed relatively reasonable, although New York had a lot of cops on the take and we never had to play an arrest to that degree. Then again, New York is a city of 10 million.

There was also that second little matter of the umbrella that I wanted to know about. Coming in when the operative says the code word, or gives the signal, is the most critical aspect of an undercover operation. It can often be a matter of life or death.

Abrahams brushed that off like a Paris waiter growing tired of an American trying to decipher a menu. He said they decided that they didn't want to make the arrest in the sacred plaza, and waited for another opportunity.

The fact that the area they chose was terribly dangerous to all involved didn't seem to faze them.

Van Derveer and his crew were, of course, greatly amused by our misery. It's an FBI guy thing.

At that point, all we wanted to do was get back to our hotel, shower, shave, burn our clothing, and get something decent to eat. Don now had a bad stomach to go with his runny nose and pounding head, and was ready to AK-47 everybody in Canada and at the FBI. Since I was the one who had goaded him into 'getting back into the action,' the first bullet was reserved for me.

After cleaning up, we decided to get the hell out of Dodge before the Montréal cops found a reason to arrest us again. On the bus to the airport, Don coughed up most of his expensive lunch, further plunging his already rock bottom mood.

The story, unfortunately, didn't end there. Since it was such a headline grabbing case, Washington wanted us to return to Montréal to testify against The Goon at his trial. As an attorney, I knew that could be a disaster because Canadian law doesn't offer the same protection to informants as in the American courts. That meant The Goon's defence attorney's first question would be the identity of the informant who sold his client out. Since that would put the informant's life in danger—and freak out every mole from Anchorage to Key West—we naturally didn't want to be put in that position.

From a personal perspective, I didn't want to be put in the position of having to refuse, and then be sent back to my old familiar jail cell. Been there, done that. Don't want the French T-shirt.

My pleas fell on deaf ears at the 'Puzzle Palace' in DC. They were still wrapped up in the public relations game, and wanted us to appear in Montréal like good soldiers.

Angry, I called van Derveer and told him that I wasn't going to spend another second in that stinkin' rat hole French cell, and if he didn't do something, I was going to serve up his snitch on a platter.

That might seem harsh, but it's routine law enforcement behaviour. We'll protect our own angelic snitches with our lives because we've given our word and formed a personal bond. On the other hand, everybody else's snitch is just some low-life scumbag hustler who doesn't deserve being spat on, much less going to jail for. Which explains why cops are so reluctant to give up the identities of their informants, even to their bosses.

Van Derveer made his case to DC, but was blown off as well. Next thing we knew, we were back on the plane to stinkin' Montréal. Everything was different now. Suddenly, Don and I were conquering heroes. Abrahams and the prosecutors promised the judge, jury, and media that two big-time superstar undercover American FBI agents were going to appear in court, reveal themselves, and put on a show. It was as if Melvin Purvis, top FBI agent, and Efrem Zimbalist Jr, of TV show *FBI*, were coming to town.

We arrived at the courthouse and were literally pacing in the hallway outside the courtroom when van Derveer fielded an emergency call from DC. 'Get out of Canada, now!'

We were whisked downstairs, stuffed inside a waiting car, taken to the airport, and plopped on a jet.

Meanwhile, back at the courtroom, the prosecutors dramatically announced our appearance, opened the door, and ta da—we're gone like the von Trapp family in *The Sound of Music*. They could have fed the entire courtroom breakfast with all the eggs that were on everybody's face. The cops went nuts and were ready to track us down, throw us in our waiting cells, and weld the doors shut.

Van Derveer, our compadre who had found it so amusing that we were jailed overnight, was left in Montréal to take the heat. He tried to explain the predicament we were in regarding the snitch; mostly to no avail.

The only explanation I received was that somebody in DC finally woke up to the fact that there might be an international incident in the courtroom regarding informants, and pulled the plug at the last second. That wasn't unusual. Agents in the field work at warp speed, while Washington grinds along like snails on thorazine. The same phenomena occurred, tragically, in 2001 when field agents began filing reports about Arabs enrolling at various aviation schools across America. The Arabs wanted to be taught how to fly commercial airliners, but were unconcerned with learning how to take off and land. The strongly worded warning memos were collecting dust on desks at FBI headquarters when the same Arabs staged their infamous 9/11 attacks on the World Trade Centre and the Pentagon.

Back in Montréal, despite the courtroom theatrics, Kirchick was convicted, as were the rest of the gang in America. They were given the usual probation or short sentences, with Kirchick getting 3 1/2 years. Two of the thieves, however, were initially given 20 to 30 years, a sentence aimed at getting them to cough up their share of the coins. They held out stubbornly for a few years, but with their cellmates angling to rat them out to help their own causes, they eventually saw the light, trading the coins for 20 to 25 years being shaved from their draconian terms.

The gang naturally zipped it about their other activities, and denied taking the paintings from the Montréal Museum of Art. Those remain at large.

The Fogg eventually recovered 6,773 coins and 105 medals, which they estimated to be nine-tenths or more of what was taken, and virtually all of the most valuable ones. According to *Harvard Magazine*, they're now kept at a secret location in the Slacker Museum across the street from the Fogg.

I would question the need for that. With the astounding amount of priceless paintings the Fogg has on display at any given time, I don't think they need to worry about somebody hunting down those coins again. Although, their value has probably gone up 10 times or more since then, so you never know.

In one of those 'kill all the lawyers' kickers, original thief Martin Regan filed a multi-million dollar lawsuit against Harvard. The crook who used sympathy over a child's birthday gift as a ruse to break into the Fogg Museum, hold the watchman at gunpoint, and then wave his marauding partners in, wanted $5 million for the 'injuries, humiliation, pain, and suffering' he received when roughed up by the private dick. Enraged, Harvard, an institution with a literal army of influential alumni judges, attorneys, and politicians, vowed to defend itself with vigour. The suit faded away.

To combine Harvard's motto 'veritas' with a famous quote from Jesus: 'The truth set the famed university free.'

.10.

THE PEEVED PEPPERDINE PROFESSOR

A POPULAR JOKE I heard a thousand times among the art fraternity goes like this: Monet created 100 paintings in his lifetime—500 of which are in America.

Monet wasn't always the artist in the straight line. That was interchanged with whoever happened to be the *faux du jour*. The French Impressionist was a popular choice, however, because his misty dabbed style is easy to forge. Picasso's *Mona-Lisa*-on-acid abstracts are also frequent targets for half-baked fakes because every talent-challenged hack believes he or she can produce one of those—and can pass it off as the real thing.

Whatever the skill level, copies of great paintings are everywhere. Some are rudimentary. Others are near perfect, works of art in their own right. Most are sold as just that, duplications, violating only a muddle of complicated and hard-to-prosecute copyright statutes that differ from country to country.

The trouble arises when a skilled forger, or his agents, try to pass off copies as the real thing. Aside from the criminal fraud involved, these bogus Rembrandts, van Goghs, Rubens, Manets, ad infinitum, pollute the market, befuddle law enforcement, and throw a wrench into the worldwide registrations and location guides. It's exasperating to try and produce an accurate book or listing when you can pinpoint six identical *Adoration of the Shepherds* in different museums, each one claiming to own the original Rubens. That's on top of dozens of others sharing the same title produced by different artists.

During my career as a masterpiece tracker, I always felt a special sense of accomplishment when I removed one of these brilliant fakes from the international art gene pool. When I was able to shut down a forgery factory, the feeling intensified.

One of the biggest counterfeit operations I ever came across was a bustling business headquartered in a huge apartment outside San José, California. We were tipped about it in 1989 when a Pepperdine University business professor thought he stumbled upon the buy-low, sell high score of a lifetime. The professor purchased a series of drawings and sketches signed by the likes of Rembrandt, van Gogh, Rubens, Edgar Degas, and Marc Chagall.

Degas was a 19th century French Realist/Impressionist also known for his sculptures. His best paintings sell in the $10 million range. Chagall was a whimsical, Russian-born, France-living, 20th century artist who gave the world magnificent, childlike visions on canvas and stained glass, among other mediums. His upper-tier paintings retail for about a million dollars. Rembrandt, van Gogh, and Rubens, are, well, Rembrandt, van Gogh, and Rubens.

The Pepperdine instructor came away with 13 works from the magic hands of such esteemed masters for a paltry $9,600. While drawings don't carry the same weight as oil on canvas, anything from these superstars is gold. A van Gogh pencil sketch can sell for more than a million. The professor could have increased his investment

50 to 100 times over by selling a single one of the Rembrandts, van Goghs, Rubens, or Degases.

Eager to confirm his good fortune, the professor took photographs and sent them to Sotheby's, the famed New York auction house. The news was not positive. The experts at Sotheby's deemed them all fakes.

Getting ripped off on oil paintings is one thing, but drawings are something entirely different. A fake oil can be a magnificent work of art in its own right, having been laboriously created by a talented artist. If someone can score a brilliant copy of the *Adoration of the Shepherds* for $500, they really shouldn't complain when it turns out to be bogus. Hang it over the fireplace and tell your friends it's the real thing. They won't know any better anyway.

Drawings, however, are all about an artist's fame. Might as well make a paper airplane out of that bogus $1 million van Gogh scribble and toss it out the window.

Royally ticked, the professor screamed to the FBI. Often, such complaints are put on the back burner, if not tossed right into the circular file. A $10,000 art con is no big deal in the scheme of things, and the FBI probably didn't have Federal jurisdiction to begin with. Fortunately for the professor, his luck had changed. He had randomly reached a special agent I'd worked with on another case, someone who suspected this might be of interest to me. That was especially true when the professor mentioned that the sellers had an ongoing operation that spilled beyond the boundaries of California.

The case caught my attention for an even more important reason. I had recently moved from New York to Oklahoma because things had gotten too hot for me in the Big Apple. Aside from being outed to the media one time too many by the brass in Washington following a sensational art recovery, I'd moonlighted on a Mafia investigation that turned into the biggest FBI drugs-and-organised-crime case in history. In 1986, we busted a billion dollar heroin smuggling operation known as 'The Pizza Connection,' so named because the foreign-born mobsters were selling their poison out of pizza joints and other businesses around the nation.

The crooks were mostly Sicilian, and were reminiscent of the old country Italian gangster who tried to assassinate Vito Corleone in *The Godfather* because he wouldn't agree to sell their drugs. This was real life, not the movies, and there were 19 similarly deadly defendants who wanted me and my associates similarly out of the picture. They included the boss of the Sicilian mob, his top henchmen, and a home-grown pack of New York's Bonanno family goons. I testified at the trial regarding my participation in wiretaps and surveillance activities, and had to point my G-Man finger at a number of the goombahs in the courtroom to identify them.

The Pizza Connection was front-page news week after week. We confiscated 600 kilos of heroin, and virtually destroyed an entire mob family. One of the Assistant US Attorneys, Louis Freeh, was a friend and former special agent who later became the Director of the FBI. My testimony was necessary considering the scope of the crime, but it's sure difficult to keep one's clandestine alter-egos alive under that kind of attention.

Afterward, despite a wealth of convictions, the bosses felt it was best I head west until things cooled down. Even in Oklahoma City, I worked in a secret special operations office away from the main FBI headquarters.

I enjoyed Oklahoma as before, but quickly found that I missed the adrenaline rush of banging around in the stolen art capital of the world. There's not a whole lot of $25 million paintings that get filched in places like Norman, Oklahoma. There's a surplus of $25 million football players grown there, but Oklahoma's version of a work of art is a sculptured linebacker with a crimson Mohawk who can run a 4.3 second 40-yard-dash and bench press 300 pounds 20 times.

Faced with that reality, I was more than eager to jump on the professor's case. I rang him and listened as he related his sad story. He hesitated, however, when I said I'd be happy to put some serious

The infamous ABSCAM crew. Few remember that the biggest political sting in American history started out as an art theft case involving a Rubens and a Ter Borch. I'm standing to the left of the phony sheik, played by Special Agent Michael Dennehy, brother of actor Brian Dennehy. *(FBI photo/ No credit needed)*

Standing with the multi-million dollar Rubens and Ter Borch at the FBI offices. *(FBI photo)*

Left: The long lost Purple Picasso that's been missing from Texas since 1976. The huge painting could be worth anywhere from $25 to $100 million today. Anybody know where it is? (*FBI photo*)

Right: The Tinteretto pilfered from a German museum by Russian army officers during WWII. It materialised in New York more than three decades later. (*FBI photo*)

Above: Educating my FBI cohorts on the *CSI*-like art of authenticating ancient masterpieces via the flaws, cracks and composition of the paint, along with the aging of the backing materials and canvas. (*FBI photo*)

Above: Van Gogh's *Le Petit Pont*, in the centre, and a Grandma Moses were among the paintings worth up to $15 million that I successfully retrieved from New York Mafia henchmen. Among the cache was a drawing of a man beating a dog with a stick, etched by French caricaturist and satirist Honoré Daumier. Only a crew of bent-nosed gangsters would have snatched that off a gallery's walls. *(FBI photo)*

Left: The chase for Harry Jackson's famous *Gunsil* took me from Long Island to a real-life gentleman cowboy out west in Phoenix, Arizona. *(FBI photo)*

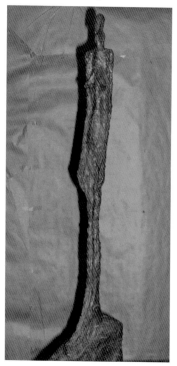

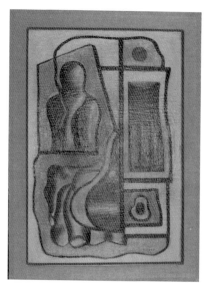

A chance encounter with a beautiful woman at a New York art museum library led to the recovery of eight valuable paintings and sculptures stolen from a private collector on Long Island. Included was Tom Wesselman's *Great American Nude* (above left), a painting by Willem de Kooning (above right), a Giacometti bronze (below left), and an abstract by French cubist Fernand Leger (below right). Because the recovery was after hours, I had to bring the entire $5 million haul home for the night, and schooled my son on art appreciation. *(FBI photos)*

Left: Con man extraordinaire Harold von Maker, aka Prince Harold von Hohenloe, lounges with a prop dog in front of a mansion he pretended to own. Such photos enabled him to fleece galleries nationwide out of untold millions worth of historic art. He based himself in residences rented from such luminaries as Marlene Dietrich and Jackie Gleason. *(FBI photo)*

Right: Among the authentic paintings found in von Maker's home gallery were pricey works by Jackson Pollock, Thomas Hart Benton, Norman Rockwell, Degas, and 16th century Flemish master Pieter Brueghel. *(FBI photo)*

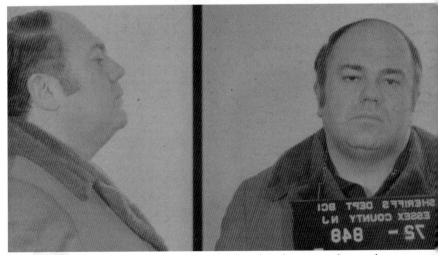

Above: Harold von Maker's mug shot. Shortly after this photo was taken, mob sources say he tried to swindle famed Mafia art aficionado Carmine 'The Doctor' Lombardozzi by pawning off some of the bad fakes I left behnd after the bust. Rumour has it Lombardozzi's henchmen tied von Maker to a Volkswagon and drove it into New York's East River. He was never seen again. *(FBI photo)*

Right: Sacrilegious thieves invaded a 12th century Roman Catholic church in Abella de la Conca, Andorra, and made off with a massive four-panelled altarpiece. The work by the Serra brothers was nearly eight feet tall and six feet wide, depicting the Virgin Mary, infant Jesus, the crucifixion, and other historic Judeo/Christian imagery. (*FBI photo*)

Left: I flew to Andorra to bring the Serra back to its rightful owners — Roman Catholic Bishops who double as the political leaders of this tiny nation. They gave me a sculpture to show their gratitude. (*FBI photo*)

Left: Telly Savalas lookalike 'Don Kojako' and the 'Lady from Spain' check out the recovered Serra in New York. As with most thieved art worldwide, the massive Serra ended up in Manhattan—the stolen art capital of the world. (*FBI photo*)

Above: This busy Rubens, an oil on wood entitled *The Judgement at Cambyese*, was one of two stolen paintings that kicked off the ABSCAM political sting. *(FBI photo)*

Above: Old West themed sculptures by Frederic Remington, similar to the one above recovered in a Florida theft, were among 53 works of art stolen from the Woolworth Estate in Maine. Highly specialised professional cat burglars are suspected, and most of the score remains at large. *(FBI photo)*

Above: Rembrandt's infamous Rabbi, as photographed for FBI files. The cranky old man's nine-year, globe-trotting misadventure at the hands of various thieves reads like a Hollywood movie. Some suspect he cursed everyone who dared possess him. *(FBI photo)*

Above: I worked with well-known NYPD art detective Robert Volpe many times. Volpe was one of the best undercover 'art pimps' in the business. *(FBI photo)*

Left: Vermeer's *The Concert* is generally regarded as the most valuable missing painting in the world today. One of only 30 Vermeers that remain in existence, it is estimated to be worth more than $100 million. It was stolen from Boston's Isabella Stewart Gardner Museum in 1990. There's a $5 million reward for information that leads to the return of the art taken from that theft. *(Courtesy of the Gardner Museum)*

Right: Enjoying a day at the beach with my daughter, Marianne. She was almost a victim of the Oklahoma City bombing while I was in hiding there. I was also in New York for the 9/11 World Trade Centre attacks. I've seen too much drama.

time and effort into it, but I needed some hands-on help from him. As with most people, he was afraid of getting involved.

Using a little psychology laced with good old Catholic guilt, I laid out that it was bad business to let this fraudulent activity continue, and as a business management professor, it was his duty to help nip it in the bud. After hemming and hawing, the professor was finally convinced that along with being his civic duty, it was his only shot at getting his ten grand back—not to mention a solid measure of vengeance as well.

Actually, all I needed from the professor was for him to vouch for me, and to introduce me to the sellers. He could do it in person, over the phone, via arranging a meeting, or simply by having them call me. I instructed the professor to praise the works he'd purchased instead of venting his displeasure, and say that he knew a heavyweight buyer who might be interested in purchasing a substantial amount of their remaining inventory. Although he was a nervous wreck, the man did as instructed. His contact, Tony Barreiro, 39, told him to have me call.

My first impression was that this Tony guy had to be pretty confident, or pretty stupid, to give out his phone number so readily.

The problem I had on my end was my new office location. What kind of art buyer would be in Oklahoma City? If I called from there, it would be a joke. Thinking fast, I decided to pay a visit to an informant I knew in Sun Valley, Idaho. Although that might sound even more jerkwater than Oklahoma City, it's actually one of those strange Hollywood East getaway towns popular with celebrities. The glitterati frequently fly in to ski at the resorts, or just to breathe in the crisp, fresh air. There are numerous film industry related events, music festivals, and conferences held in Sun Valley to keep their guests entertained.

Many celebrities who visited Sun Valley over the years liked what they saw and bought homes there. Ernest Hemingway arrived in 1939 and wrote *For Whom the Bell Tolls* at the Sun Valley Lodge. Demi Moore, Bruce Willis, Ashton Kutcher, Arnold

Schwarzenegger, Clint Eastwood, Jamie Lee Curtis, and Jean Claude van Damme call the place home at least part-time.

Sun Valley, population 1,500—less than a small New York building—was the exact kind of place a hotshot New York art dealer would be hanging, rubbing elbows with the stars.

I hopped on a plane piloted by an FBI special agent with his own Hollywood name, Dick Powell, hit my informant's pad, and dialled Barreiro, pouring it on thick about hanging with Eastwood, Robert Redford, Jamie Lee, and Jean Claude, all big art connoisseurs. Redford is actually a resident of another Off-Broadway Hollywood enclave, the Park City/Provo area of Utah, where he holds the annual Sundance Film Festival. If Barreiro caught the distinction, he didn't mention it. Instead, he was eager to sell me his paintings.

Ready to deal, I informed Barreiro that the next stop on my whirlwind tour just happened to be San Francisco, which is a short drive from San José. What a coincidence!

In San Francisco, I reunited with Barry Mawn, the Special Agent from the van Gogh case (See Chapter 8) who arrested the guy in the middle of our sting for selling bogus watches. He had had a pretty wild going-away party when he was transferred from New York to be the Number-Two man in the City by the Bay. We reminisced a bit about the party, and the van Gogh hunt, then got down to business.

Mawn hooked me up with an ambitious young female agent who looked like a soap actress called Susan Lucci. The agent, Susan Alford, knew the San José area, having recently transferred from that paradise field office to the hectic big city to seek more action. Eager to get a taste of undercover work, she readily agreed to be my assistant, for both Tom McShane and Thomas Bishop. She had studied art in college, and had a strong interest in the field.

I shared some war stories about my career, then outlined the similar undercover work we would be doing in San José. To my amusement, Alford blurted out, 'Wow, do you get paid extra for this?'

'Sadly, no,' I explained. 'It's all part of the big bucks they give us.'

We motored to my hotel, where I called my ol' pal Tony Barreiro. I decided to pull back on the high-flying schmooze a bit so as not to scare him off. If he was a counterfeiter, as we expected, I had to be more of a dupe than a black light-carrying expert. It was best I leave all the fancy equipment behind and simply play an unscrupulous wheeler-dealer. Barreiro swallowed the bait and invited us up the following day.

My new Girl Friday drove us through the pretty California countryside until we reached the address we were given. I'd previously advised her how to dress, upscale art world bimbo chic, and told her I'd be in my usual striped 'Artefact Pimp' suit accented by the phoney jewellery. She was naturally nervous about what to do, so I instructed her to just sit there like arm candy and take notes.

'What kind of notes?' she inquired, ever-diligent.

'Names of the paintings. Artist. Medium. That kind of appraisal stuff. I'll let you know. You can put that high-priced college education to work.'

We pulled into a luxury apartment complex that was actually in Sunnyvale, not San José proper. We rang the bell and were greeted by a shaggy man and a shaggy dog. The man was about 5-foot-8-inch, 250 pounds, and reminded me of comic actor Dom DeLuise, but with more hair. The dog was shorter, hairier, and weighed about half as much. Barreiro was wearing a tan leisure suit that had caused the death of a hundred polyesters, as the old joke goes.

The hefty guy led us to a large conference room with a huge, glossy, rectangular table surrounded by leather chairs, the kind of set-up you'd find in a law firm, not someone's home. It was impressive. He was obviously eating so well because he was rolling in the dough.

He was not, however, rolling in good health. He advised us right off that he had hepatitis, 'but not the catching kind.' That gave us the creeps. I could sense my young trainee already starting to regret volunteering. After making his medical announcement, Barreiro served soft drinks. I signalled to Alford to drink directly from the can, and avoid the provided glass. This was obviously a bachelor pad, and bachelors with hepatitis, whether type A, B, or C, aren't known for their cleanliness.

Two additional men were wandering around the place as well. They popped in and out, and appeared to be at home, so I made them for partners and roommates. One was a short guy who looked like actor Dustin Hoffman from his *The Graduate* days, while the other was a tall and lanky *Napoleon Dynamite* clone. They didn't appear threatening, so I basically ignored them.

We decided to go in unarmed because we were playing on their home court and didn't know if we'd be frisked. We were wired via the briefcase, and had some backups outside. If by chance anything went wrong, I'd toss 'Clint Eastwood' into the conversation as the signal for the agents to break in and rescue us. That was just a precaution. I didn't expect any hanky-panky at this stage because we weren't carrying any cash, and this was just a preliminary meeting. My main challenge was to survey the scene, and make sure Clint Eastwood didn't come up naturally in the conversation.

Barreiro kept moaning about his illness and rambling about everything and anything, so I had to push the issue along. I told him my time in the area was limited because I had to get back to my work with Redford and the glittery gang back in Sun Valley, stopping myself from disastrously dropping the name of the *Fistful of Dollars* actor. 'They're interested in your stuff as well,' I baited.

Brightening, Barreiro began rattling off a mental inventory of what he had, which was virtually everything you could think of. Name an artist and/or work, and he either had it or could get it. Oils, watercolours, pastels, charcoal drawings, etchings, sketches, sculpture, prints, pencil, ink, crayon, chalk sticks, he had it all. I asked how he happened to be in possession of such a J. Paul Getty-like stash. Smiling, he launched into his well-rehearsed spiel. He had contracted with a young Arab sheik who had travelled the world collecting fine art, but had since fallen on hard times and needed to unload it at pennies on the dollar. Nice story, I thought to myself, suppressing a laugh. This guy was sitting there dumping a bullshit Arab sheik story on the FBI agent who created the characters and scenario that fuelled the ABSCAM political sting.

His sheik, however, had crapped out and was in need of cash? Ummmm, I guess an alternative fuel was discovered and oil was no longer a hot commodity?

Actually, Barreiro's story wasn't totally preposterous. There was indeed a whacked out Arab sheik running around America back then raising all kinds of hell. The little brother of the wife of one of King Fahd's zillionaire brothers, Mohammed al-Fassi first hit Hollywood in the late 1970s and tried to buy his way onto the B list by tossing money around like a drunken sheik, and throwing lavish parties. He bought one of Beverly Hills' most prominent mansions, a 38-room palace on Sunset Boulevard know as 'The White House.' It's the same wildly audacious and tacky home that can be seen in the Steve Martin movie, *The Jerk*, and was used to symbolise Martin's exaggerated version of the good life. The sheik caused an international uproar when he later painted the house pea green, then hired an artist to highlight the genitalia and add pubic hair to the Italian marble statues surrounding the place.

When Hollywood tired of its crude, 5-foot-4-inch, perpetually unshaven pet, he took off in a huff, touring the world with his 65 servants, eventually landing in Miami, Florida. There, he raised another ruckus, spending money like he had an oil well in his backyard, which he apparently did, and buying high-priced waterfront property. He was tolerated by the locals until he was cut off back home, began bouncing Godzilla-sized cheques everywhere, and ran up million-dollar tabs at area hotels.

Meanwhile, back in Beverly Hills, a former chauffeur looted the mansion of more than a million dollars worth of art, then torched the place to cover it up. Neighbours gathered around the flaming monstrosity chanting 'Burn, baby, burn.'

Al-Fassi was eventually recalled home by the royal family and wasn't heard from afterward.

Although Barreiro wasn't specifically saying it, this was no doubt the genesis of the load of crap he was handing us. Since it was my job to set the hook, not challenge his story, I played along.

There was a slight chance that Barreiro had some of the missing al-Fassi art, but I doubted it since we already had the professor holding nothing but junk, and this guy claimed to have far more than what was reported in the al-Fassi theft. Heck, he had more than was reported in *any* theft.

The three men briefly escorted us around the spacious apartment, showing us assorted works of art on the walls in the various rooms, including the bedrooms of the other men, confirming my suspicion that they lived there. I made a conscious effort to search for a workroom, which Barreiro and associates could have easily explained away as being artists themselves, but there wasn't one. Whoever was duplicating the paintings was doing it offsite.

We were additionally brought various works from an unseen storage room. It was a cornucopia of media, everything from Rembrandt etchings, an entire sketchbook from the surrealist Joan (Jo-an), some watercolours and chalk stick pastels from Degas, and a large 3-by-4, signed and dated (8 June 1968) Picasso of a King Henry the VIII-like character. I thought the Picasso looked childish and terrible—which didn't necessarily rule it out as authentic. It just lacked the usual exuberance I saw in real Picassos.

The Rembrandt was good, but an obvious fake, which I could ascertain with the naked eye. Of course, I had an advantage because I'd studied Rembrandt extensively, and even travelled to his preserved studio in Holland and spent time with the curator. I knew the markings Rembrandt included on the edges of his engravings, which were absent here.

I didn't know anything about Miró's sketches, being more familiar with his splashy, brightly collared, childlike paintings. The others were pretty much on the mark, with the Degas being especially good. The Degas chalk pastels had the same powdery, glowing appearance found in the originals.

My approach differed with these con men, as with forgers in general, than with crooks in possession of genuine articles. In the latter cases, even if I was thunderstruck, I'd find fault with the paintings and emphasise the microscopic flaws in order to beat the seller down on the price. That was expected, and was how the game was played. With fakes, one takes the totally opposite tack. I freely oooed and aaaahed and praised the works so as not to tip the seller that I knew they were bogus.

In line with this strategy, I boldly announced to Barreiro that I'd take the whole lot, which he claimed to consist of 400-plus items when counting all the sketches and drawings. He initially agreed, but when we started haggling over price, he wasn't hearing what he wanted—$250,000—and pulled back. We eventually agreed on 100 for $150,000, which included the good stuff, i.e., Picasso, Degas, Miró, Rembrandt, and anything else of note I spotted.

The haggling was essentially meaningless, since we were going to take him down without any money changing hands, but it was necessary to make him believe we were legit. Nobody buys everything. And nobody sells everything, even when they claim they have. The more you haggle over the money and details, the more real the deal appears.

The buy was set for the following day because I needed to secure the cash and rent a truck to cart off the goods. We drove back to San Francisco, turned in the tapes, and filed all our required paperwork on the day's activities—the dreaded 302 forms. I commandeered a computer and double-checked the items I had seen to make sure none were actually listed on any of the worldwide stolen art registries. Nothing matched, as expected. There was also nothing in the records of a recent large theft or sell off from an Arab sheik, just the old stuff noting the al-Fassi fire.

Double-checking Barreiro's background to make sure I hadn't missed anything earlier, I remained unsurprised that he came up clean. An operation of this magnitude had to be pretty fresh. It doesn't take long for someone to complain to the police after being ripped off, as the professor had, or for an angry mark to come after the guys with a baseball bat.

Digging further, I stumbled upon something very interesting. Barreiro's mother was a noted area artist of considerable skill. Could she be the source producing all of the high-class fakes? Was the son conning the mother into it? Or maybe Barreiro himself had trained at the feet of his mom, and was having trouble keeping himself in sprawling California apartments on a budding artist's wage? The possibilities were endless.

The following morning, we were bogged down with more paperwork, mainly getting a Federal prosecutor to draft the proper search warrant needed to comb the fat man's home for all his phoney art. My idle chatter about selling the stuff to Robert Redford in Sun Valley brought in the interstate transportation of stolen goods statutes needed for the Feds to be involved. Actually, they weren't stolen goods, so it was more akin to devising an interstate scheme to defraud. The trouble was, we were having a hard time finding a judge on a Friday who wasn't too busy to deal with us. Seems they were all eager to break early, dash over to the country club, and get in nine holes before the sun went down.

My new partner said she knew a magistrate in San José who was on vacation, so she gave him a call. He must have had a Susan Lucci fetish because he surprisingly agreed, summoning us to his home. Greeting us in a sweater and slacks, the stately gentleman with thick, curly hair went over the warrant line by line, questioning me extensively about the details. Thankfully, he determined we had probable cause to believe these con men scam artists were con men scam artists.

With warrant in hand, we boomeranged back to San Francisco to rally the troops for the take-down. We needed trucks, vans, surveillance teams, arrest squads, the whole parade. It was late on Friday afternoon before all the ducks were in order. As we cruised back to Sun Valley, I kept complimenting Alford on her work, trying to calm her down. She was not only going to be in on her first undercover bust, she was going to be arrested along with the perps.

'The guys are going to manhandle you like every other dirt bag criminal, so don't expect to be treated like Princess Diana,' I warned. She nodded that she understood, which she didn't. Nobody does their first time out.

Me? As long as they didn't leave my butt in a stinking rat hole Montréal prison overnight, I didn't care if they bounced my hard Irish head off the pavement a few times.

At the apartment, we were met by the trio, all of whom appeared to be wearing the same clothes as the day before. No secret why hepatitis was rampant there. To avoid any temptation for a rip-off, it was arranged that we would do some final selections of the paintings, then wire the money in from San Francisco. Since it was so late, that would have to be accomplished via a bank that opened on Saturday; no easy trick. Despite that little flaw, they agreed and began lugging out the goods. There were stacks of paintings, sketchings, drawings, etchings: an entire museum full, virtually all in beautiful, expensive frames.

Among the new arrivals was another alleged Picasso, this one a much better copy of a freaky looking woman from his abstract period. There was also a dead-on Degas nude of a woman with her back turned, and a van Gogh sketchbook full of pencil drawings of trees, sunsets, and vineyards. Had the van Gogh collection been real, it could have been worth $250,000 to a million dollars alone.

It took us nearly three hours to sort through it all as a real buyer would. I was trying to get Barreiro to expose everything he had, so time wasn't of the essence from my perspective. Meanwhile, the troops were all sitting on their duffs, waiting for me to drop Clint Eastwood's name into the conversation. Finally, the sickly Barreiro grew weary of the ordeal and cut us off, saying that was all we could have for $150,000. I protested for a few moments to make it look good, then dropped the Dirty Harry bomb. 'I bet Clint Eastwood will really go for that one,' I said, pointing to the Degas nude. 'Clint Eastwood likes that kind of thing.'

We were in the conference room talking over the details of the payoff when there was a loud banging at the door. 'This is the FBI! Open up!'

Barreiro nearly crapped in his leisure suit. The skinny *Napoleon Dynamite* guy ran to the kitchen for some reason. The Dustin Hoffman musketeer simply went to the door and let the Feds in.

Taking the initiative, I kept asking Barreiro, 'What's going on? Why is the FBI involved?' It was a valid question since this was supposed to be an above-board sale. Barreiro took the same tack with the invading agents, challenging them on their right to blast into his home.

'This is a legitimate transaction,' he insisted. 'Nobody's breaking the law.'

'Conspiracy to defraud,' somebody said, flashing the warrant and advising us of our right to personal silence and chatty attorneys.

I glared at Barreiro. 'Just whom were you trying to defraud?'

'Nobody!' he said, pretending to be in the dark.

Despite our continued protests about the bad, bad Feds trampling our civil rights, we were all roughly arrested, including my delicate young assistant.

Outside, after the others had been taken away, an agent came over and showed me a massive handgun inside a plastic evidence bag. 'What the hell was going on up there? Is this yours?'

'Hell no! Where'd you find that?'

'Under the table, at the end.'

I replayed the scene in my mind and realised with a shiver that the clone of the guy from *Napoleon Dynamite* had a gun secretly trained on us at crotch level the entire time. The trio figured we might be angling to rip them off, and were ready to shoot our nuts and ovaries off at the first sign of trouble. That explained why he bolted to the kitchen, to distance himself from the weapon.

'You must look like a bad *mujer*,' I cracked to Alford, who had turned ghost-white at the prospect of taking one in the panties for Uncle Sam. 'I've never given off those kinds of vibes before.'

The troops stayed on the scene until 3am, tagging, cataloguing, photographing, and carting out all the fakes. The neighbours, who had no idea who we were, started yelling and threatening to call the police. We filled two panel trucks, and uncovered a cache of Renoirs, Matisses and Gauguins the twerp was holding out on me. (Paul Gauguin was a 19th century French impressionist painter, and noted pal / adversary of Vincent van Gogh, known for using bold, unrealistic colours, and travelling to the South Seas for inspiration. Van Gogh cut off part of his own ear with the same razor he earlier tried to slice and dice Gauguin with during one of their endless arguments over the nature of art.)

At the field office, the agents grilled the trio about their source, but they lawyered up and zipped it. With clean records, they faced little more than probation or short jail terms, giving them no motivation to deal. Even the gun-wielding *Napoleon Dynamite* guy skirted the serious weapon-possession charge by claiming the weapon wasn't his. They no doubt claimed it was mine.

Our inability to smoke out the entire operation was very disappointing. If the source of a forgery factory, i.e., the creative golden goose producing the copies, isn't rooted out, their production will continue. If, however, it was Barreiro or his mother, there was a good chance they had now retired.

Either way, we had taken 200 to 300 high-quality fakes off the market, doing our part to help purify a polluted pool and restore a modicum of order to the fine art universe.

Every little bit helps.

As an aside: Mohammad al-Fassi, the nut-job sheik who was the basis for Barreiro's cover story, died in Egypt in late 2002 aged 50, from an infected hernia. His death left his vast holdings in a snarl of legal red tape. Famed palimony attorney Marvin Mitchelson won a $216 million judgement against the Saudi royal family in a divorce settlement action filed by one of al-Fassi's wives, Dena. The ex, however, had no better luck collecting than she had with an earlier $80 million judgement. Her new attorney, Helen Dorrah-White, offered the settlement for sale at a substantial discount. White says they've fielded offers, and one has progressed to the option phase with the purchase money held in escrow until the legalities can be ironed out.

Dena al-Fassi did collect nearly a million dollars as an insurance settlement for the stolen art, which has never been recovered, and the specifics of which nobody seems to remember. Easy come, easy go.

11

THE GUNSLINGERS TAKE THE GUNSLINGER

I WAS BUSY doing research at the Frick Museum's library one afternoon when a beautiful woman with an angelic face and chestnut hair sat down at my table. When I could tear my eyes away from her, I stole a few glances at what she was perusing, searching for a conversation point. She spread open a large book that displayed a reproduction of a painting by Michelangelo Merisi da Caravaggio, a 16th and 17th century Italian pre-Baroque artist who lived a rowdy life. A hot-headed gambler and carouser, Caravaggio carried a sword and a dagger, which he used to literally cut a swath through Rome.

Before his time was up, Caravaggio had built a criminal record nearly as impressive as his masterful Catholic-themed religious paintings, stunning creations that focused on human movement and realism.

Among art connoisseurs, the woman's action was the equivalent of dropping a sensually scented pair of black panties. I broke the ice and found that we had a lot in common. We were both attorneys interested in ancient art, although I was more G-Man than lawyer. She knew about the headline making stolen paintings I'd tracked, and seemed fascinated with my melding masterpieces with master thieves.

Aside from being a classy knockout in a Faye Dunaway, *The Eyes of Laura Mars* way, she was a French Canadian from Montréal with an accent that made my heart flutter. This was in 1978 before the Fogg Museum caper soured me on our neighbours to the north.

We met again a few days later at the bar inside the Metropolitan Museum of Art. After that, our busy careers got in the way of the budding springtime romance, and we drifted apart.

She called a month later, but unfortunately had business, not pleasure, on her mind. She lived in a nice apartment building on York Avenue and 72nd Street in Manhattan. In her soft French accent, she told me that there was a great deal of suspicious activity going on in and around a unit down the hall from her. Strange men kept passing her doorway late at night carrying paintings wrapped in brown paper.

Most people would have said 'packages' but this lady knew her stuff and identified them as paintings. By the way they were gingerly transported, she suspected they were extremely valuable.

It was certainly worth checking—if only to drop by her place in the process. Those caddish thoughts were soon cast aside as my bloodhound nature took over. Everything she described screamed of a major heist.

I had a friend, Tommy Hagen, who knew her part of town inside out. He ran a lumberyard near Coney Island, the once-glorious City of Lights amusement park that was badly showing its age prior to yet another much needed renovation. Tommy furnished the wood needed to make backroom gambling tables, among other nefarious things, and through that had wired himself into everything shady going on in the area—mob activities, prostitution, drugs, and crap games.

'What do you know about the building on 72nd Street?' I asked. Tommy knew exactly what I meant with the vague question. Were the doormen, superintendent, and managers on the take? Would they rat me out in a New York minute, or was there someone around I could trust? Tommy smiled brightly and said the super, Patrick Reilly, was a fellow Irishman like us and a straight shooter.

Hopping on the subway to 72nd Street, I watched the place and sure enough, spotted some crusty men taking slender packages in and out. When things quietened down, I introduced myself to Reilly, who came as advertised. He was more than willing to help, promptly giving me the name of the occupant of that particular apartment, Jeffrey Shore. Reilly had noticed all the 'fishy' activity, and pointed out the man's vehicle. I wrote down the plate numbers and returned to the office to run a check. The plate matched the name, but not the apartment building. Shore's listed address was an exclusive area of South Hampton, Long Island, dotted with five-million dollar estates.

Very interesting.

The fact that a rich young man kept an apartment in the city didn't set off any alarms in and of itself. Those who have the money frequently keep 'crash pads' in the city to avoid the traffic and long commutes, and/or to pick up lovers in the classy Upper East Side bars and art galleries. Still, there was something about the address that nagged at me. I searched through my files of recent art thefts and bingo, there it was. Shore lived near J. Daniel Weitzman, a retired banker and noted art collector. Weitzman, a hip fellow with long brown hair and round, John Lennon glasses, had been robbed at gunpoint in his house on 28 April 1978, a few weeks short of a year earlier.

Weitzman was home alone around 8pm that evening when his doorbell rang. A friendly, personable sort, he answered it. A man standing outside said his car had broken down and asked to use the telephone. Weitzman thought nothing of letting him in. Before the door closed, two masked bandits leaped from the shadows and burst inside. They were armed and wearing stockings over their heads. The first man quickly slipped on a nylon stocking as well, working on the theory that Weitzman's memory imprints wouldn't kick in until the robbery was revealed.

The trio tied the banker up, taped his mouth, and tossed him inside his bathroom. Struggling to inhale enough air through his narrow nasal passages to remain conscious, he signalled his attackers that he was in distress. They ignored him.

The gang then proceeded to slowly and selectively go through the mansion room by room, taking specific paintings and sculptures. 'They were very professional,' Weitzman told *Newsday* reporter Christopher M. Cook. 'They went from one work to another, skipping the less-valuable ones. They knew to take the [Alberto] Giacometti over the other sculptures that I have.'

Despite lingering in the home for more than an hour, the bandits chose to steal only eight pieces. They left with six paintings and two sculptures worth a total of a half million at the time, and considerably more today. The paintings were by Willem de Kooning, a contemporary, Dutch-born American abstract expressionist who lived on Long Island; Jean Dubuffet, a contemporary French pop artist: Fernand Leger, a contemporary French cubist known for mosaics and stained glass; Alexej von Jawlensky, a 19th and 20th century Russian post-Impressionist; Tom Wesselman, a contemporary American pop artist; and John R. Grabach, a contemporary American known for landscapes and nudes.

The sculptures were a bronze from Giacometti, a Swiss surrealist, and another from Harry Jackson, a well-known American who sculpted images of the Old West, including the much reproduced gunfighter known as *The Gunsil*, of which Weitzman had an original. Or more precisely, formerly had an original.

While these paintings and sculptures were no Rembrandts or van Goghs, they were all highly respected modern artists whose works were destined to explode in value over time. Some of Giacometti's sculptures, for example, have recently been auctioned for nearly $10 million. Jawlensky's and Leger's best oils are closing in on the $10 million figure as well. De Kooning's top paintings are nearing $5 million, while Dubuffet's oils and Wesselman's pop art are approaching $1 million. Jackson's popular Old West bronzes are starting to top six figures, as are Grabach's nudes.

This all pointed to investment-minded thieves who were extremely knowledgeable about the market and the coming art value explosion. Either that, or they were working for somebody who was.

It's always amused me that there's been, and remains, a strong sense of denial in the art world that there are wealthy masterminds out there orchestrating made-to-order thefts. I keep coming across them, but no matter what I say or do, the denials continue. It's almost like these haughty gallery owners and museum curators can't accept that one of their fraternity could ever do something so pedestrian as resort to theft.

Weitzman, who knew what he had, what he had lost, and what was left behind, was labouring under no such illusion.

'In a way, I'm glad they were professionals because I have less fear that the paintings will be damaged or mistreated,' he lamented to *Newsday*. 'I just hope whoever gets them enjoys them. I wouldn't be surprised if they contacted me and tried to sell them back, but maybe they'll end up in the hands of someone who goes up to his attic and sits with them for hours on end.'

It's those kinds of sentiments that tore at my gruff, special agent heart and made me want to bring the treasures home to their loving owner. So did the fact that Weitzman had an extensive security system wired throughout his house, but had it off at the time because he was home, and was trying to help what he thought was a stranded motorist. If he hadn't been home, the alarms would have been active and would have undoubtedly thwarted the burglary.

That spoke of an inside job, or someone who knew Weitzman's habits. Someone like a wealthy young neighbour.

What I needed at this point was for a clever person to slip inside Shore's Manhattan apartment and get a peek at the goods. I beat around the bush with my hoped-to-be future art crime-fighting partner, figuring Shore's neighbour could use her considerable feminine wiles to gain entry, but she was too terrified to consider it. Some of the brutes hanging around the place didn't appear to be too big on chivalry.

The building superintendent, by contrast, was gung ho. Supers are snoops by nature, and can dream up a million reasons why they need to check out somebody's pad, from the sound of running water, to electrical wiring routes, to complaints about televisions left on too loud with nobody home. I showed him some photographs of the stolen paintings, and told him to pay particular attention to the easy-to-remember Wesselman. It portrayed an eyeless nude lady with her hands behind her head standing near an American flag, and a television set with actor Victor Mature of *Samson and Delilah* fame on the screen in the background. Intrigued by that alone, the super took it upon himself to use his passkey to check it out.

Reilly phoned me afterward and reported that the Victor Mature painting was indeed in the apartment, along with what he believed were most, if not all, of the others.

'I also saw Victor Mature's son,' he said.

'His son?'

'Yeah, Pre Mature.'

The super laughed heartily at his own silly joke. While his comedic skills may have been lacking, his sleuthing was dead on. It enabled me to get a search warrant to bust into the place and grab the goods before Shore could move them. Since we had not established Federal jurisdiction, I would have to recruit the assistance of the local police precinct, always a high-wire act considering these were the Serpico days of rogue cops on the mob's payroll.

While waiting for the warrant paperwork to go through, I did some background on one Mr Jeffrey Shore. He lived on a sprawling thoroughbred horse farm complete with a track and luxury stalls.

His gentleman horse-breeder father owned, among other things, Shorewood Publishing, a book company which published, insert drum roll here, expensive art history books. Aside from being an editor of such tomes, rich young Jeffrey was a certified art appraiser.

And, if this case wasn't already being tied with a giant psychedelic ribbon, one of Shore's first clients after he hung his appraiser shingle was his neighbour, J. Daniel Weitzman.

I could hardly believe how amazingly this case fell into place. Wealthy masterminds contracting out thefts are by far the hardest thieves to corral because everybody scatters. The gunmen usually don't know who they were really working for and therefore have no one to trade when caught, and the art vanishes instead of popping up for resale. If not for trying to hit on a pretty girl in a museum library, I'd have been just as lost as everybody else. Instead, all I needed now was a warrant, combined with an honest NYPD Blue cop, and I'd soon be bathing in accolades for solving my latest 'crime of the decade.'

Naturally, nothing ever happens that easily. As I was leaving the courthouse, warrant in hand, I heard a famous line from a classic cowboy movie ringing through the corridors. 'Come back, Shane. Come back, Shane.'

Baffled, I stopped and turned around. Instead of a little blonde boy, it was the prosecutor, a beautiful woman who was a dead ringer for a young Lauren Bacall. She was running after me, seemingly in slow motion. 'Come back, McShane,' she was saying in her girlish voice. 'The warrant is not valid.'

Unwilling to accept what she was saying, my mind wandered to the real Lauren Bacall, who I had observed while lurking around The Dakota apartment complex trying to keep a lunatic from killing John Lennon. The former Beatle had been receiving threats, so the FBI detached a team to watch the building and hang around inside with him and Yoko, his Japanese avant-garde artist wife. We all jumped at the chance, even the strict nine-to-fivers.

My ABSCAM cohort, Mike Dennehy, pulled the short straw and got to be with John, Yoko, and little Sean. I pulled a longer straw and was stationed outside, where I watched Bacall, Howard Cosell, Art Carney, Roberta Flack and other celebrity residents and visitors breeze in and out.

Sadly, we couldn't stay on the stake out indefinitely. Two years later, a crazed fan named Mark David Chapman did shoot and kill Lennon outside the Dakota.

For whatever reason, my thoughts focused on the ultimately futile Lennon stakeout as the Lauren Bacall look-alike prosecutor floated toward me bearing her bad news. Due to some bizarre technicality over the Clintonesque meaning of the term 'peace officer', the warrant wasn't good. Apparently, under New York state statutes, FBI agents aren't considered 'peace officers'. Only state, county, and city police come under that umbrella, and only peace officers can acquire a warrant.

'For goodness sake,' I exclaimed. 'You'd think that with the FBI being in existence for more than half a century, this issue would have come up before now?' I couldn't friggin' believe it.

We argued over that for a few hours until a judge agreed to allow a New York City detective sign the bottom and vouch for me. Great, I was used to having my sleazy alter-egos Robert Steele and Thomas Bishop vouched for by street hoods, but now squeaky clean FBI Special Agent Thomas McShane had to be vouched for like I was some punk trying to get an audience with John Gotti?

After clearing up that red tape mind fry, we finally got back to the business of fighting crime. A team comprised of the NYPD detective and two backup FBI agents joined me in visiting the apartment building on East 72nd Street. We badged the doorman, found the super, then took the elevator to the sixth floor. I sighed deeply as we passed my attractive friend's apartment, then steeled myself, no pun intended, to get down to business.

Since we were dealing with a sophisticated, well-educated rich kid from 'The Island', we didn't expect there to be any cops and robbers gunplay. The strategy was to simply knock on the door and grab him—taking an ironic page out of his own little gang's robbery book. Unlike with Weitzman, however, there was no answer. Relying on the power of the headache-inducing warrant, which was properly served on the door by a bona fide NYPD Peace Officer, we let ourselves inside.

The place was, as expected, a well-kept, if sparsely furnished, big-city playpen for a rich suburbanite. It was a studio apartment, which is a fanciful Manhattan way of saying a tiny kitchen, a living room, a bathroom, and no bedrooms. There was the prerequisite television, couch, end table, lamp, and expensive stereo. It was obvious that nobody was actually living in the place, as there was nothing but wine and snack food in the fridge and cabinets. Small wonder, because a single horse stall at young Mr Shore's South Hampton palace was bigger than this mouse hole—which nonetheless probably cost $2,000 a month way back in the late 1970s.

The only thing notable about the flat was the art. Mr Shore had exquisite taste in art. Actually, Mr Weitzman had exquisite taste in art because virtually everything in the place belonged to him. The funky Wesselman was on the couch. The soon-to-be-worth-millions Giacometti was sitting on the end table. The Dubuffet, Leger, and de Koonings were on the walls, while the Jawlensky and Grabach were leaning against a table. The only thing missing happened to be the one I was most interested in seeing, Harry Jackson's Shane-like gunfighter.

It struck me that the entire apartment had been rented for no other reason than to store, preserve, enjoy, and possibly sell this art. An apartment, interestingly enough, that was three blocks from the FBI's then-New York headquarters at 201 East 69th Street.

Only someone with an astute understanding of the art world, and the coming price explosion, wouldn't blanche at investing $2,000 a month, possibly for a decade or two, waiting for the value of the art to dwarf the pricy storage costs. That was another giant foam finger pointing at Jeffrey Shore.

Because of the absurd warrant snag, it was now too late to take the art to my lady friend in the FBI evidence room, so we inventoried, recorded, and tagged the materials, gently placed them in my car, and I drove home—making doubly sure I didn't park in any tow away zones en route.

That evening, I studied the works closely, learning everything I could about these rising-star modern artists just in case I'd one day be called upon to authenticate one of their creations. They were all top-notch, as their multimillion-dollar price tags now attest.

The next morning, I brought them to the office, then recruited Special Agent Jim Sangello to join me on a nice spring afternoon drive to the Hamptons. As before, we weren't expecting any trouble in the land of the *Lifestyles of the Rich and Famous*, so there didn't appear to be a need to bring in the SWAT team. Besides, we still didn't technically have Federal jurisdiction, and after what I'd been through the day before regarding the warrant, I didn't want to trip over any more annoying technicalities—especially with a guy who could afford the best legal assistance in the world. No, this would be a friendly visit between educated gentlemen.

We arrived at the impressive Shore estate and knocked on the big, stately door. A well-groomed, well-bred young man in his late twenties or early thirties greeted us. He was a Basil Rathbone/Al Pacino type, with a narrow face and long brown hair worn in a shaggy 1965 Beatles style. He was wearing corduroy pants, an Izod alligator shirt, and a suede jacket—probably his lounging-around-the-house clothes.

We introduced ourselves and he went white with fear. It was as if something had been eating at him for a long time, and he knew this day was coming. Ever the gentleman, he invited us into his luxuriously furnished home, one that was filled with legitimately purchased art.

Gently, I spelled it out for him. 'We know about the apartment on 72nd Street. We have the paintings and sculptures, seized through a warrant. We know where they came from, close by as a matter of fact. The apartment is rented in your name. I surveilled the building myself, and observed you coming and going with packages shaped like paintings. It's an airtight case. You are in a lot of trouble.'

At this point, he should have screamed for his law firm to send in the troops. Surprisingly, he didn't. He just sat there, frozen, as the world was collapsing around him. There's nothing like seeing someone with so much to lose on the verge of losing it all. I almost ached for the guy.

'Is, is there anything I can do?' he stammered.

'Matter of fact there is. We have everything but the Jackson piece, the gunfighter. Give us that, and it's a start.'

Shore explained that he had already sold it for $10,000 to a big construction tycoon in Phoenix, Arizona. Bingo, I thought to myself. We had jurisdiction. I also gave myself credit for believing that would be the most popular work in the batch, especially to a bigwig builder in Arizona.

'Help us get it back, and that would really look good in your favour.' Shore pondered that for a moment, then agreed. I was amazed how he was doing this, all without an attorney. I credited our gentle, respectful, fatherly approach.

'I had intended to get it all out of state,' he offered, deepening the Federal hook. 'Guess I should have.'

'Do you know where FBI headquarters is?' I inquired.

'Not far from the apartment?'

I nodded.

When we started asking him about the theft itself, the more serious armed robbery, assault, and kidnapping aspects of breaking in with guns and tying up the homeowner, something finally clicked in Shore's head. He advised us that it was probably wise that he speak to his attorneys. We allowed him to make the call, told him where he was going to be taken, then officially arrested him.

Suffice it to say, the Shore family, and their long-time lawyers, were not pleased with young Jeffrey. It turned out that his father was elderly and frail, and his sister was very ill. His attorneys, the expected heavyweights, began hammering the US Attorney for probation. The US Attorney, yet another talented young woman, stood firm, reminding them that it was a serious armed robbery and poor little Jeffrey was obviously the mastermind. She generously offered a year in prison and five years probation—if Jeff gave up his accomplices and helped retrieve *The Gunsil*.

No go, said the defence. Jeff was too refined a young Izod-wearing Hamptonite to spend any time in some wretched prison with all those desperate poor folks. The impasse lasted for months. Finally, we all agreed that rounding up the gunman and getting back *The Gunsil* took precedence over putting some rich kid in jail for a few months. The prosecutor reluctantly offered probation.

We were promptly hosed on the first part of the deal. Jeffrey coughed up his accomplices all right, but had no doubt warned them what was coming down. They were Dominicans and Puerto Ricans he recruited from his publishing company's warehouses and shipping docks. One turned up dead, having already gotten himself killed by an angry liquor store owner he was trying to rob. The others were long gone, either back home, in another state, or had changed their names and filtered into the illegal alien underground.

We had better luck with part two, setting up a sting to grab *The Gunsil*. Jeffrey called the buyer, Phil, and said a big offer had come in and he'd pay the man $15,000 to re-purchase it. Usually only a quick-kill horse trader will go for that kind of Indian Giver deal, but Phil swallowed the worm. The exchange was set for Sky Harbour International Airport in Phoenix.

I hooked up with a tall, strapping Arizona FBI agent with the central casting name of Reno Walker, and put the plan in motion. The commercial airliner stopped in Chicago, and I called Phil to let him know I was on the way with the cash. He said he'd meet us at a certain section of the airport parking lot, and would be driving a black Cadillac—probably with steer horns tied to the grill.

Cowboy Phil met me at the gate. He was a big guy dressed, as expected, in his cowboy get-up—string tie, flowery shirt with embroidered shoulders, faded blue jeans, big belt buckle, leather, two-toned boots. He herded me toward a covered parking garage. It was early spring, so it fortunately wasn't 150 degrees in there.

Strolling through the catacombs like a bow legged wrangler, he led me to his Caddy, popped the trunk, and pulled out *The Gunsil*. It was a really nice piece, a thin, road-weary, sun-wrinkled, Old West gunslinger ready to emotionlessly plant another person on Boot Hill.

The moment I had the bronze sculpture in my hands, Reno Walker and crew swarmed in, tossed us against the vehicle, and snapped on the cuffs, removing the last layer of skin I had there from being arrested so many times. We were placed in separate vehicles, and I was released at the field station. New city. Same dance. Cowboy Phil was processed and walked out on his own recognisance, tagged with the usual toothless interstate transportation of stolen property charge.

Reno kept *The Gunsil* until the legal case cleared, then sent it to New York to be reunited with Weitzman. When I handed it over, I advised him to keep his alarms set 24/7, and not to let stranded motorists inside his home anymore. Better to bring them a portable phone outside.

Meanwhile, Jeffrey Shore had been bitten by the law enforcement bug. He gave us additional information on his remaining at-large accomplices, but we still couldn't find the guys. He offered to give me an entire set of expensive art books from his publishing company to support my recovery efforts. They would have been a big help, but I had to decline due to strict FBI policy. For obvious reasons, the agency frowns on criminals giving their arresting officers expensive gifts.

Occasionally, Jeff would call me with a hot tip on some stolen artefact. Odd that he'd do this, but as I said, he was a thrill-seeker and must have gotten off on being on either side of the law. One of his tips, about a $350,000 mushroom-shaped Tiffany lamp stolen from a Madison Avenue gallery, was definitely worth pursuing. Singer/actress Barbra Streisand was said to have the matching lamp, so the theft made some media noise.

The thief was a mid-level gangster type. We wired his apartment and set up a buy, but he spooked and vanished. Far as I know, that lamp is still out there, probably in the bedroom of another singer/actress with more of an eye for bargains.

Jeffrey later named a racehorse after me, 'Rembrandt McShane'. I never got around to seeing it run. I was far too busy winging around the world chasing after art thieves and their stolen masterpieces.

12

COME BACK TO THE FIVE AND DIME, REMINGTON, RUSSELL AND WYETH

ONE OF MY first cases after transferring to the New York office in 1972 was a tangled web that bloodied my rookie art sleuth nose like a solid right cross. Talk about trial by fire. Even my seen-it-all mentor, Don Mason, came away emotionally bruised and battered.

It began when we received a call from Jim Mellows, an investigator for Chubb & Son, a specialty firm that insured both public and private fine art collections. Mellows, a dignified man who resembled broadcaster Edward R. Murrow, told us he had an informant with a lead to a painting that was among more than 50 taken earlier that year from the F.W. Woolworth estate on the shores of Lake Cobbosseecontee in Monmouth, Maine. Mellows wanted to know how to proceed.

Mason was energised by the call because the theft had stuck in his craw since it had occurred on 24 April 1972. It was a clean job performed by professional cat burglars who slipped inside the 1,000-acre grounds, went straight to the correct 'art' building among the

26 structures on the site, broke in through a glass door, and climbed a stairway to a specific second storey gallery. With no sense of panic or rush, they lingered inside for an estimated three hours, carefully selected the paintings they desired, and gently removed them from their frames. They vanished with their haul, leaving few traces of their presence aside from the shattered glass by the entrance, and the 53 missing paintings, sculptures, antiques, and other artwork worth $500,000 then, and more than $10 million today.

Woolworth's descendants, especially Pauline Woolworth and her son, noted New York art dealer and gallery owner R. Frederick Woolworth, were fans of contemporary Western and rural-themed art, particularly the works of Charles Russell, Frederic Remington, Andrew Wyeth, Andrew's father N.C. Wyeth, Grandma Moses, and Howard Helmick.

Most of the 174 paintings and other artwork housed on the property had been personally purchased by Pauline Woolworth. She was the wife of Norman B. Woolworth, who was the son of Fred M. Woolworth, who was the cousin of Frank W. Woolworth, the founder of the international chain of stores. Cousin Fred established the company's lucrative overseas branches throughout Great Britain.

Pauline Woolworth viewed the compilation as a colourful history of America as seen through the eyes of influential artists. She was naturally devastated by the loss.

'The house has been open for years to anyone who wanted to see the collection,' R. Frederick Woolworth lamented afterward. 'Losing this many paintings takes a bit of the heart and soul out of the display.'

Charles Marion Russell was a 19th and early 20th century Montana cowboy, painter, and sculptor of bears, buffalo, cowpokes, Indians, Texas longhorns, and the like. In 2005, one of his oils, *Pieqans*, sold for $5.6 million.

Frederic Sackrider Remington was a 19th century Yale art student who went west to Montana, Texas, and Arizona for inspiration. His cowboy-and-Indian themed oil paintings today sell for up to $2 million, while his sculptures have climbed over the half million mark.

Anna Mary Robertson Moses, or Grandma Moses, the mother of ten children, was a 20th century folk naturalist who started painting in her 70s and lived to be 100. Her best works would reach half a million dollars today.

Andrew Wyeth is a still-living 20th century impressionistic watercolorist, and the most revered member of the Wyeth artist dynasty. One of Wyeth's temperas on a panel, *Battle Ensign*, sold for nearly $4 million in 2005. (Tempera is a type of water-based paint that uses egg yokes, glue, or casein to create a luminescent quality.)

Andrew's father, Newell Convers Wyeth, was a commercial artist and illustrator noted for painting *Saturday Evening Post* covers, along with murals on buildings such as the Missouri State Capital. His daughters, Carolyn and Henriette, son-in-law Peter Hurd, and grandson Jamie, are also bankable artists.

Howard Helmick was a 19th century illustrator who favoured portraits of dancers. His works sell in the five-figure range.

Huddling with Mellows, we developed a game plan. Mason would fall into the role he was most familiar with, a wealthy art collector willing to toss money around with little or no inspection of the product. Don wasn't a gadget guy, and because he spent most of his career strangled by J. Edgar Hoover's ban on undercover investigations, he didn't need to be. On the other hand, I was coming up during the heyday of FBI stings and undercover activities, so I had to learn all the highly technical CSI stuff.

With Don as the lead agent, we were going to keep this one simple. Don was the buyer, and I was his bodyguard assigned to carry the money. That, of course, made me the target if anything tricky happened.

Our alter-egos were a not-so-private joke. He was Don Norton. I was Thomas Gleason. The names were taken from *The Honeymooners*, the popular Jackie Gleason TV show. (Norton was Gleason's sewer-worker buddy played by Art Carney.) Normally, it's not good to choose such obvious handles, but we thought the mixing of a fictional character, Norton, with a real actor, Gleason, would be enough of a cover. (Gleason's character in the show was Ralph Kramden.) In-house, we often used silly names to deal with the tinfoil-on-the-head types who called reporting space aliens in their gardens and ghosts on their roofs. The callers would be transferred from Special Agent Laurel to Special Agent Hardy, or Agent Martin to Agent Lewis, and endless variations. Whatever got us through the day.

The bad guys we were planning to spring Norton and Gleason on were in Philadelphia, so we had to drive down there, connect with the Philly field office, and have the insurance man's informant set up the sit-down.

We hit our first snag when we tried to register at the luxury hotel that was to be our base of operations. Attempting to pay with cash, we were told that form of currency was no good there. They wanted a credit card to cover our room service, telephone calls, and any other overpriced add-on they could think of. The trouble was, thanks to Hoover, we didn't have any credit cards bearing our undercover identities. The hotel wouldn't budge for love or green money, and we were thoroughly plastic challenged. An entire operation was going down the tubes because we couldn't check into our stinkin' room.

After a rash of panicked calls, we finally located an FBI supervisor who knew the hotel security chief. Strings were pulled to get us booked. Of course, that widened the circle of people who knew about our operation and may have compromised the effort, but we had little choice.

With that ridiculous hurdle removed, we regrouped. The insurance guy's informant, who we never knew, set up a dicey meeting where we were to flash some serious cash right from the get-go. That's always a high-wire act in first contact situations, but we were playing by someone else's rules.

Noting the obvious dangers, I was wired and packing, this time a Smith & Wesson .38 Detective Special 'belly gun' tucked in a waist holster. The nickname derived from the fact that you couldn't actually hit anybody with the snub-nosed weapon unless you were brawling in a phone both and had the barrel jammed inside your opponent's belly button. Actually, I was pretty good with the little stinger, qualifying at -60 yards. I wasn't, however, looking forward to having to use it that afternoon.

Right from the start, I had a bad feeling about this operation. The original thieves were pros, the kind of ninja-like cutthroats who would alter their plans in a flash if they spotted a weakness. Why sell a painting when you can simply steal the flash money? Despite my misgivings, I was given specific instructions to let the money walk.

Specifically, that meant we'd fork over $7,000, as a down payment, and allow the subject to wander off, ostensibly to get the first painting. From what I was told, it was expected to be the Helmick, *His Favourite Meal*, which pictured an old guy praying over a loaf of bread. It wasn't remotely the most valuable of the stolen stash, but was believed to hold some special meaning for the Woolworth family, possibly being one of patriarch Frank W. Woolworth's favourites.

The plan from there, devised by the Philly squad, was to follow the money and hope the seller led us to additional paintings and sculptures, particularly the more valuable Remingtons, Russells, and Wyeths. To this end, I was instructed to hand over the cash and not dick around with negotiations. It was a strategy I wasn't comfortable with, fearing that despite our orders, any screw-ups would fall on me.

We waited in our room for the guy to show at 1pm. The hour passed, and so did another before he finally called and informed us he wasn't coming up. He wanted us to meet him in the lobby. Smart move for him. Major hassle for us as we had the place wired, with agents in the surrounding rooms. Instead of playing on our turf, I suspected we were about to go on a road trip with a potentially deadly stranger.

Before heading downstairs, I went into the bathroom, took the $7,000 out of the envelope in my breast pocket, stuffed the cash into my pants, and put a folded washcloth in the envelope. It was precisely the kind of ad lib I was advised against doing, but my instincts were screaming that something about this smelled. If everything was cool, I could still hand over the money from my pocket. I just wanted that extra layer of security—against both crooks and office politics.

Because I was acting on my own, I didn't tell Don about my unauthorised subterfuge. If the shit hit the fan, I didn't want him to have to go down with me.

In the lobby, we were greeted by an average-looking guy in his early thirties with wavy brown hair, no moustache or beard, and a medium build. He was about 5-foot-8-inches, and didn't appear threatening. He told us he was going to take us someplace to see the art. No doubt—either that or shoot us and snatch the money. I glanced around to determine if any of the shadowing agents were monitoring the rapidly changing situation.

Milling about the lobby was Special Agent Robin Smith, a rare female G-Woman who had once worked security for eccentric billionaire Howard Hughes. I was glad she was our shadow because the contact was jumpy, and women attract less suspicion. Up until the 1970s, we invariably had to resort to clerical staff when we needed a female undercover, so a trained special agent who knew self-defence and could handle a weapon was a big plus. (Agent Smith, sadly, was destined to die in a plane crash four years later while on her way to testify in a mob case.)

I could see by Smith's expression that the Philly squad wasn't with the turn of events. Them and me both! Don and I talked it over and decided what the hell, we'd take the chance. We did this in character right in front of the suspect, which was weird because there were so many different personalities and thought processes involved. FBI agents or shady art dealers, nobody wants to be lured into a trap.

The man, James, escorted us to a brand-new 1973 Cadillac El Dorado, a giant land boat gleaming in the sun. I hopped in the front and Don spread out in the spacious back. Off we went to who-knows-where. We were in a different city, didn't know the lay of the land, and were desperately hoping that we were being followed and monitored. To make sure, I expressed a keen interest in Philadelphia geography, asking our driver what this landmark and that was, which bridge we were crossing, and what satellite city or suburb we were travelling through. It was all broadcast via body mike back to the troops—at least I hoped it was.

It turned out the shadows lost us a number of times because James had been 'dry cleaning' himself, meaning he was backtracking and driving in circles to shake any tails. That wasn't a good omen of what was to come. Thanks to my travelogue, however, the agents were able to keep relocating us.

We left Pennsylvania and crossed over to Cherry Hill, New Jersey, another move I noted on the air. James pulled the Caddy into one of those old silver bullet style diners. Inside, he advised us that he had to make a call to arrange the viewing. At the table, Don and I were shaking our heads, half pissed off that we were in some greasy spoon hash house instead of a fancy hotel, but relieved that we had been taken to a public place instead of the end of a dark alley.

James returned from the pay phone and laid it out. 'Give me the money, and I'll go get the painting.' It was the oldest trick in the world. Con drives you to an unfamiliar, uncomfortable place—the tougher the neighbourhood the better—asks for the money so he can get or buy the goods, then vanishes, never to be seen again.

'You've got to be kidding,' I argued, once again going against my instructions. 'We give you the money, you take off, and we never see you again. What kind of dunces do you think we are?'

I could all but hear the Philly guys cursing—if they were still listening—but I knew enough to know you can't give in that easily. We argued some more, then James had an idea. He said he'd give us the keys and leave the Caddy at the diner. It wasn't a bad trade, but it meant that the guy had his own shadow or shadows waiting nearby. Regardless, I had my instructions, so I agreed. Worst came to worst, we end up with a really fine luxury vehicle.

I took out the envelope and reached out my hand to give it to him. Before I fully extended, his fingers shot over, snapped it up like a starving dog grabbing a hambone, and literally ran out the door.

'What the hell?' I exclaimed to Don. 'I got his keys. Where is he running?' Don merely shrugged.

Outside the window, James jumped into a beat up Chevy and roared out of there. The bastard had stashed his own wheels for the drop. Wonderful. This case was getting messier than a Jackson Pollock splash painting.

Regaining my senses, I described the vehicle and situation out loud so our shadows could keep James in sight. I said nothing about my little secret; that James had run off with a 50 cent hotel washcloth, payment for a screaming white, $9,000 El Dorado with a black vinyl roof.

The car, of course, turned out to be stolen. Everybody was screwing everybody.

We phoned the Philly squad and learned that they were on top of it. They nailed James down the road and had him in the bag. The painting was on the seat beside him. That meant he made us for a couple of saps and opted to rip us off instead of selling the art. Beautiful.

The arrest of our ex-friend James did nothing to end the insanity. Back at the hotel, we learned that while we were being played for fools, James' accomplice—another guy named James—was trying to shake down the insurance company for $50,000 to deliver additional paintings. Next thing we knew, Don and I were portraying insurance agents at Chubb & Son's Philly office, waiting for James II to march in and rip us off again.

At the appointed time, around 5pm, in walked a well-groomed, well dressed, and fast-talking character with black hair who looked like an advertising executive—which he was. After introductions and small talk, James II tried to pull the same ruse as his accomplice. We were to hand him $50,000, and he'd return tomorrow with the good stuff from the burglary: the Remingtons, Wyeths, whatever we named he said he had it and would bring it. I tried to get him to reveal where they were, how they were stolen, what they looked like, etc., and all he would say was there were 'lots of cowboys and Indians.'

A secretary walked in and informed me that I had a call in another room. That was odd, but I had a sinking suspicion regarding what it would be about. Sure enough, I was told the Philly squad had enough of these clowns and were going to pop the guy. I argued that we didn't have any lead whatsoever on the rest of the paintings, and I was willing to play it out a day or two longer to see if we could get some better information. They wouldn't go for it. I got a sense that these were nine-to-five-guys who wanted to punch out and make it home in time for dinner. They were going to bust the guy then and there, and squeeze him for the information later. Within seconds, they swooped in and arrested James II.

On the way back to the field office, I went over what we had and didn't have. We had one small, relatively insignificant painting, a stolen car, and a couple of goofballs who didn't appear to be remotely skilled enough to have carried off the original theft. We didn't have 52 other works of art worth a half million dollars, any indication of where they were, or any information about who had knocked over the Woolworth estate.

With the expected interstate transportation of stolen goods charge so weak, and the actual thieves skilled and fearsome, I predicted that the James boys were going to lawyer up and zip it tight.

My head was full of these depressing thoughts when I strolled into the Philly FBI headquarters and was introduced to a tall, stately, Claus von Bulow-looking man in his forties wearing a classy cashmere coat. It was R. Frederick Woolworth, the department store heir with the greatest love of art. Buoyed by reports that we were close to breaking the case, the owner of New York's Coe-Kerr Gallery had flown in to monitor the situation. I shook his hand and tried to put on a happy face, expressing our hope that the suspects would sing. He graciously thanked us and repeated that the recovered Helmick was indeed one of his family's favourites. He also mentioned how thankful he was that a solid contingent of his impressive collection was on tour at the time and therefore was not stolen.

As expected, the two Jameses, Thompson and Lloyd, hired lawyers and wouldn't cooperate. With clean records—Thompson was a meter reader and Lloyd indeed worked in advertising—they weren't facing serious jail time and had no motive to trade. Whatever they knew they kept to themselves. I wrote it off as a major lesson learned about sticking with a case until the bitter and often-fatiguing end. Unless we had a major hammer on a suspect, we could learn a whole lot more while they were wheeling and dealing than we could by arresting them and trying to do the bare bulb and rubber hose routine before they screamed for an attorney.

My mentor, Don Mason, took this case hard. He liked Mr Woolworth and worked on it diligently up to and beyond his retirement. Despite the yeoman effort, he couldn't make any headway. With that many paintings on the loose, the tips come in fast and furious, and can send investigators chasing wild geese full-time.

There were, however, some subsequent successes. The following year, in May 1974, the Wyeths were recovered via an FBI sting on Cape Cod. As an added bonus, the agents nabbed infamous New England cat burglar Myles Connor Jr, a scrappy Irish redhead with a talent for slick and ingenious art thefts. Connor led the Massachusetts agents to a U-Haul that contained one Andrew Wyeth painting and three by N.C Wyeth. Depending on who he was speaking to and what the perceived advantage was, Connor alternately claimed and disavowed being one of the original burglars.

Incarcerated cons will confess to anything if they can arrange to be 'temporarily' released to recover the stolen merchandise from the 'secret location' where the goods are allegedly stashed. Although such recoveries come with deals to shave considerable time off an inmate's sentence, in the history of the world, I don't recall that any prisoner released on his own under such an arrangement has actually returned with the stolen items. Or returned at all.

My guess is that since Connor was offering only the Wyeths, that's probably all he had. He either gained possession through contacts in the art underworld, hit the Woolworth place a different time, or simply pinched the Wyeths from whomever had them— stolen or purchased.

Ever the slick hustler, Connor later orchestrated the theft of a Rembrandt from Boston's Museum of Fine Arts and used that as his 'Get Out of Jail Free' card. It wasn't the first time he traded art for his freedom, and it wouldn't be the last.

Mason thought he had a solid lead three years later in 1977 when an informant reported that two notorious East Coast safecrackers and cat burglars, Allison and Cliff Williams, were trying to fence some of the Woolworth art. The brothers were dangerous characters who once rigged a Plymouth Fury with a homemade shotgun booby trap that blew away a former associate planning to testify against them. Another turncoat was shot in Florida during a fishing trip, while a third was blown away by a shotgun blast to his face during a bogus robbery.

Although the brothers never physically hurt any of their rich and famous society victims, they were sure murder on their partners.

A meeting was set to try and sting the pair, but nothing came of it. The informant smartly cut things off before he was forced to eat a mouthful of buckshot.

Following that flurry of excitement, things remained quiet for more than a decade. Then, in 1988, that crazy Irishman Myles Connor resurfaced again, this time in the unlikely location of a farm in Lexington, Kentucky. He had moved there to escape the heat in Boston. Connor, however, was a human torch who created heat wherever he went. He was soon starting bonfires in the Bluegrass State, and sending up smoke signals across half the South. It wasn't long before he fell into another FBI trap headed by a crafty undercover agent named Thomas Daly. For $10,000, Connor sold Daly an 18th century grandfather clock constructed by American master Simon Willard. Once they had the brilliantly crafted antique, the Kentucky agents had a hard time trying to figure out where it had come from. They eventually traced it to another Woolworth Estate robbery 16 years earlier.

Little by little, the Woolworth family's possessions were trickling home.

More recently, in 2004, *The Philadelphia Inquirer* printed a memoir-like story about Allison Williams, now in his eighties and serving a life term. Williams decided to come clean before he checked out, owning up to a half century of famous thefts, including million-dollar jewellery burglaries of Cornelius Vanderbilt Whitney in New York, Campbell Soup heiress Elinor Dorrance Hill at her mansion in Rhode Island, and the Yamron Jewellery Store in the Traymore Hotel on Atlantic City's boardwalk. Almost as an afterthought, Williams confessed to hitting the Woolworth Mansion in 1972. However, he didn't claim to be in on the original robbery, but instead said he read about it in the paper, figured the huge place was an easy mark, went there himself a few weeks later, and took six more paintings. He was so smooth that the art missing from his theft was credited to the first one.

Despite his newly loosened tongue, Williams didn't detail what specific paintings he took, and where they are today. Known to fence things quickly, he had no doubt pawned them decades ago.

As for the remaining Woolworth art, the Remington and Russell paintings and sculptures may still turn up, as their monetary worth today is astronomical. The lesser-known but still highly valuable remaining works, from Thomas Waterman Wood, Charles Rain, Cleveland Rockwell, Childe Hassam, Samuel Lancaster Gerry, and Xanthus Russell Smith have no doubt simply filtered back into the $100 billion art world, emerging sparkling clean like stonewashed drug money, with nobody being the wiser about their history.

Until, that is, they are stolen again.

Those with an artistic eye can be on the lookout for a few others in particular: Grandma Moses' *The Mail is Here*; Samuel F.B. Morse's *Reverend McKinstry*; George Catlin's *The Smoke Shield*; William R. Leigh's *After the Hunt*; Alfred Jacob Miller's *Sioux Indian Reconnoitering*; William W.A. Walker's *The Cotton Field;* and George B. Wood's *Home Sweet Home*.

If you spot one, call or e-mail co-author Dary Matera at 602-351-8684, dary@darymatera.com, or contact the FBI.

. 13 .

AND AWAY THEY GO

*O*NE OF THE most clever art thieves I ever encountered during my decades as an FBI stolen masterpiece tracker never carried a pistol, nor did he lug around a set of burglar's tools. His weapons were a silver tongue and a cunning mind. After hearing his celebrity-studded rap, gallery owners from coast to coast were falling all over themselves sending him million dollar paintings.

To twist the ancient cliché, sometimes in the art world the mouth is mightier than the Uzi.

The strange saga of Harold von Maker, aka Prince Harold von Hohenloe, aka Dr Harold J. Maker, aka Peter Wertz, aka David Patterson, aka a dozen other aliases, began in 1973 when a retired NYPD officer turned security consultant alerted me to another con man. He was a suave and cultured young man running around the Big Apple posing as an Austrian prince. The guy's scheme was to get close to the rich and famous, and then steal their luxury automobiles.

The cop, Ted Bielefeld, had an interesting story of his own. He was a Bronze Star Army vet who saw action in both Germany and the Pacific Islands during World War II. Returning home and joining the police force, a bank robber shot him through his hat on his very first day in the blue uniform. The razor's-edge brush with death, ironically coming after surviving the deadly war for so long, earned him instant entry into the prestigious NYPD Legion of Honour.

Ted, who lived in my neighbourhood near Kennedy Airport, and whose daughter, Kathy, also became an NYPD cop, spoke fluent German, and had worked as a translator in Germany and Austria during the war. That's how he knew this other con man, this Prince Michael von Harrach character was a fraud. The 'Prince', whose full European-styled name and title took up an entire sentence (Prince Michael Balthasar Karl Friedrich von Hohensiegen du Zunger und von Harrach), couldn't even speak German that well, and certainly didn't use the upper class dialect of the royals. The flaw didn't stop him from parading around in a pseudo-military dress uniform complete with seven rows of shiny heroism awards.

A small detail lost or overlooked by those he charmed and conned was the fact that an Austrian military officer so awarded during World War II would have earned his honours by killing Americans and Russians for Adolf Hitler.

Americans, even rich Americans, aren't generally history buffs, so that little kink didn't slow him down at all. Nor did the fact that the Prince was actually a gay Miami Jew named Michael Goldbaum. Playing a royal Austrian military hero was no doubt a private joke Goldbaum relished.

His Highness Goldbaum used his princely moniker to infiltrate high-society types dwelling in New York's Upper East Side. Once on the party circuit, he'd case their Rolls Royces, Jaguars, Mercedes, and Maseratis, then have his ring of gay thieves in Greenwich Village steal them. The vehicles were shipped to Florida, where their titles were scrubbed by insiders there—probably more gays.

The re-born chariots were then sold to wealthy Floridians of all sexual preferences.

After being tipped by the ex-cop, we infiltrated Goldbaum's operation and quickly turned his personal assistant, a young art student named Marianne Oluluma. The eager employee had no idea her boss was a total fraud, and that her dream job was a house of cards. Goldbaum was eventually caught with 18 stolen cars and his operation was put into park.

In the process, Ms Oluluma informed us that there was a second gay Austrian operating with Goldbaum, a Prince Harold von Hohenloe. This prince was said to be into pricey art instead of pricey automobiles. Guessing that he too was a fake, and was similarly up to no good, I began to investigate.

Right off, I picked up a familiar pattern in the Twin Princes' behaviour, and pinpointed the inspiration for their colourful aliases. Few remember anymore, but the famed Walt Disney Castle used as the ultimate Cinderella fantasy symbol was once the actual abode of a flamboyantly gay 19th century Bavarian ruler known as Mad King Ludwig II. His audacious, turret-topped mansion near the Austrian border in Bavaria, Germany, is known as *Neuschwanstein,* or *The New Swan.*

King Ludwig ascended to the thrown of the largest German state at the tender age of 18, in 1864. He was eventually judged insane for his wild, foppish lifestyle. It seems the King paid more attention to art, theatre, music, clothing, seducing gay lovers, and building extravagant castles than he did to the more manly activities of warring with rival nations. He lived wildly until the Elvis age of 42, when he and his doctor were found drowned in Lake Starnberg in 1886—either by accident or by design.

The delicate king spent part of his childhood in *Hohenschwangua Castle* near Füssen. That was, no doubt, where New York's Prince von Hohenloe derived his name.

Putting aside their odd but understandable idolisation, these gay con men had a keen sense of German and Austrian history. I suspected that my new target would know his art as well. Fascinated, I made him a top priority. If Prince von Hohenloe was anything like his car-stealing partner in crime, I expected him to be hip-deep in hot masterpieces.

The more I investigated, the more intriguing the story became. Prince von Hohenloe used his associate's overflowing supply of top-shelf stolen vehicles to establish his identity as a wealthy international art dealer. To complete the picture, the 5-foot-9-inch, balding, pudgy, 42-year-old grifter leased various mansions, which he resided in for only a few months, rarely paying the high rent.

Sometimes, he'd do nothing more than gain temporary access to one under the guise of buying it, and would hang around just long enough to have someone photograph him on the grounds. To complete the picture, he usually wore a royal blue jacket with an Ivy League family crest stitched on it. He'd then show prospective marks the photos to support his claims of wealth and power.

It didn't take long to discover his real name; the equally impressive sounding Harold von Maker. Instead of a castle in Austria, however, the 42-year-old hailed from the decidedly unimpressive city of Newark, New Jersey.

For an art loving homosexual, Harold had some very interesting macho man friends. Among the pals and associates he had been arrested with in past schemes was a feared Mafia Capo named Carmine 'The Doctor' Lombardozzi, a long-time Colombo and Gambino family cutthroat. Other cohorts included Vinnie 'The Human Fly' Leone, a noted cat burglar, and Bernie Howard 'The Dirty Little Coward'—a hustler with a reputation as a backstabbing rat.

The Doctor, so nicknamed for his dignified air, was Mafia royalty, having been among the nationwide cadre of mobsters arrested at the infamous 1957 Commission Meeting in Apalachin, New York. One of the richest and most powerful mobsters of all time, he survived the treacherous life long enough to die of natural causes in his late 70s.

I had the book on The Human Fly as well because I'd recently arrested the little gnat for scaling a 30-foot drainpipe, breaking into the second story Manhattan apartment of Standard Oil heir Peter Salm, letting in a team of accomplices, and carting out 29 of Salm's paintings. The haul was worth $250,000 in 1970 dollars, and included works by 19th century French artists Eduard Vuillard (*A Japanese Vase Filled with Red Roses*) and Henri Fantin-Latour (*Vase with Flowers*). I was in the midst of squeezing The Fly for the location of the goods and names of his cronies when the von Maker tip came in. (We eventually recovered most of Salm's art and swatted The Fly and his partners. Vuillard's and Fantin-Latour's best works go for $2.5 million today.)

Following the arrests of Goldbaum and The Human Fly, von Maker was smart enough to shed his princely façade, but not smart enough to stop conning. He borrowed the identity of a Madison Avenue delicatessen owner, Peter Wertz, and fast-talked his way into leasing a historic brownstone at 116 East 95th Street near Park Avenue that had once been owned by legendary German actress and Frank Sinatra paramour Marlene Dietrich. The home was now in possession of Dietrich's daughter. It was the exact kind of celebrity-tinged base of operations that von Maker could make work for him. (Marlene Dietrich once insured her trademark raspy voice for a million dollars.)

I phoned the younger Dietrich in Germany and received a raspy earful about what a no-good sleaze ball her tenant was, apparently a reputation earned by defaulting on too many $2,500 monthly rent payments. I informed her that instead of being reputable businessman Peter Wertz, he was actually a scoundrel named Harold von Maker. She, of course, offered to help us in any way, mostly because she wanted him out of the brownstone.

Picking her brain further, I determined that von Maker had conspired with Wertz to rent the place under the deli owner's name, and that Wertz had willingly helped him. That meant Wertz would not be a good contact because his loyalties no doubt remained with von Maker.

Continuing to dig, it soon became apparent that von Maker had been a very busy boy. He had acquired art catalogues from the major auction houses and galleries, and went down the list of great masterpieces for sale around the country. He then contacted the sales agents, gave them his celebrity spiel and nifty address, and somehow convinced a few of them to send him the paintings on consignment in return for full payment within 30 days.

Once he gained possession of a valuable painting, he used it in various ways, often as the centrepiece to pawn dozens of fakes he had in inventory. In this sense, he was 'art kiting'— stealing the concept of 'cheque kiting' which follows one good cheque with dozens of bad ones.

Working the phones, von Maker hit gold with the Maxwell Gallery in San Francisco. It was owned and operated by a novice who had inherited it from his uncle, Fred Maxwell. The New York con man convinced the heir to send him three notable paintings: *Susanna*; a nude by Thomas Hart Benton; *Portrait of Madame Cordier*, by Mary Cassatt; and *Crucifixion* by Jackson Pollock. All three were artists whose works, then worth about $200,000 collectively, were about to mushroom in value.

Mary Stevenson Cassatt was a 19th and 20th century American Impressionist who trained and lived in France. She favoured scenes of chaste women in ladylike poses. Her oils are currently approaching $2 million. Benton, a 20th century American regionalist, focused on life in the Midwest and South. His gouache style paintings are nearing $1 million. (Gouache, pronounced gwash, is an opaque watercolour mixed with gum for a thick, creamy effect.)

Pollock, known as 'Jack the Dripper' for his wild, 20th century abstract expressionist splattering style, not to mention his colourful, booze-soaked East Hampton, Long Island, lifestyle, would have fitted right in with the twin Princes von Maker and Goldbaum— except in a more heterosexual way. His body of work, encompassing everything from pencil drawings to enamel, is nearly off the charts. One of Pollock's oils sold for $11.6 million in 2004 (*Number 12, 1949*).

Anyone seeking these three promising but mostly overlooked artists in the early 1970s, whether to buy or to steal, was no neophyte. Later that same year, the art world would be galvanised by the sale of a Pollock for $2 million, at the time the highest price ever paid for a work by an American.

Once in possession of such paintings, von Maker had numerous ways to profit from them. The Pollock, bought for $30,000, was promptly used to secure a $75,000 loan from the Central Valley Bank of New York. The transaction, enacted by von Maker's attorney, came with a fake bill of sale from a New York gallery to authenticate von Maker's ownership claim.

It was a shell game von Maker had pulled on banks numerous times before, including the pimping out of *The Marriage Feast of Jan Brueghel*, by 16th century Flemish master Pieter Brueghel the Younger. Von Maker used the same Brueghel to secure more than half a million dollars in loans from different banks and development companies in New York and Pittsburgh. (Pieter Brueghel's oils sell for as much as $7 million today. He was the son of Pieter Brueghel the Elder.)

Flush with the Pollock cash, the con man set out to finance his latest scheme, luring investors to buy a piece of a non-existent sugar cane factory and plantation in Santo Domingo.

What he didn't do with the cash was pay for the paintings as promised. He did send the Maxwell Galleries two cheques for $45,000 to cover the consignments, but both bounced higher than the Golden Gate Bridge. Alarmed, the new Maxwell owner, Mark Hoffman, first flew into a rage, then flew to New York. Doing his own investigation, he learned that Wertz was really von Maker, and that his Pollock was at the bank—not on the wall but in a vault. Hoffman came to us to protest, and was immediately sent to me. I informed him I was already on top of it.

'You know, I've only had this gallery a year and a half and I've made a lot of mistakes,' Hoffman said. 'But I'm learning fast.'

Indeed he was. With a victim screaming loudly that he'd been ripped off, and Federal jurisdiction established via the San Francisco connection, I could now bring my alter-ego Robert Steele into the picture. Our first target would be von Maker's attorney. He was doing his client's dirty work, which made him equally culpable. I did some background on the guy and discovered he was a legitimate lawyer who had offices in both Manhattan and Westport, Connecticut, a wealthy enclave of the bordering state. Why this obviously successful barrister was hooked up with the likes of Prince Harold von Maker was yet another mystery I wanted to solve.

Posing as an art investor, I set up a meeting with the mouthpiece, Martin Schwartz, Esq. He readily agreed to discuss the sale of *Crucifixion*, for $40,000. Mind you, this was a painting which, A, his client didn't own, and B, was already being used as collateral on a $75,000 loan. This told me that the attorney was more than just another of von Maker's dupes.

Prior to the meeting, I spent four hours at the Metropolitan Museum of Art with a Mr Rosenberg, billed as the world's foremost expert on Pollock's work. I wasn't sure if I was going to have to do a verification task, but just in case, I wanted to know my stuff.

Rosenberg patiently showed me dozens of examples, from Pollock's earlier straightforward realism studies, to his Jack the Dripper, toss, splash, and crush period when he was known to place a canvas on the floor and throw everything at it from paint gobs to Coke bottles. Rosenberg showed me Pollock's manic brushstrokes— when he used a brush—the modern paints he favoured (white oil, black enamel, brown and blue lines), how his works differed when he was feeling melancholy, depressed, or drunk (from manic to mellow), how the drip style meant the scenes were centrally focused with the edges often bereft of paint, and similar tip-offs. Preferring a heavy impasto (peanut butter-like) style, Pollock was partial to sticks, trowels, and knives rather than brushes in his later years, and often added sand, broken glass, and other foreign matter to his creations. The man was definitely a nutcase, but he was also a genius who created stunning beauty out of chaos.

I was especially intrigued when Rosenberg informed me that the key to spotting a Pollock fake was not in the paint, strokes, or style, but in the canvas. Pollock, for all his crazy abstracts, was a fanatic about canvas quality and preparation. A student of fellow 'theftee' Thomas Hart Benton, he used only the best, and prepared them to make certain that the subsequent paintings could withstand the abuse of his passionate style and last for centuries. Even the way he stretched the material, and the marks that the process left, were unique because unlike most artists, Pollock didn't stretch the canvas until after the painting was finished.

Knowing that I needed some seriously upscale suits and accessories to play Robert Steele on Park Avenue, I pleaded poverty to some high-end men's clothiers and found a sympathetic owner with a detective bug. He slid me inside a highly discounted, $1,500 dark blue suit with alternative red, blue, and green pinstripes. It was perfect art dealer chic. I borrowed an alligator briefcase and a Tiffany watch from a wealthy gallery owner, and checked out some Italian wing-tipped shoes from evidence. All I needed was Sonny Crocket's Ferrari Testarossa from *Miami Vice* and I could have negotiated a $50 million cocaine deal on the way to Schwartz's office!

Actually, I probably could have taken one of the Rolls Royces Prince Goldbaum had hotwired that were now decaying in an evidence lot. If the meeting had been in Westport, I would have. (Although once in Chicago, I used an impounded Rolls Silver Cloud and was promptly pulled over by the nosey local cops before making it to a critical buy meeting. Deeply undercover, I had to fast-talk my way out of it.)

The extra care with my clothing and wheels was essential because this wasn't some street vagrant I was doing business with. This was a big shot Westport attorney who would have an eye for such details. One wrong cufflink can expose an undercover agent in the flash of a .38 muzzle.

Granted, it wasn't a good situation having to scramble for the outfit on my own, as it could have exposed me to a reprimand for not following proper protocol. On the other hand, I didn't have a choice. One can't pose as a wealthy art collector going after Pollocks and Cassatts while wearing a leisure suit from Wal-Mart.

Schwartz's office was on Park Avenue around 53rd Street: no cheap real estate there. I recruited a tall, blonde, female agent from the office to pose as my wife, draped her with a mink coat supplied by another sympathetic clothier—along with tons of 'bling bling' as they say today, provided by a friendly jeweller. Slender and refined, she looked the part of the trophy bride.

Neither of us wore a wire or a gun. This was Park Avenue. I didn't expect to be shooting it out with a Jewish lawyer.

We waltzed just like the Gettys into Schwartz's mahogany-embedded office and introduced ourselves. I could tell he was impressed with our money-dripping appearance. He was equally adorned in his stately attorney's uniform, dark blue suit, powder blue shirt, red power tie, and slicked-back brown hair. After the standard small talk, we got down to business. He wanted $50,000 for the painting, small change for a high-powered couple like us. That was, of course, a $20,000 profit over what they were charged for it, and a $50,000 profit considering what they paid for it, which was zilch.

The Pollock was actually on-site. After the gallery owner from San Francisco made his stink, the attorney had managed to retrieve it from the bank. As I mentioned, in the world of Westport types, you can indeed steal more with a pen than with a gun—especially if you have a law degree.

As we continued to chat, I searched for signs that would explain why this man was throwing away his reputation and hard-earned, high-class life by getting involved in this mess. Drug habit?

Gambling? Women? What was his Achilles heel? Nothing leaped out at me.

The Pollock was smallish, about four feet by three, and appeared to be a gouache, basically a watercolour on steroids. It was a nice piece, but was more colourful, artsy, and abstract than emotional or inspiriting. Virtually every major artist did a crucifixion scene, and every one I'd ever come across was cleaned up as to the torture and brutality involved. It wouldn't be until the 21st century when Catholic actor/producer Mel Gibson broke through the unspoken guidelines and gave the masses a stunningly realistic depiction in his controversial movie *The Passion of the Christ*.

After years of up-close viewings of scores of crucifixions painted over the centuries, I found myself desensitised to the act, but discovered that I couldn't sit through the stark reality of Gibson's gut-wrenching film.

Pollock's vision was more to show Jesus' ascension to heaven than to depict his suffering. The Saviour's face and body were muted by the swirling abstract nature, and the nailed hands and feet were unclear. It was a relaxing, comfortable depiction, which was odd because Pollock's life and other works were anything but relaxing and comforting.

Inspecting the art with my naked eye, it appeared to be legit. The telltale signs regarding the canvas preparation and stretching that Mr Rosenberg had tipped me off about were easily noticeable. Satisfied, I nodded to my 'wife' and said that we'd take it. That was our signal that the attorney was going down. We pulled our 'bling bling' badges from our expensive pockets, flashed Schwartz, and told him he was under arrest for the proverbial interstate transportation of stolen property.

He immediately expressed shock and indignation, claiming to be working for Peter Wertz of Antiques Investors, one of the phoney companies von Maker hid behind. Schwartz was not helping himself with those revelations. I informed him that we knew all about the bank scam, and that the Pollock's legal owner was in New York raising a ruckus. After being read his rights, he smartly zipped it.

Prosecuting a wealthy lawyer is no easy task. This one fell upon the sturdy shoulders of US Attorney Henry 'Pete' Putzel III, whose father, Henry Putzel II, was the long-time Reporter of Decisions for the Supreme Court at the Library of Congress. Putzel had no sympathy for his peer, wouldn't budge on a plea bargain, and took the case to trial, winning a conviction on mail fraud and receiving stolen property charges.

We bagged the attorney, but the real bad guy, Harold von Maker, was still very much on the loose. In fact, as with the bust of his Austrian Prince partner, his attorney's arrest did nothing to slow von Maker down. He just kept speeding along like one of Thomas Hart Benton's famous train portraits. That's not surprising. Con men are so deep into the flim-flam life, they can't stop themselves. They usually have high overheads, spend money without thought, and don't know any other way to survive. Unless we killed the head of this snake, more people would be swindled, and the art world would continue to be polluted.

Putting my nose to the trail, I uncovered the disturbing news that von Maker had now taken up residence in legendary comedian Jackie Gleason's summer mansion on Furnace Dock Road in Cortlandt, New York. He'd changed his name yet again; this time forever muddying the handle of a friend named Dave Patterson, and used the new ID to convince yet another eager real estate broker that he was a dream tenant.

Von Maker started wheeling and dealing again the moment he settled in, dropping Gleason's name to impress more feckless gallery owners. This time, he snowed the Jasper Gallery in Houston out of, among others, a huge, 6-by-4-foot feline, *Le Lion* from Kees van Dongen, another Vuillard, *La mere de l'artiste*, and a Degas, *Portrait Presume Achille Degas*, which was a stunning depiction of the great artist's brother. The sky was the limit on the turnaround for those, at least a million then. As noted in previous chapters, Degases now go for the big bucks, $10 million and up, and that includes his sculptures and pastels as well as his oils.

Van Dongen was no slouch either. The 20th century Netherlands-born, Paris-living illustrator and satirist's best oils are rapidly approaching the $10 million mark as well.

They were all sent to the Cortlandt mansions on consignment, meaning von Maker paid nothing for them. And why not? This was, after all, the home of 'The Great One', Jackie Gleason. Who wouldn't trust Ralph Kramden?

Trouble was; the Jasper Gallery would have an easier time finding *The Honeymooners*' Alice Kramden on the moon than they would of ever recovering a dime from von Maker or getting their masterpieces back. (The same Jasper Gallery would later lose a giant Picasso in shipping. See Chapter 4)

If this wasn't bad enough, the name-dropping grifter conned a Boston Gallery out of New Hampshire native Maxfield Parrish's *Jason and His Teacher*. The 19th and 20th century American traditionalist's oils have recently passed the half-million-dollar mark.

Continuing to live artistically large, von Maker began throwing lavish parties at the Gleason estate, inviting in his latest lambs, which included everyone from the local idle rich to international jet-setting adventurers.

Von Maker told his future marks that he had a $7 million art, jewellery, and artefact collection, and passed out a detailed listing of more than 150 works, complete with price tags. The list, a study in salting a dead gold mine with a few shiny nuggets, offered everything from an Edouard Manet for $850,000 (*Still Life with Fish*) to a Norman Rockwell, (*Life and Works*) for a bargain basement $1,000. Virtually all were fakes, some copies of existing paintings, while others were completely fabricated.

The list itself was a fascinating document, which incorporated everyone from mega-stars like Remington, Degas, Picasso, Manet, Dalí, and Rubens, to lesser-knowns like Reginald Marsh, Arthur

Davies, Carel Fabritius, Percy Moran, and Jean Arp. The products were priced accordingly.

Among the jewellery on the list was 'Mountain of the Immortals'—a '939'carat emerald carving that von Maker was offering for $375,000. That one caught my eye because I had a file on its theft. Closer to 700 carats, it was the largest emerald in the world, and was destined to nearly destroy my life and career. (More on this later.)

I had an excellent flow of accurate information on von Maker's activities because we had turned his associate, Bernie Howard 'The Dirty Little Coward,' who was a Woody Allen-like forger. Bernie, 52, was caught in California with $2.5 million in fake Los Angeles treasury warrants, which are a type of bond. As his nickname attested, Bernie was eager to deal his pals to lighten his own load.

In spring 1974, we decided to take von Maker down. I couldn't do it personally because Schwartz was out on bail and had no doubt warned him that I was an FBI agent. In fact, Schwartz could have very well appeared at any meeting set up with von Maker. We instead recruited a young special agent named Bob Spiel and prepared him to get his undercover feet wet. I dressed him properly, advised him what to do and say, then convinced the brass to have $100,000 wired into a safety deposit box at Manny Hanny—Manufacturers Hanover Bank on Madison Avenue—so Spiel could flash some heavy cash. Sensing another news making bust, the bean counters at the Puzzle Palace in DC cooperated.

Spiel, introduced to von Maker by The Dirty Little Coward, took his new business partner to the stately old bank to view the stacks of hundreds. Von Maker was all but having an orgasm as he caressed the bills. Spiel stroked him even harder by saying there was a lot more cash where that came from—which wasn't a lie since it had come straight from the United States Treasury! The following day, von Maker invited Spiel to his New York residence, the Dietrich home, to do some serious business.

Going over von Maker's list prior to the meeting, we were careful to pick out some fakes along with the real ones we knew had been stolen. We also instructed Spiel to make no mention of the Jasper and Maxwell galleries. This was being played as if von Maker was a legitimate art broker, which explains why we had to display so much money. We were buying retail, not 10 cents on the dollar as we would have with a fence.

Spiel called von Maker and relayed our selections. The con man set the total price at $250,000. Spiel agreed, and went to the Dietrich brownstone on East 95th Street to check out the goods. He went in alone, unarmed but wired, while I sat in a car down the block with a team of other agents. Spiel, a California boy who came from a well-to-do family, chose his own code word, 'Pasadena', the location of the famous Rose Bowl parade and football game.

The Dietrich house was as impressive as the artworks inside. Considerably larger than it appeared from the outside, a number of its spacious rooms had been set up as galleries. The three Maxwells and four Jasper paintings were all on prominent display, as was the Parrish from Boston. Von Maker certainly knew how to seed a gold mine. Interspersed among them were fakes, and some unexpected originals from Frank Stella (a contemporary American minimalist and innovator), Pieter Brueghel (16th century Belgian) Louis Valtat (French, 19th and 20th century), Frank Myers Boggs (19th and 20th century American) and Jack Levine (20th century American.)

Valtats were worth around $25,000 then and $250,000 today. Stella's fluorescent lights, mixed media, metals, and alkyds (sticky resin), once easily owned favourites in the psychedelic 1960s and '70s, are closing in on a million today. Boggs' oils now approach $50,000. Levines are closer to $100,000, while Brueghels are rarely available on the market and are difficult to price.

All the sorting and figuring, however, would be done later. We still had to put von Maker in the pen, and shut down his very strange operation. To that end, Spiel and von Maker began bickering over how Spiel was going to deliver the rest of the money, which had now leaped to $300,000 due to the new discoveries. I could sense the con man growing frustrated because Spiel didn't have a good rap down as to the method in which the transactions would be handled, and where the extra $200,000 was coming from. At one point, the pressured agent said, 'I'll just have an armoured truck pull up.'

We burst out laughing at that. Apparently, Bob thought he could toss bags of cash on Dietrich's stoop with the morning newspaper. Fortunately, von Maker had already touched the first $100,000, and Bob was able to recover enough to convince him the rest would similarly be made available. Before von Maker had a chance to ask for more-specific details again, Bob changed subjects. 'I'm going out to Pasadena to play golf tomorrow. It's beautiful in Pasadena. Have you ever been to Pasadena?'

I don't recall hearing von Maker's answer because we were out like rockets at the first Pasadena. Within seconds, we were banging on the door announcing our presence. Inside, von Maker took off, retreating deeper inside the brownstone. He left it to Spiel to let us in, which the agent did. The others arrested Spiel, and I took off to introduce myself to my long-unseen prey. He had pranced through a second gallery area and trapped himself in the kitchen like a cockroach.

I wasn't impressed, with either his behaviour or his appearance. He was just another chubby little balding hustler—like Jason Alexander from *Seinfeld*—and was acting rather Bernie Howard cowardly to boot. I flashed my badge, announced who I was, and told him he was under arrest.

After recovering from the shock, von Maker's hustler side finally emerged, and he gave me a little show. He insisted he was a legitimate art dealer, that he was the esteemed president of Antique Investors, that they were doing above-board business, that we were jackboot goons violating his civil rights, that he was going to sue us and own the whole United States. Amused, I asked him how he acquired all the paintings. He kept saying they were his, repeating the words 'mine, mine, mine' like a child. I mentioned the problems with the

Maxwell and Jasper galleries, and he quickly spat back that he paid Maxwell with the two $45,000 cheques, and the Jaspers were on consignment.

'Those Maxwell cheques bounced months ago,' I reminded him, commenting on the rubber quality of his currency. Brushing that off, he continued to babble, telling me that I'd made a horrible mistake and my career was toast.

'By the way, what's your name?' I asked him. He paused for a moment like the question caught him off guard. 'I thought so.'

'I'm Harold von Maker,' he said defiantly.

'That so? Then who is David Patterson? Who is Peter Wertz? Aren't they the owners of the paintings? Whose name is on this lease?'

Von Maker stuttered for a moment, then spat, 'I want my lawyer.'

'We already busted him weeks ago,' I said, telling him what he already knew. Von Maker professed to know nothing about the nasty Pollock incident.

'He's not my lawyer. I have a different one now.'

'I'll bet.'

Although I was enjoying the banter, I pawned von Maker off on another agent so I could inventory the art. We took everything I thought was good, and left the obvious junk fakes. We had to summon a truck to haul them out of there. Among the 'treasures' I did take was an ancient Bible manuscript that turned out to be phoney. Von Maker was probably marketing it as being written in God's own hand.

What I didn't take, or even notice at the time, thankfully, was another 'valuable' stash in the Dietrich house. The New York sanitation department's eviction squad unearthed reams and reams of elaborate homoerotic sex toys, pornographic videos, books, magazines, anal probe vibrators, along with a closet full of leather-and-whips S&M gear. Mad King Ludwig would have loved the place! Harold von Maker, on top of everything else, was one kinky cherubic boy-toy.

It was a role, however relished, that he had no plans of playing in prison. He was taken to the 'Downtown Hilton'—the name we gave the Metropolitan Correction Centre because the cons were always said to be too busy taking dance, cooking, and ceramics classes, and seeing their doctors and shrinks, to ever talk to us. Von Maker, right at home, put up 10% of his $50,000 bail and was out the next day. Then zoom, just like that, he vanished. Nobody ever heard from him again.

One might question why a judge would grant bail to such an obvious flight risk as a skilled con man with multiple identities, but judges do things like that all the time. That's the American justice system. We street grunts work months, sometimes years, to put a crook away, and he's in jail a single day. That's why I learned very early on that in the art sleuth dodge, it's all about recovering the masterpieces. The thieves are just the chaff.

Which is not to say that von Maker had the last laugh. The most common story regarding what happened to him was that desperate for a stake to re-establish his life in a new location, he sold the remaining paintings he had—the junk I wouldn't even consider taking—to his ol' bent-nosed pal Carmine 'The Doctor' Lombardozzi. The Doc had them checked, and was told there's no fool like an old Mafia fool, and grew furious with rage.

'Yer buddy von Maker's in the East River with a Volkswagen tied around his left leg,' a knowledgeable informant told me. If so, the Beetle sank deep because the con man's body was never recovered.

A few years later, I received a Telex from Interpol saying they were tracking a scoundrel who was travelling around Europe, leasing castles, then selling all the contents. His description fitted, but we were never able to confirm that it was von Maker risen from the East River dead. My guess is that the Luxembourg Looter in Europe was someone else, and that The Doctor fed von Maker to the fishes.

Dead or alive, von Maker's legacy lived on because his case didn't end there. The wily con was destined to reach a decomposed hand from the depths of the river like Jason Voorhees in those *Friday the 13th* teen slasher movies and nearly pull me down with him.

Among the relics we didn't find at the Dietrich house was the previously mentioned Emerald of the Immortals, then the largest emerald in the world at nearly 700 carats. The carved, cantaloupe-sized green gem, worth about $400,000 back then, had been stolen from a well-known Chinese artefact collector and author named Warren E. Cox. I put out the word that we were looking for it. One of my long-time favourite informants, a grizzled street hustler named Chappy, came up with yet another big hit for me. He told me it had been fenced for $10,000 to a high-class antique dealer on Third Avenue. I visited the place, and sure enough, there it was, right in one of the display cases. I called in the troops and we seized it, eventually giving it back to Mr Cox.

I explained to Cox that Chappy was the key, and said he'd be coming by so Cox could thank him personally. I never mentioned money—sometimes my law degree came in handy—but the implications were clear. Cox offered Chappy $150 for finding the massive jewel that's worth millions today. Chappy was upset at both the financial and personal diss, and came to me and complained. I agreed with his assessment and called Cox and reminded him how instrumental Chappy was in the recovery, stating that he deserved to be treated with more respect, again careful not to specifically mention money. Chappy paid Mr Cox a second visit and came away happier and $1,500 richer.

Cox, though, was not so happy. He went straight to the Knapp Commission, the King of All Police Rat Squads. The Knapp Commission was in the process of ravaging the New York City police force following the fallout from the Frank Serpico case of book and Al Pacino movie fame. The commission started off doing a good job cleaning up corruption in the police ranks, but soon became a beast with a raging appetite, stretching the bounds of sanity for its next meal. For years afterward, cops were afraid to accept an apple from a fruit stand, or a free beer from a bartender for fear of being painted as dirty and splashed across the headlines. Knapp Special Prosecutor Maurice Nadjari raised the tension further when he told the media that getting a guilty verdict against a dirty cop was better than sex.

Naturally, when Cox complained about me and Chappy, the headline-grabbing Knapp prosecutors jumped on it. Bagging an FBI special agent would have been the cherry on their cake. They wired Cox and had him call me, trying to get me to implicate myself in extorting him or some such nonsense. The shoe was now on the other foot. Somebody was using a tape on me.

Cox caught me when I was up to my neck in stolen alligators and started blathering about Chappy, the 'reward', and sending Chappy over to collect. He seemed to be beating around some bush, and I didn't have the time to deal with it so I blew him off by saying, 'Look, I'm sorry but I have no time to talk. I've got to go.'

Truth was, it was 10.30am, and that meant the busty Russian bombshell in the apartment directly across from our offices at 201 East 69th Street was doing her nude breakfast routine. Every morning at that time, she pranced around in front of her windows, naked as the day she was born in cold, cold Moscow, driving us all nuts by flipping her eggs. That, of course, was the point. The Russian Embassy was a few blocks away, and she had been stashed there to lure an FBI agent into her, uh, trap so he or she could be turned and used as a spy. The Russians were well known for arranging such temptations. American soldiers guarding overseas US embassies sometimes fell victim to similarly stunning Russian vixens.

We were ordered to ignore her, and not to go to the window for fear of being photographed by telescopic cameras, catalogued, and identified—another common Russian espionage technique. We didn't go to the window, but we certainly didn't ignore her. Her appearances were a mid-morning treat.

My interest, of course, was purely professional. The lady was a true work of art!

Long story short, with that distraction going on, combined with all my other work, I didn't have the time or energy to listen to Cox's complaints. That's why I blew him off.

The Knapp Commission, in their blood fever, took my response as a confession that I was extorting Cox. They opened a file and began the process of trying to prosecute me. A copy of the tape was sent to my bosses. I was summoned to the Principal's Office, where I was grilled as to whether I had ever taken money from a victim, ever shared reward money with an informant, ever ordered a victim to pay an informant, the whole gamut.

I denied it all, which was the truth. They asked if I'd take a lie detector and I said, 'Hell yeah!' Satisfied, my boss tossed the tape into the trash.

Later, a US Attorney ruled there was nothing incriminating on the tape, and even if I had admitted sending Chappy to Cox for a reward, there was nothing criminal about that either.

Regardless, I get chills to this day thinking how one casual comment offered during a conversation I wasn't even paying attention to could have destroyed my life. And thank goodness the Knapp Commission didn't go sniffing around my jewellery, clothing, shoes, and fake identification friends, or they could have painted me as the Dr Evil of FBI agents.

The von Maker epilogue also pounded home playwright Clare Boothe Luce's classic statement that 'No good deed ever goes unpunished.' Here I'd recovered this guy's prized King Kong gonad-sized jewel, and he tried to hang me in return!

On the other hand, I imagine all the crooks I'd conned during my years undercover would have no doubt considered it poetic justice.

The Case That Wouldn't End didn't finish with that near booby trap either. After sorting through the rest of von Maker's stash, we were left with a single painting that couldn't be traced to its rightful owner. Try as we might, we couldn't figure out where Frank Stella's *Brooklyn Bridge*, came from. We would have been forced to give the potentially million-dollar work back to von Maker, but he, as noted, was sleeping with the mullets. The brass in DC eventually presented it to the National Gallery of Art in Washington.

After that, the case spun in a bizarre and bloody direction. In September 1976, a troubled socialite, who wasn't identified at the time, drove into Manhattan one afternoon to raise some funds needed to maintain her lifestyle. Her green Jaguar was loaded with four important modern paintings, along with some jewellery she wanted to sell.

The lady, another Barbara Hutton-like, hard-living member of the E.F. Hutton investment banking and stock brokerage clan, parked on East 70th Street near Midtown Manhattan. Tipped by one of von Maker's cronies, that ol' goombah art fancier, Carmine 'The Doctor' Lambardozzi, sent his boys over to swipe the latest 'Poor Little Rich Girl's' car and everything in it. The vehicle was subsequently found in Brooklyn charred to the frame.

The torch crew had removed: *Boat in Early Morning* by William Zorach, a 20th century water-colourist and abstract sculptor; *The Wave* by David Levine, a 20th century California and Mexico realist; *Deer Island, Maine* by 20th century water-colourist John Marin; and *Ann*, by Robert Henri, a 19th and 20th century Nebraskan who was a leader in the 'Ashcan School' noted for painting scenes of everyday life in poor American neighbourhoods. Also stolen was an $8,000 diamond brooch. The total take in 1976 dollars came to $400,000.

Zorach's sculptures bring close to that alone today. Marin's oils are closing in on $750,000. An Henri oil was sold for $3.6 million in 2005. Levine's works have not been on the market recently.

We received a lead that the theft was schemed by the woman's insurance broker and estate manager, a high-flying social climber named Michael Escott, 35. I went undercover as a collector in need of insurance to try and see if he'd set me up as well. However, before I could make any headway, The Doctor took care of the problem, Mafia style. Less than three months after the theft, Escott was shot five times in the head and body as he sat in his silver Jaguar in the Ironbound section of downtown Newark, New Jersey. He was discovered the next morning by factory workers, still wearing his 18-carat gold cufflinks, a gold medallion, and with $400 cash in his wallet. The Doctor wasn't after Escott's money or metals. He was insulating himself from the theft.

The ritzy Jag that became Escott's tomb had been purchased by the socialite. Escott's experience reiterates the danger of amateurs teaming up with professional gangsters. If you ain't one of them, you're the loose end. The paintings, worth untold millions today, were never recovered.

And that, at last, put a fork in the life and times of Prince Harold von Hohenloe. May he rest in peace with the fishes.

.14.

THE CASE OF THE VANISHING VIRGIN

*O*N 6 JUNE 1972, a team of sacrilegious thieves invaded a 12th century Roman Catholic church in Abella de la Conca, Andorra, the small principality in the Pyrenees that sits between Spain and France. Their target was a massive four-panelled altarpiece nearly eight feet tall and six feet wide depicting the Virgin Mary, baby Jesus, the crucifixion, and other historic Judeo/Christian imagery.

Entitled *Scenes From the Life of the Virgin*, the irreplaceable $3 million retablo was created in the 14th century by the Serra Brothers, mostly Jaume Serra with an assist from his brother Pedro. (Retablos/retables are Spanish/Mexican art painted on panels depicting the saints.) The most renowned of the Catalonian artists of the late 14th century, the Serra Brothers were students of the Sienese tradition, and favoured magnificent altarpieces. Their inspiring religious works, which are rarely on the market, are of incalculable value today.

None of which meant anything to the thieves. They were believed to be part of the band of radical Basque separatist terrorists known as ETA (*Euskadi Ta Askatasuna*—Fatherland and Freedom). They took the masterpiece to finance their bloody campaign to free themselves from Spanish rule and become an independent nation.

The group hailed from a region of Spain that is better known to Americans like me for supplying the world with professional jai alai players. *Jai alai* is a game similar to handball or racquetball played on a much larger court. The athletes use a narrow, banana-shaped wicker basket known as a cesta to first catch, and then toss a hard, rubber pelota against a wall at speeds of up to 160 miles per hour. The sport is popular in Nevada, Connecticut, and Florida solely because of the legalised gambling associated with it.

The Basque radicals, however, favoured bombs and guns over cestas and pelotas. Their trek into Andorra was in keeping with a worldwide wave of political and terrorist groups kidnapping great art both to finance their activities, and to bring a hated enemy to their knees.

In Ireland in 1974, a band of Irish Republican Army (IRA) soldiers headed by Dr Bridget Rose Dugdale raided the estate of Irish millionaire Sir Alfred Beit in Blessington (near Dublin) and made off with 19 paintings worth $20 million, including works by Goya, Rubens, Metsu, Velasquez, Gainsborough, and Vermeer. Bridget Rose and associates had previously stolen another Vermeer in London and used it to try and have fellow IRA soldiers imprisoned there, including two fellow females, transferred to jails in Northern Ireland.

The London Vermeer, *The Guitar Player*, snatched from Kenwood House, was so valuable that Dugdale farmed it out to other terrorist groups. A baffling assortment of demands soon poured in, including one calling for $1.15 million to feed the people in the faraway island nation of Grenada, and another for kerosene, food, and money to be provided to the poor and elderly of the Highgate and Archway districts of London—two thriving areas that weren't known to be impoverished.

The 20 paintings were eventually discovered in a cottage in Glandore, County Cork, and the radicals were arrested. Bridget pled 'proudly and incorruptibly guilty' to the theft charges and was sentenced to nine years in an Irish prison, where she raised constant hell through hunger strikes, rebellions, and recruitment of additional art-stealing 'freedom fighters'.

Whatever her politics, Dr Bridget Rose, the daughter of a wealthy British art collector of Irish descent, had excellent taste. The works of the 17th century Dutch artist Johannes (or Jan) Vermeer are some of the rarest and most coveted paintings in the world, as only 32 are said to remain in existence. For one feisty Irishwoman to have stolen two was extraordinary.

Although Vermeer died broke and left enormous debts, his few paintings in circulation today go for around $50 million. The ones in museums might even bring in double that—enough money to finance a small-scale war.

Even back in a bygone era, art and politics were intertwined. The last time the *Mona Lisa* was stolen, in 1911, it was taken by an Italian appalled that Leonardo da Vinci's great masterpiece was in possession of the snooty French. In a similar vein, the Russians and Germans have been fighting for nearly a century over art taken as booty in World Wars I and II.

More recently, Edvard Munch's *The Scream*, worth about $70 million, was stolen on the eve of the 1994 Winter Olympics in Lillehammer, Norway, ostensibly by another politically minded group. Anti-abortion forces claimed responsibility, and demanded that a film favourable to their cause be shown on Norwegian television while the eyes of the world were on them. The Norwegian government refused, suspicious of the claim. The masterpiece was recovered three months later during a sting at a hotel 40 miles south of Oslo. (A second version of *The Scream*, as well as another Munch masterpiece, *Madonna*, was stolen in Oslo in 2004 and only recovered in late August 2006, but no reasons for the theft were ever given by Norwegian police.)

Stealing masterpieces benefits rebel groups because it makes front-page news and publicises their cause. Even if they don't profit monetarily from the heist, the attention is worth its weight in gold.

Learning from their fellow revolutionaries, the Basques jumped into the game by targeting their home-grown masterpiece in tiny Andorra. However, just like the other groups—and art thieves everywhere—the Basques found that selling such a massive retablo was a lot harder than stealing it. Years passed and little was heard about the panels. The Basque revolutionaries didn't appear to be flush with newfound financing, so the suspicion was that they had the *Virgin* on ice.

In 1977, the head of Spain's version of the FBI arrived in New York carrying a 'Letter Rogatory,' which is an official request from one government to another to co-operate in a major criminal investigation. It was received in that 'woo, woo' way we Americans have of reacting to anything that sounds royal, stately, or Olde European. Officially presented to the FBI's New York office, I hovered around it like everybody else, thinking it was really neat. In my case, however, it was about to become personal. Spain's version of J. Edgar Hoover was on our shores tracking the missing Serra. When the hoopla died down, he was assigned to partner with me.

At first, I thought it was a practical joke because the Spanish top cop, Inspector Miguel Nuñez Ferrer, was a dead ringer for bald Greek actor Telly Savalas, then at the height of his 'Who loves ya, Baby?' Tootsie Pop sucking fame, playing NYPD Detective Theo Kojak.

It was no joke. Despite his Hollywood appearance, Spain's chief crime fighter was very real and very determined. Huddling in my office, he emotionally brought me up to speed on his five-year quest for the Serra, which he termed a matter of national pride. After years of chasing false leads all over Europe, things had suddenly heated up. The previous month, an art dealer in the Netherlands attempted to shake down Spain for a $1.5 million ransom. The deal fell through when the Dutch representative spooked and broke off communication.

The suspect, some kind of pseudo con man dignitary— probably another phoney prince—had switched directions and was currently attempting to broker the altarpiece in a safer, less intense environment. Translation—he wanted to pawn it in America, where he felt tempers were cooler, the bald cops operated under tighter restrictions, and the European legal statutes didn't apply.

My new buddy, dubbed Don Kojako, appeared to be as straight-laced a cop as the incorruptible Kojak himself. He was a loyal Spanish subject with a good heart and a dogged sense of responsibility to his work, people, country, and the Pope. Although I found him to be far too optimistic for my cynical New Yorker tastes, I liked the guy and we hit it off.

He soon loosened up over a few shots of Scotch and gave me the inside details on how the American angle had developed. The Netherlands suspect had contacted the Metropolitan Museum of Art and offered to sell the Serra through them to the National Art Institute of Madrid. The Met just happened to have a knowledgeable Spanish national on their staff, a middle-aged Catholic woman we dubbed 'Consuela' who was an assistant curator responsible for Spanish art. The caller was referred to her, and she naturally showed a passionate interest in acquiring the Serra. She immediately contacted the Spanish police, and Don Kojako was on the next plane to New York.

We reconvened at the Met to enable Consuela to give me the story straight from the horse's mouth. She was a refined woman who looked like she could be pretty if dolled up, but had no interest in such superficialities, instead favouring the makeup-free, horn-rimmed glasses, tight-bun uniform of the stereotypical librarian. She spoke in a soft, perfectly enunciated Spanish that was so elegant

I could almost understand it, a far cry from the machinegun-paced Puerto Rican, Dominican, and Cuban dialects heard in New York.

Consuela explained in English that the caller had identified himself as Robert Roozemond of the Cultural Institute of the Netherlands, and as the President of the Netherlands Chain Christian Arts International Group of Panama. That second title raised my eyebrows. If anything ever sounded like a front for stolen art, especially stolen paintings of a religious nature, that was it. In fact, any European company that ended with the words 'of Panama' was immediately suspicious.

Roozemond, 44, told Consuela that he was acting as an intermediary for the current owners, and professed that his interest in the matter was solely to return the great masterpiece to the nation of its creation. That, and $1.5 million, which, naturally, was merely a small finder's fee for their troubles.

Don Kojako later informed me that the Interpol background check on the refined Mr Roozemond revealed that he lived in a Dutch castle. That sounded noble until it was further explained that he was participating in a generous government programme that allowed people to live in area castles rent-free in return for their promise to restore them. Interpol reported that Roozemond, as far as they could determine, had not so much as put a splat of grey rock putty into one of the chipped stones.

The wily Roozemond was also listed in various documents as heading the Cultural Institutes of Norway and Holland, and in another, to change things a little, the Netherlands.

Here I go again, I sighed to myself. Roozemond was just a Dutch version of Harold von Maker and Mel Weinberg, two notable American con men of chapters past.

Meanwhile, Don Kojako outlined a plan that was right out of Disneyland. They'd contact Roozemond and set up a meeting. We'd all agree to his outrageous demands. He'd bring us the altarpiece. We'd flash our badges, arrest him, confiscate the Serra, and send it back to an overjoyed Spain. Just like that, everything would fall into place perfectly without a snag.

I thought the guy was absolutely nuts. Nothing ever goes that smoothly in New York. For one thing, how was Roozemond going to cart an eight-foot painting halfway around the world, and hand it to us for inspection like it was a bag of crack cocaine? The Spaniard's optimism was beyond belief. My guess was that Roozemond was just playing a shell game, and planned to take the money and run.

It was, however, Don Kojako's show, and he did have that outstanding Letter Rogatory and all, so I had to Rogatory along with the program.

We set up Don Kojako at the Sheraton on Lexington Avenue across from the famed Waldorf Astoria hotel, which would be our base of operations. Consuela called Roozemond in his castle and advised him that the Spanish government was ready to deal, and had contracted with an American art expert to verify the work and make the payment. She said we were willing to meet with him anywhere in the world. He responded that he'd be in New York in a few days to get the ball rolling.

The American expert, of course, was Thomas Bishop. I'd been expecting to road trip across the continents, and was relieved that first contact was going to be in my home ballpark. I still expected to hop the ocean and inspect the Serra in Europe or South America, but having the initial sit-down in New York was one less headache.

The Flying Dutchman winged in as promised, so fast that he caught us a bit off guard. I had to set up the flash money, which was astoundingly $500,000 in cash. Suddenly, after years of being tighter than a chipmunk's butt, the FBI was so wowed by the Letter Rogatory that the purse strings were not only loosened, but ripped apart.

This caused problems in its own right. Citibank refused to accept so large a sum in the fabricated name of Thomas Bishop, and made me use my own personal account. It was a simple-sounding process that would actually cause me colossal headaches with the IRS for nearly a decade. Unaware of the future ramifications, I agreed. The money was wired in, transformed into stacks of ice cold cash, and was stashed inside four safety deposit boxes.

So there I was, a G-Man who started out making $9,000 a year, and had slaved my way to $25,000 per annum a decade later by recovering more than $250 million in stolen art and artefacts. I now had $500,000 packed inside four safety deposit boxes, and a quartet of little keys jangling in my pocket. Talk about temptation.

This was the exact kind of situation that fuelled J. Edgar Hoover's distaste for undercover operations. Because of Hoover's policies, we weren't psychologically screened as FBI agents and police officers are today to see if they can handle the stress, anxiety, and temptations that come with leading a double life. This explains why many of the early undercover agents fell into drinking, drugs, shoplifting, and graft as they struggled with the constant tension and stark contrasts of their dual existence. One FBI agent finally cracked in the mid 1980s and took off with 90 pounds of pure cocaine, worth $2.5 to $5 million on the streets, depending upon how it was cut. After being caught and convicted, he sued the bureau on the grounds that he wasn't properly prepared to face such enticements.

My fantasy figure had always been $5 million. If I somehow found myself in possession of a painting, cash, or whatnot worth that, then I'd have to think about taking a hike. Of course, I never would have done it. Too many years of Catholic schools and High Masses made that a psychological impossibility. Still, one has to dream. Although I've had more than $5 million worth of paintings in my possession on occasion, and even in my home, somebody always knew about it.

The closest I ever came to a possible clean score was during the 'Pizza Connection' Mafia case. My assignment one evening was to join a team of agents tailing Joe 'The Whale' Ganci, a massive, 5-foot-7-inch, 350-pound gangster high up in the heroin smuggling business. The Whale shook everybody but me. I was the only agent who discovered his hidden lair in Riverside, New Jersey. That meant, according to the devil on my shoulder, that I could have hit the place for the two to three million dollars worth of jewels, furs, and cash he was known to be hiding there. Nobody would have been the wiser.

Instead, the angel on my other shoulder shrieked and vanquished the evil demon. I radioed in the location, cashed my $500-a-week pay cheque, and caught a movie in the Bronx instead of drinking Pina Coladas on a beach in Tahiti.

Damn that Catholic guilt and squeaky clean G-Man brainwashing. Point being, the half-million dollars worth of tax money in my safety deposit boxes, however tempting, still fell $4.5 million short of my 'off to Tahiti' fantasy.

Even if I couldn't live like a king, my alter-ego Thomas Bishop was allowed to visit various kingdoms on occasion. The Bureau sprung for a $1,000-a-night suite at the Waldorf, complete with a conference room. I'd barely settled in, kicked off my shoes, and put up my feet when the tech squad booted me out. I wanted to stay and solve the gnawing mystery of where they planted their bugs, but they would have none of it. As mentioned in previous chapters, that's a secret they guard with their lives because they don't want agents spilling their guts about it in court. The less we knew, the better.

To this day, after scores of undercover operations, I still don't know where the bugs are placed. All I know is what I see in the movies like everyone else.

The meeting with The High Flying Dutchman was set for 2pm. Earlier, I was pleasantly surprised when I didn't have any trouble recruiting backup agents, even for potential after-hours duty. Usually, one had to go begging. I finally pushed my luck and asked somebody why I wasn't receiving the normal cold shoulder.

'Are you kidding? It's the Waldorf!' I was told. 'Everybody wants to hang out there. Some of that money, glamour, and celebrity might rub off!'

Don Kojako eagerly volunteered as well, but I insisted that he stay out of sight. The guy was far too recognisable to be of any surveillance use. If Roozemond had any knowledge of the Spanish police force, he'd recognise the big bald cop in an instant. On top of that, people on the streets were starting to stop and stare, as if he were indeed Kojak. If I gave the guy a cherry lollipop, he would have been mobbed.

Consuela arrived on time, looking just as 'librarian understated' as ever. We certainly weren't a matching couple because I was decked in my art pimp gear. Ten minutes or so later, in walks this tall, lanky guy who looked like actor Danny Kay playing Hans Christian Andersen, complete with a thick, guttural Dutch accent that was difficult to understand. He was dressed like a mortician, all in black save for a white shirt.

Consuela had met with him the day before in the Waldorf dining room, so she made the formal introductions. We shook hands, small-talked, then focused on the issue at hand. In between, I fielded calls from Sotheby's, Christie's, the Kennedy Galleries, all the major art players. They were actually other agents, but Consuela answered the phone and announced the phoney callers with a flourish to impress Roozemond. I had to stay in character and keep up the fake art world banter while some agent was telling me dirty jokes or dicking with my head on the other end of the line.

Roozemond launched into his I'm-a-legitimate-art-dealer-helping-out-Spain dance, reciting his suspect credentials and acting like he was doing the world an enormous favour. We played along, making sure not to drop the crass 'S' word: stolen. I asked him whom he was representing, and how the massive Serra travelled from the dry highlands in Spain to the soggy, dyke-protected lowlands of the Netherlands. He bobbed and weaved, claiming his 'investors' and their travels had to remain confidential.

A half-hour in, my head began spinning from European accent hell. Between Roozemond's Dutch and Consuela's Spanish, I was getting a pounding headache trying to make sense of all the unfamiliar pronunciations. After the words 'chiaroscuro' and 'craquelure' were tossed around in competing versions completely foreign to my ears, I made a mental note to push the meeting along before I completely lost it.

The Flying Dutchman fished around in his briefcase and withdrew a professionally prepared portfolio on the Serra, complete with vivid colour photos, its history, bios of the artists, the whole enchilada. It was by far the most elaborate prospectus a thief or fence had ever presented to me. I noticed that both Roozemond and his materials referred to the Serra as comprised of four parts. The common belief, reported in the media and some art books, was that it was in three sections. The fourth bottom panel was frequently overlooked. Roozemond not only mentioned it, he had photos of that section. It was obvious that he had the real deal.

Getting down to the nitty gritty, Consuela told Roozemond that she was authorised by Spain to pay him what he wanted, and added that we were prepared to show him the first payment if he would then allow us to inspect the work. No matter how she sugar-coated it, this was still back alley Crack Cocaine Dealing 101. Legitimate businessmen on Roozemond's level should have blanched at the 'Show me the money' aspect. A man doing such an enormous favour for the 'Esteemed Country of Spain' should have accepted a government-issued cheque or bank draft without question.

Not The Flying Dutchman. He showed his crass and nibbled at the bait. Not yet ready to swallow, he said he'd consult with his people and get back to us. I thought for sure that sanity, or a smarter partner, would prevail and he'd tell us later that the money feel was 'Not necessary among gentlemen and gentlewomen.'

As Consuela, Don Kojako, and I dined that evening, I marvelled at the layers of bullshit involved in such dealings. Logic gets tossed aside when negotiating with thieves and con men, no matter how upscale they pretend to be. Highly intelligent, or dumb as an ox, they always do something that tips you off to their criminal intentions.

Roozemond reported in the next day with the news that his 'investors' wanted him to view the money. Yep, this guy was a sleaze, but then again, that's why we had gone through all the trouble to wire the cash to Citibank.

While waiting outside the financial institution on Park Avenue and 52nd Street, I was certain the deal had shifted to something entirely different. Once he sniffed the money, I expected Roozemond to morph even deeper into con man mode and implement some scheme to rip us off. We'd be asked to cart the suitcase full of American dollars to some godforsaken part of the world, a Dutch or Panamanian mean street, where we'd be waylaid. Suffice it to say, I wasn't in the best of moods as we ventured down into the dungeon of Citibank. I felt like grinding The Flying Dutchmen into mincemeat and stuffing him inside a pair of wooden shoes!

Hiding my true sentiments, I was all smiles as we put on the show. The magic keys produced four long, narrow stainless steel boxes, numbers 14, 15, 16, and 17, packed with 5,000 one-hundred dollar bills tied in stacks of $10,000. Roozemond, like the cons before him, was practically orgasmic at the sight and smell of the money. He tried to maintain his 'ho hum, been there before' air of castle-dwelling dignity, but it was obvious he felt on the cusp of the score of a lifetime.

Actually, I was rather overwhelmed myself. It was by far the most money I'd ever seen, and I had to admit, it was intoxicating. I found myself thinking again about when that next flight to Saint Tropez might be leaving. I took out of few of the weighty stacks and handed them to Roozemond to let him cop a feel. He was in con man's heaven.

'This is just a third of it, remember,' I baited, setting the hook deep into his stomach. 'We'll be paying you in three easy payments,' I joked, copying the ads shown on late-night television. Roozemond didn't get the joke, but he understood the point.

Consuela interrupted the monetary orgy and reminded Roozemond that since she had showed him hers, it was time for him to show her his. Here it comes, I thought. Call my travel agent and book a flight to Back Alley, Panama.

'Okay,' Roozemond said. 'We can see it now. It's at the Day and Meyer warehouse.'

Did I hear that right, I thought? The Day & Meyer, Murray & Young warehouse was on second Avenue and 61st Street, eight blocks from the FBI building. A beehive of self-contained, fireproof steel vaults, it was the precise kind of a specialty warehouse where one would store giant sized masterpieces. Still in operation, it's used by all the top galleries and auction houses. Could it be this easy? Was Don Kojako's absurd fantasy actually going to materialise without a hitch? This I had to see.

Buying into Don Kojako's eternal optimism, I had taken the liberty of bringing my portable inspection kit, complete with the X-ray machine from the bomb squad. It was all in the trunk of the FBI-owned mock Chequered Cab parked out front, driven by a special agent posing as a cabbie. We piled in and headed toward Day & Meyer. On the way, Roozemond expressed a keen interest in the X-ray device. After we arrived, I pulled it out and gave him a little demonstration.

The box, about the size of two Bud Light 30 packs placed side-by-side, was topped with an old Speed Graphic camera. They're the big ones with the accordion fronts and cracking flashbulbs seen in all the period movies. This throwback enabled the operator to rear load a large, 5-by-4-inch negative.

Innovative FBI techs had created the machine to enable the bomb squad to make on-the-spot inspections of suspicious packages. It allowed them to literally see inside the boxes for telltale signs of wires, detonators, clocks, and explosives.

The moment I saw it, I knew it could also be used to similarly see inside paintings to help determine age, restorations, corrections, previous drafts, the underpinnings of the canvas or wood, lead in the paint, glue or egg in the gleaming tempera, and various other critical factors. It could additionally reveal the type of nails used in the frames or wood panels, and even the skeletal remains of long-dead burrowing bugs. The possibilities were endless.

Protective of their invention, the techs were loath to let me take it, but I was complimentary and persistent. They finally agreed to do so under the radar, meaning no official sign-outs for nosy bosses to question.

Roozemond was totally absorbed, not because the machine might reveal that the Serra was fake, but more likely because he wasn't above foisting the occasional forgery on an unsuspecting 'Christian' buyer. He wanted to know what he might be up against in the future. He kept repeating that he'd never seen anything like it, which was true because it was the only one of its kind in existence. I didn't tell him that, however. I just put it off as state-of-the-art American ingenuity.

'I bought it for $15,000,' I fibbed. 'Best investment I ever made. You wouldn't believe what it reveals. Some artists, even the biggies like Rembrandt and van Gogh, become upset with their progress on a painting and simply cover it up with a white, black or brown base and start over. Well, this baby reveals the lost masterpiece under the found masterpiece!'

It truth, it was something from the dinosaur age of bomb detection, but in 1977, it was hot stuff.

We proceeded to lug the magic box into the Day & Meyer building. Roozemond produced all the right paperwork, and we were escorted to a padlocked, walk-in vault on the second floor. The workers opened the locks and swung open the heavy doors, revealing a space 5-feet wide, 10-feet high, and 10-feet deep, about the size of half a garage. Inside were four wooden crates crafted from pine that gave off a fresh, herbal aroma foreign to New York.

The crates were wheeled to a workroom area at the end of the hallway. Using crowbars and hammers, the skilled labourers popped open the nailed shut tops, dug through the artificial straw packaging materials, and pulled out the contents—four narrow varnished wooden cases with hinged tops.

Roozemond took it from there. He selected the middle panel, sliding it out and unwrapping the plastic. The first thing I saw and heard was Consuela gasp, cross herself, and start mumbling some kind of prayers or rosary in Spanish. She was having a religious epiphany, and would be in a trance from that point on. It was as if she was experiencing the resurrection.

Admittedly, the painting was a stunner. It was a thrill to be able to see it and touch it. The colours were as vivid as if brushed on the day before, from the Virgin's blue gown to Jesus' flowing brown hair. When the remaining panels were similarly revealed, we were bathed in a sea of New Testament, Biblical, and Catholic spectacle. There was the Virgin looking majestic, the Virgin's coronation, baby Jesus, young Jesus, adult Jesus, Jesus crucified, the Pentecost, shepherds, wise men, the three kings, new Christians, Roman soldiers, you name it. I could all but hear a choir of angels in the background. Even the crusty warehouse workers were moved. One of them made a sign of the cross himself and whispered something that sounded half-curse, half-prayer.' Mother of God, wouldya lookit that! Holy Toledo!'

Holy Andorra, more accurately. I knew instantly it was the real deal. Heck, Consuela and the workers wouldn't be on their knees doing the 'we're not worthy' wave if it weren't. Still, Roozemond was expecting a show with the newfangled X-ray machine, so I had to perform.

The panels, while large, could still be hand held. I took one over to the window to see it under the sunlight. All the expected signs of 500 years of aging were present, from the wood in the panels, to the ancient nails, to the spider web craquelure' of the paint, the chiaroscuro, and the era pigments.

I started with the ultraviolet black light wand, but it was too bright inside for that to reveal much of anything. What I accomplished was all show. Then, the moment Roozemond was waiting for, I set up the X-ray. He watched my every move as I loaded it and flashed a couple of panels. 'If a picture is worth a thousand words, an X-ray is worth a thousand pieces of provenance,' I told him.

The Dutch dealer naturally wanted to see the negatives and be taken through all they revealed. He correctly assumed they'd be ready on the spot, as they would need to be during bomb investigations. I had to duck him because it was the first time I'd used it myself, and I wasn't really sure what I'd find or how to interpret it.

'Nah, we've got to take it back to the lab to develop it fully and study it closely,' I dodged. Before he could argue, I pointed to some flaws in the more exposed bottom panel where the paint flaked off in spots, and the wood was nicked. Taking the bait, he claimed that the blemishes were hundreds of years old and were there before the work came into his possession. Considering the care with which it had been stored and packaged, I believed him.

Deeming it legit, I announced our satisfaction and summoned the workers to repack it.

We took the phoney cab back to the Waldorf, where we ditched Consuela before the fireworks went off. No sense getting her smacked around by my heavy-handed co-workers. I took Roozemond back to my suite and said my assistant would be coming for the X-rays. I also told him that I needed to verify his story about the pre-existing damage to the bottom panel. After that, we'd be good to go.

While explaining this, I flicked on the television and searched through the channels. 'Do they have the show *Kojak* in the Netherlands?' I asked.

He seemed dumbfounded. '*Kojak*. It's a big hit here and around the world. A cop show. Bald guy. *Kojak*.'

'Kojak,' of course, was the code word to send in the troops. In this instance, it was designed to be deliciously ironic because the first man in would be the look-alike, Don Kojako. The fun was spoiled, however, when The Flying Dutchman professed no knowledge of either *Kojak* or Telly Savalas.

Within minutes, Don Kojako indeed burst into the room, surrounded by FBI agents Terry Cox, Fred Berins, Ed Murphy, Bill Roemer, and Larry Kennedy. I advised my cohorts to keep close tabs on the Spaniard, because I sensed he wanted to rip Roozemond to shreds with his bare hands. Don Kojako was another in a long line of Catholics whose blood boiled over the kidnapping of the great national religious treasure by the godless Basque rebels and their godless Dutch agents.

We were thrown up against the wall, frisked and cuffed. Roozemond let out a steady stream of protests, reiterating ad nauseam that he was a respected, castle-dwelling citizen of the Netherlands, president of Chain Christian blah blah in Panama, that this was an outrage, that he was going to sue for the Statue of Liberty and Fort Knox, that he wanted us to call the Dutch Consulate, his attorney, F. Lee Bailey, Perry Mason, on and on.

At the FBI offices, we let Don Kojako have a go at Roozemond to see if he could get him to roll on the Basques, but miraculously, Roozemond suddenly lost all ability to speak or understand English. Don K wanted to bring out the cattle prods, but we advised him that, Letter Rogatory or not, that kind of thing was frowned upon in America.

Roozemond bonded out the following day. He immediately skipped.

It didn't matter, because we had the Serra. The afternoon of the arrest, we banged on the door of the United States Attorney in the Southern District of New York, explained the situation, flashed the all-powerful Letter Rogatory, and were awarded a warrant to snatch the Serra from the fireproof vaults of Day & Meyer. It was moved to Special Agent Lynn Shorski's FBI evidence room, which thankfully had a big freight elevator near the back entrance on 70th Street. Shorski, a Polish Catholic, stayed after hours to make sure it was secured in a safe, respectful place.

Interestingly enough, because of the chain of custody procedures, I had to initial the back of the panels with a 'T' for Tom written in pen. That made my marks an official part of the historical provenance of the 500-year-old painting.

Way cool!

The US Attorney selected to prosecute the case, Peter Murphy, was an unusual character with shaggy blond hair worn under an applejack hat, headgear more apt to be found on a jazz musician or a Rastafarian reggae singer than on a Federal prosecutor. It looked like a baseball hat with a shorter bill and a larger, fatter top. Instead of the usual Harvard/Yale Ivy League law degrees framed on his wall, he had a diploma from St Peter's Catholic Middle School in the Bronx. I had no idea how he slipped through the staid federal prosecutor cracks, but he certainly was a breath of fresh air.

That was an especially good thing because in late 1977, I travelled to Amsterdam, Rotterdam, and the old Zeider Zee area with the guy to try to find somebody to prosecute. We were assisted by a Dutch detective named Jon Cosell who looked like his American namesake, broadcaster Howard Cosell. Somehow, they must have been related.

Roozemond had pretended to be the ultimate nobleman, yet every lead we had on the guy took us from one sleazy low-rent joint to another. Amsterdam was full of hippies, dope dens, red-light districts, live sex shows, cathouses, and all those kind of fun things. It was a criminal's paradise, and nobody wanted to cooperate with an American prosecutor or a G-Man.

Zeider Zee, a vast shallow lake now called Ijsselmeer, offered more of the same. We searched for Roozemond, and attempted to track down any of his Basque rebel and gunrunning associates. We kept reminding ourselves that we already had The Low Flying Dutchman in New York, but the judge had kicked him loose on a cheap bond, which meant we were now halfway around the world trying to smoke him out of some wretched, lakeside wormhole.

We were warned about laughing at any of the old salt sailors in the proverbial rough-and-tumble waterfront bars dotting Zeider Zee, but weren't told why we'd find them so humorous. The mystery was solved after entering our first tavern. The Dutch Navy uniforms have normal tops, but are completed by kilts. The beer and knuckle sandwich palaces were packed with rugged sailors who looked like hairy Catholic school girls from the waist down. It was indeed strange to the American eye. What would Popeye and Brutus think?

Then again, I'm sure the Dutch sailors didn't know what to make of Murphy's applejack hat either. The prosecutor insisted on wearing the snazzy thing all over Europe.

The situation was pretty much the same in Rotterdam: all sex, drugs, rock and roll, and seamen in skirts, with little regard for 'The American Man.' Without any informants or sources, we were pretty much up the Ijsselmeer without a paddle.

I did take the opportunity to visit Rembrandt's still-preserved home and workroom in Amsterdam, and study with the curator there. I also viewed *Cuyp's Cow*, a giant mural of the cud-chewing farm animal painted on the wall of a government building in Den Haag (The Hague) by Aelbert Cuyp, the 17th century Baroque master known as the 'Michelangelo of the Netherlands.' Cows were big there, depicted to the point of redundancy by Cuyp, van Gogh, and other artists great and small. The doe-eyed beasts were also allowed to graze in fields of beautiful first-generation tulips. Only the second- and third-generation tulips, I was told, were fit for export, so the cows could have their fill of the newbies.

After a few weeks of great history, cows, windmills, dykes, and frustrating police work, the Mad Hatter and I were fit to be tied. We ended the futile search and returned to New York.

In early 1978, the Serra was officially handed over in New York to Don Rafael de los Casares, Consul General of Spain, and Juan Pique Vidal, Consul for the Diocese of Urgell, Andorra. A few days later, I was back on a jet to Europe, this time heading to the Pyrenees to be feted by Bishop Joan Marti, the ruler of the principality's 70,000 people. The brass in DC, still giddy over the Serra recovery and Spain's subsequent elation, insisted that I go and reap the accolades.

I flew into Madrid and reunited with Don Kojako. He told me he was stuck in a snowstorm after leaving New York, diverted to Lisbon, Portugal, and had to do the planes, trains, and automobiles number back to Madrid. It took him a harrowing week. The next day, I returned to the Madrid airport where we were greeted by more than a dozen representatives from Andorra. When it was time to catch my flight to Seo de Urgel where the Bishop awaited, they all left me on the runway and hopped back on their bus.

I walked up the stairs and entered a completely empty prop plane. Curious, I asked one of the flight attendants why none of the Andorrans had taken the opportunity to fly back with me. She explained matter-of-factly that it was British Airways' inaugural flight to Seo de Urgel, and the airport runway was on a small plateau between the mountains. Nobody was certain the pilot could safely make it.

Say what?

Here I was, supposedly the Honoured Guest of Spain, and instead I was really the Dumb Gringo Guinea Pig. Thanks to that classic 'too much information,' briefing, it was white knuckles all the way. The flight was indeed scary, and if there was a runway down there in between the peaks, I never saw it. Fortunately, the crack ex-British fighter pilot put us down on a dime, which was about all he had to work with.

I was greeted by a large crowd, complete with a band and newspaper photographers—all of whom had driven in. They were celebrating my arrival, the return of the Serra, and the opening of the tiny airport. I was handed a bottle of wine and was asked to take the first ceremonial sip. Not knowing what else to do, I put it to my lips, took a good ol' New York swig, then handled it to the priestly dignitary next to me. He proceeded to stick his fingers in the hole and squirt it into his mouth from eight inches away without touching the glass. All the others did it that way as well. I once again felt like the dumb ol' germ-spreading uncouth Ugly American.

Those missteps aside, it was truly the experience of a lifetime to be an honoured guest of this quaint European nation where religion and politics are mixed to a dizzying degree. The Bishop of Andorra doubles as the country's political leader. Everywhere I went, nuns and priests catered to me as both representatives of the government and of the church. I was given the rock star treatment because, thanks to the local newspaper, everybody in town seemed to know who I was and what I'd done. Many stopped to thank me on the streets with tears in their eyes.

The official presentation of the retablo was at the magnificent Cathedral of Seo de Urgel. The Bishop decided it would be easier to secure and guard it there than back at the ancient church in Abella de la Conca.

That evening, there was a state dinner in my honour inside a castle that looked like something out of Prince Valiant. There was a massive table with 30 people on either side, mostly Catholic clergy of various ranks. We dined on heaping portions of roast pig and lamb, and drank from jewelled chalices.

Doing a little scouting of my own, I discovered that the staunchly Catholic Andorra, so pristine and deeply religious on the surface, had a few ugly skeletons in its seemingly chaste closet. Andorra is widely regarded as a proverbial smuggler's paradise, dotted with thriving markets offering stolen and/or tax-free booze, cigarettes, leather goods, you name it. I guess there's no escape from organised crime, even in idyllic nations run by Catholic bishops.

After five days of lavish attention, I was back on a jet to New York. Upon my arrival, a cab splashed muddy water on my leg, and somebody laughed and flipped me their middle finger. Nothing like coming down to earth, New York style. Obviously, these people didn't understand what a celebrity I was in Andorra!

Neither did the IRS. A few months later, I was hit with the first of five straight years of complete and comprehensive audits by the feared tax collection agency. Seems the $500,000 that had been wired into my personal account at Citibank triggered resounding alarms that were nearly impossible to shut off. Every year, I had to schlep down to their office with all my receipts and paperwork, and explain once again that the money was part of a temporary undercover assignment, and had immediately been sucked right back into the US Treasury from whence it came. And no, I therefore did not owe them $300,000 in back taxes, including interest and penalties. Of course, every stinking time, after they confirmed my story, they went ahead with the rest of the audit anyway.

As the decade turned, the Serra remained safe and sound, but the rocky relationship between terrorists and art continued to plague Europe. Nine years later, after the IRS finally got off my butt, it was believed that a new generation of IRA rebels, no doubt using the Dr Bridget Rose Dugdale handbook, hit the Sir Alfred Beit collection yet again, making off with additional Goyas, Renoirs, and the same Gainsborough, *Madame Baccelli*, that had been stolen in 1974. I was dispatched to the United Kingdom in 1986 to help Scotland Yard with the investigation. The direction quickly shifted from the IRA to the infamous Irish gangster Martin Cahill, who was known as 'The General' for his meticulously planned heists.

Before I left, I checked out Vice President George H.W. Bush's Rolex watch from the US Treasury and slapped it on my wrist. The $12,000, top-of-the-line 'Presidential' timepiece was a gift from the King of Bahrain. Bush wasn't allowed by law to accept it, so he had to hand it over to Uncle Sam. As with the literal pirate's den of other valuable gifts, it was just languishing on a shelf collecting dust. Undercover G-Men are allowed to borrow the items on occasion to help properly accessorise our high-rolling alter-egos. I took the fine-crafted box as well, and popped a fake Rolex inside that I bought on Canal Street in New York for $30.

In London, I hooked up with some of The General's lieutenants, showed them Bush's watch, let the leader feel it, smell it, rub it like a magic lantern, and try it on for size. I then pulled out the box and dramatically announced that I had one just like it for him. All he had to do was lead me to the paintings so I could buy them cut-rate and cart them off to America. Lusting after the hypnotising watch, he agreed, saying he'd take me to the paintings. Unfortunately, the London FBI Bureau Chief, Darrell Mills, the former Boston honcho frequently named in Tom Clancy books, refused to authorise it. He adamantly declared it was too dangerous to go off to parts unknown with the lethal Irish mobsters.

'We can't protect you,' I was lectured. 'You could end up dead, and we don't want an FBI agent's bloated body popping up in the Irish Sea.'

I argued that I was willing to sign off on taking the risk, but he wouldn't relent.

That ended up being the best lead we had. With my hands thoroughly tied, there was no point sticking around much longer.

Most of the paintings were eventually recovered, with some once again ending up in Holland. The Holland batch were quietly ransomed back to Ireland. Sadly, more cases end like this with governments caving in than police agencies like to let on.

Returning to New York, I was flagged at customs because of the two Rolexes. I was still on the wrong side of the border, in the Virgin Airlines no man's land, so I couldn't drop my cover. Actually, the only identification I had on me was for Thomas Bishop, so I had nothing to show them that stated otherwise. The frowning Customs agents whisked me into the little room with the bare bulb and interrogated me about the watches. I told them the one on my wrist was mine, that I'd purchased it in America and wore it over there, so that wasn't a big deal. I didn't tell them that it actually belonged to the freakin' Vice President, or the Treasury. That would have really blown their minds. The real Rolex wasn't the problem anyway. At issue was the one neatly packed in the box. Thinking fast, I pulled it out, admitted that it was a fake, and fibbed that I was going to use it as a gag gift at a party. They eventually bought the story and allowed me to proceed.

Whew! Between the IRS and US Customs, the Serra case and its spin-offs were almost more trouble than they were worth!

While it was fun doing all this international sleuthing, it was frustrating working out of my element, unable to rely upon the extensive web of informants and sources I'd developed over the years, not to mention teams of reliable fellow agents shadowing me as backups. Fortunately, there was enough art thievery going on in the good ol' USA to keep me grounded for a while.

.15.

Ben-Hur Hits the Swedish Embassy

ONE OF MY oddest, but most-reliable informants was a part-time deliveryman named Tommy Joe who was the embodiment of Ratso Rizzo, the lame, sickly street hustler and information conduit Dustin Hoffman played so memorably in the movie *Midnight Cowboy*.

When we first met in the early 1970s, Tommy Joe was typically unkempt and didn't smell like roses. One day, however, after he hopped into my vehicle to give me the latest word on the street, I noticed a strikingly uncharacteristic minty-fresh smell. I was pleased, figuring he was changing his ways.

After paying him a sawbuck or two for his info, he asked me to give him a lift to a nearby drugstore. I was curious to see what he was up to so I hung around. He returned with a case of Listerine mouthwash. He cracked open one of the bottles and drained it to the halfway mark.

He wasn't gargling.

It turned out the guy had devised a way to kill two birds with one stone. He fed his booze addiction with the alcohol-infused mouthwash, while at the same time showering himself from the inside out.

Although the concept wasn't doing his liver or brain much good, I had to admit it was a major aromatic improvement.

'The Listerine Kid' slid into my car one crisp fall day in 1973 with a bottle of bitter yellow dental antiseptic in one hand, and a minty tip on his lips. Tommy Joe said there was this big gnarly military-type guy hanging out at the Kon-Tiki Lounge inside the Plaza Hotel whispering that he had some hot painting to sell that came from an embassy in Washington, DC.

That certainly raised my antennae because something about the weird tale sounded familiar. I went back to the office and looked through my files. Sure enough, seven months before, 11 paintings had been spirited away during a burglary at the Swedish ambassador's residence near Embassy Row.

The regal home, undergoing renovations at the time, was empty following the retirement of the previous ambassador, Hubert De Besche. President Richard Nixon was blocking the arrival of the new ambassador, Yngve Möller, because Sweden had stung the oversensitive Nixon with harsh criticism regarding the floundering Vietnam war.

With the embassy and home abandoned, and workmen drifting in and out, the place all but had a bulls eye painted on it. The paintings were lifted from a storage area by thieves who knew what they were after and where to find it. A notation in the file listed one of the telephone repairmen as the suspected inside man.

Among the oils carted out on that cold, Sweden-like February evening were *Amor Som Bacchus*, a scene depicting the Roman party and wine god surrounded by love cherubs, brushed in 1784 by Adolf Wertmüller; *Draskulla*, an early 20th century portrait of a woman wearing the gaily coloured Swedish national costume, by Anders Zorn; and *Vervinter*, a winter landscape by Frans Timen.

The paintings, said to be Swedish national treasures, were worth anywhere from $25,000 to $100,000 then, and considerably more today.

Zorn was the leader of this Swedish pack. His best oils and canvases are approaching a million dollars these days, although he's noted for hundreds of inexpensive etchings. Wertmüller's paintings sell for around $50,000 now. Timen, who died in 1968, has yet to have his works appreciate in the marketplace. They can be purchased for as little as a few thousand.

I tracked down the Listerine Kid and told him to set up a sit-down between the soldier and Don Mason and myself. Don would once again play the wealthy art dealer, and I'd be his chauffeur and bodyguard.

Tommy Joe found the guy at his usual haunt, the Kon-Tiki room. The Plaza's elaborately decorated lounge was designed as a little dab of the tropics in the cement jungle of New York. It was named after explorer Thor Heyerdahl's famed balsa wood raft, which itself was named after the South Pacific islands' sun god. Tommy Joe naturally set the meeting there, which provided for an ocean of ironies. We would be gathering in a shrine to the Polynesian sun god to discuss the purchase of a portrait of the Roman wine god.

Don and I restrained ourselves from wearing loud Hawaiian shirts and kept to our Brooks Brothers art dealer look. We requisitioned J. Edgar Hoover's armour-plated Fleetwood limo out of mothballs, appropriated the chauffeur's hat used by the special agent who drove the late director around, and headed for the Plaza. Fortunately, it wasn't far away because driving that beast was a chore. The metal bullet proof reinforcements added considerable weight, and the brake system had not been fortified to compensate. I felt like I was going to crash through a nearby building every time I tried to stop.

Inside, the limo's interior was classy in an understated, functional, law office way. Notable was the lack of the standard bar with the sparkling, cut glass tumblers. Hoover was no Bacchus, and didn't want to present a decadent, party-boy appearance.

I managed to make it to the Plaza without undocking the Kon-Tiki bar and sending it sailing down Fifth Avenue.

Despite the bustling, happy hour crowd, our contact wasn't difficult to find. We introduced ourselves to this big, fit, athletic guy with red hair who looked like Biblical epic actor Charlton Heston on angel dust, a comparison that would soon take a weird twist. He was a grizzled Korean War veteran with two plates in his head, who now sold his demolition and marksmanship expertise to any person or nation in need of such talents. A dangerous fanatic, he had a simmering hatred for 'Jews, Japs, Chinks, spaghetti heads, and Fidel Castro,' for collective reasons he never adequately explained.

The Soldier of Fortune character's Nordic name, Ronald von Klassen, fitted in nicely with the Thor Heyerdahl surroundings. 'Ronnie' as he insisted we call him, lived in a studio apartment at 155 East 55th Street, right across the hall from the first widely known, mainstream porn star, Linda Lovelace of *Deep Throat* fame.

Ronnie the Red proved to be a tough nut to crack, pun intended. We tried to steer the conversation to art, but after guzzling our fruity drinks and piling up the little umbrellas, he went on various rants about minorities, cops, and all his other endless hatreds. After the initial meeting, Don turned to me and said, 'You're on your own, buddy. If I spend another minute with that racist psycho I'm going to shoot him.'

Don and I had adjoining rooms at the Plaza, and later that evening, Tommy Joe called to warn me about something he had neglected to mention about Ronnie. The guy had apparently pioneered the art of assassination via the use of tiny 'pencil bombs' which he could roll under a door and blow his targets to smithereens with while they slept or watched television. It wasn't the kind of information that promotes a good night's rest. Like two 10-year-olds who'd just been told a scary campfire story, Don and I fanned each other's fears until we resorted to stuffing towels under our doors, afraid that we'd be hit for whatever cash Ronnie felt we might be carrying.

Back at the office, I located a file on the guy. The report confirmed his Special Forces demolition background, and mentioned that he had CIA ties through his anti-Castro work in Miami. If that wasn't bad enough, an agent noted in the file that Ronnie was often 'Overcome by uncontrollable urges to kill.'

Ever the eager beaver, I suppressed my fears, and possibly my good sense, and kept hanging with the wretched guy, pencil bombs be damned. I bought him fruity drinks and listened to his constant stream of hatred. To keep from going insane, I created the image of an addicted horseplayer, meeting him in mid-to-late-afternoon, then excusing myself after 20 minutes or so to lay down my bets on the final races at Belmont. It soon got back to us that he was referring to me as 'a bleeping degenerate gambler.'

Finally, after a few months of that torture, Ronnie the Red warmed and told me about the hot art from the embassy. He said it had been heisted by some mob guys from New York and New Jersey, which I found surprising because such animals rarely venture outside their own territories. It sounded like a more worldly 'have pencil bomb, will travel' soldier of fortune did the job, then hooked up with the provincial goombahs to fence the property. Ronnie just smiled at that assertion, and nodded for me to follow him to a bank of phones outside the bar. He popped in some dimes, then handed me the receiver.

On the other end was Phil J. Murgolo, 44, a typical no-neck who spoke in huffs and grunts. He mentioned the difficulties they were having moving 'the pieces'. I assured him that we could take care of his problems. I tried to pin him down on what exactly he had, but he bobbed and weaved, saying he would give the details later.

The next day, Ronnie summoned us to a talk turkey at his apartment. I convinced Don he had to show for this one, because we were getting down to the brass tacks and he needed to be there to make decisions. Secretly, I wanted the company because I was wary of ol' Ronnie for a completely different reason. He never mentioned or noticed women: not the beautiful waitresses at the Kon-Tiki, not the parade of working girls letting their hair down, not even his anatomically gifted neighbour. Instead of going after that brand of All-American stuff, Ronnie appeared to be a bit too deep into the macho, macho man world, in a Village People kind of way. I wasn't sure what would happen if I ventured up to his little boudoir alone, and I sure wasn't interested in finding out.

Don groused, repeated how much he despised the guy, but finally agreed. We drove Hoover's tank to Ronnie's pad and took the lift to the 16th floor. I lingered in the hallway a bit, hoping to catch a glimpse of Ms Lovelace and her world-famous throat, then finally took a deep breath and knocked on Ronnie's door.

The big guy greeted us warmly and gave us the grand tour of his single room flat. In one corner, there was a literal shrine to General Douglas MacArthur. Ronnie had framed photos of the military icon surrounded by candles and a tape player. He punched the tape, and out came MacArthur's famous speech before Congress about old soldiers never dying, just fading away. We had to stand there like we were in church and listen to the whole thing, which lasted 37 excruciating, Red China-bashing minutes. The old soldier ending, which is all anybody remembers, was admittedly moving, but we could have done without the other 36 minutes.

By the time it ended, Don was once again ready to withdraw his .38 Detective Special and shoot multiple holes into this nut-job.

After properly worshiping MacArthur, Ronnie pulled out some photo albums and gave us a quick history of his life. There was mostly the expected big guns and camouflage uniform military stuff, but a second album piqued my interest. The guy had spent some time working in Hollywood as a stuntman, and had been Charlton Heston's double in various movies, including the Academy Award–winning epic *Ben-Hur*. Ronnie was the guy who drove the chariot in those famous, state-of-the-art special effects scenes of Heston battling wheel-to-wheel in the Coliseum.

Ronnie downplayed the 'Hollywood crap,' by saying it was too slow-paced, fake, and full of Jews for his agitated blood. He preferred the real thing, like killing commie chinks and gooks, and more worthwhile endeavours like that. To emphasise his point, he suddenly darted to a drawer and produced a massive Colt .45 Magnum. Not knowing his game plan, I instinctively reached for the .38 snub-nose strapped to my leg. For a terrifying moment, I considered the imbalance involved. Ronnie's *Dirty Harry* Colt could shoot a hole the size of the Holland Tunnel through our torsos. In response, my sawed-off pea shooter would sting him a bit in return.

Fortunately, Ronnie turned the barrel around and handed me the fine weapon. 'This is what I use in my work,' he said, obviously just wanting to share. He returned to the drawer and withdrew a British revolver, a Walther PPK 9-millimeter, the standard James Bond gun, along with a 9-millimeter Beretta.' They ain't exactly legit,' he informed me. 'If the cops ever raid me, boom, they're all out there,' he explained, nodding to a small kitchen window that emptied into the back service alley.

As he caressed the weapons, I could tell that Ronnie was starting to get turned on. Forget Linda Lovelace, this was obviously what rocked his raft. I also sensed the first signs of his 'uncontrollable urge to kill.'

'There are four things I really hate,' he snarled, his face reddening and his neck veins ready to pop. 'Jews, Japs, Chinks, cops, and Castro!'

That was five, but who was I to quibble?

'I don't have much use for spaghetti heads either,' he added, expanding the list.

I could feel Don's discomfort ready to reach volcanic proportions, so I moved the tour along. In between getting orgasmic over MacArthur and the handguns, Ronnie confirmed that the paintings were from the Swedish Embassy, told us the names of the artists, and claimed they were worth $100,000. His people wanted $50,000, firm, a figure that was way beyond top-dollar for stolen goods. I attempted to negotiate the price down, explaining that 10% is the normal rate, but he wouldn't budge. I then downplayed the art, saying we were used to big stuff like Rembrandts, van Goghs, and Titians, and these were all small-potato Swedes. He wouldn't bend. It was $50,000 or nothing. Since we weren't going to actually buy them, we relented. Don smoothed things over by interjecting that his wife had a special affinity for Swedish art, and that worked in Ronnie's favour.

I tried to linger around the hallway again on the way out, but Don was so eager to exit that he barked at me to get moving. I don't think it would have mattered if Ms Lovelace had appeared in the flesh at her door draped in a baby-doll nightie, mouth agape, summoning us inside with a crooked finger. Don was going to blow that pop stand.

Ronnie the Red called us at the Plaza the next day and said his pals were ready to deal. They would allow us to see the paintings—if we brought half the money, $25,000, as a show of good faith. We agreed. He phoned again minutes later and gave us an address, 296 Old Bergen Road, Jersey City, New Jersey. I knew enough about Jersey geography to guess that the location wasn't the Beverly Hills section of town. It had to be some dump near Newark. Don rolled his eyes in that 'what we do for our meagre government pay cheque' manner of a weary police vet. I got his drift. This had all the makings of a deadly swindle.

Unfortunately, the brass in DC desperately wanted this bust because of the international political implications. Relations were ice-cold between America and Sweden due to Nixon's hissy fit over the Vietnam War criticism, so DC needed these paintings ... bad. They'd use them to either smooth things over, rub it in the smug Swedes' faces, or a little of both. We therefore had no option but to play the hand.

Dispensing with all pretence, I crawled inside a shoulder holster and slid in a Smith & Wesson Military and Police Special six-shot .38. The snub-nose went to its familiar spot on my left ankle. If somebody saw or felt them, so much the better. I was the bodyguard carrying the cash, so it would be in character for me to be loaded for bear in that situation.

I was also wired, which wasn't in character, so the bug had to be taped to my chest with greater discretion.

The $25,000 in US Treasury bills was signed out and separated into four bundles, which I spread between the pockets of my raincoat and jacket. Our supervisor, a burly, white-haired Irishman named John Dooley, helped us recruit backups from both the New York and New Jersey field stations. A couple of hours before the scheduled noon meet time, I drove the monster Hoover limo to Jersey, wrestling with it the entire time to keep from flattening a half-dozen tiny Chevy Vegas and Ford Pintos along the way.

Across the border, we huddled with our fellow special agents at the Jersey shop. The plan was not very complicated. Once we saw the paintings and assessed the situation, we'd say the code word,— 'Ellie' in honour of Don's wife. The troops would swarm in and take everybody down, Don and me included, and seize the art before Ronnie the Red whipped out his gargantuan Colt .45 and started blowing donut-sized holes into Hoover's finest.

With everyone supposedly on the same page, we climbed back into the limo and ventured out in search of 296 Old Bergen. It wasn't easy to find.

The neighbourhoods grew seedier and seedier as we hunted, and it wasn't like we were inconspicuous in doing so. Limos weren't as prevalent back then as they are today, and they were unknown to those neighbourhoods. We were turning heads and stopping traffic the whole way. We finally pulled up in front of a dentist's office in an old, wooden, three-storey house built in the 1930s. I had to double and triple-check the address to make sure it was the right place. Yep. No mistake. The showdown was going to be at a drill and fill joint.

That was actually comforting, if baffling. Any time a meeting is staged at a public place, it lessens the chances of the buyers being ripped off.

Still suspicious, I left Don in the limo and went inside to see what was up. I told the receptionist why I was there, and she waved me upstairs. Instead, I returned to the limo to fetch Don. Outside, I noticed a crowd of kids starting to gather around the vehicle. I tried to shoo them away, but they were persistent. When Don emerged, looking his dignified best and chewing on a big cigar, one of the munchkins stared and asked, 'Are you da mayor?'

No, but we were 'Da Man.' Just a different kind of man.

Up the creaky staircase we ventured, not knowing what to expect. At the top, we were greeted by Joe, a grubby little man who looked like a taller version of Louie de Palma from the *Taxi* television series. We introduced ourselves, and were told that we were early. The others had yet to arrive. Despite our troubles finding the place, we had indeed appeared half an hour before show time.

Our unfashionable arrival was exacerbated by the fact that the rest of the gang didn't appear until closer to 1pm. We killed the time moaning about our busy schedules, and forcing Joe to make calls to check when the others were coming.

Finally, two cars pulled up out front, a beat-up Ford station wagon, and a dented old Chevy. Their arrival scattered the kids, who had lost their initial thrill, and were no doubt now plotting to steal the mayor's limo. After shooing them away with a blast of 'gettaouttahereyalittletwits,' six men marched lockstep into the building. I didn't notice any of them carrying something that looked remotely like a painting, which wasn't a good sign.

Our new friend Joe introduced us to their leader, Phil Murgolo, a stout, balding man with jet-black hair dressed in a New York Yankee's warm-up jacket. I had previously talked to Phil on the phone. He was backed by a quartet of interchangeable young working-class Italians in tight slacks and leather jackets. They looked like John Travolta and his disco buddies from the movie *Saturday Night Fever*.

A second older man, Nicholas Acquaviva, 41, was presented as the uncle of the dentist downstairs, solving the mystery of that soon-to-be unfortunate connection.

Surprisingly, there wasn't hide nor red hair of Ronnie von Klassen and his Colt .45. He was apparently sitting this one out. I wasn't sure what to make of that. Maybe the encounter wasn't going to be violent enough for his tastes? Whatever, he'd have been happy about the bumpy way things started. We expressed our anger over being kept waiting, and still seeing no sign of the paintings. They blamed the traffic, saying that they had to motor in from Long Island and the roads were a mess. The excuse cooked their collective gooses regarding the critical interstate transportation of stolen goods charge that we had yet to lock down.

At that point, we launched into the usual tug-of-war over what was to come first, the painted chickens, or the money to buy the eggs. They wanted to see the cash. We wanted to see the oil. We batted that around until I became so frustrated I whipped open both my raincoat and suit jacket, pulled out a pack of hundreds, and slammed it on the coffee table. Nobody saw the dough. All eyes were on the .38 handle jutting out from the shoulder holster.

'Hey, what's wit da heat?' Murgolo asked. 'We don't need dat. Dis is a legitimate transaction. Whatsamatta with you?'

'Whatsamatta with me?' I shot back. 'I'm carryin' a load of green, as you guys requested. You think I'm coming in here naked? To this neighbourhood? If there's any funny business, it's gonna get ugly. People are gonna start bleedin'.'

'No, no, there ain't gonna be no problems. No sir,' Murgolo assured me. 'We're all businessmen here. No need for dat stuff.'

'So, show us some oil.'

Murgolo nodded to Travolta and crew to go and fetch the art. I speculated that it was stacked in the back of the station wagon—that is, if the neighbourhood juvenile delinquents hadn't stolen them.

Glancing out the window, I saw the Travoltas walk to the rear of the Ford, pull down the tailgate, and lift out a series of square and rectangular packages. I kept a keen eye on them because I wanted to make sure they weren't bringing up any violin cases as well. Far as I could see, they were lugging up nothing but hot paintings.

The art was covered in padded moving blankets and wrapped in paper. They were frameless, mounted on standard wood stretcher bars. Despite the tension and danger involved, it was always thrilling to see a classic painting that I'd been tracking in pictures and descriptions materialise in front of me in living colour. You always hope you're getting what was advertised, but you can never be sure. In this instance, there they were, lined up in the den and kitchen. Wertmüller's soused god and winged cherubs. Zorn's pretty Swedish lady. Timen's winter wonderland. The others, by lesser artists, were variations of the same Swedish scenes.

If writers are told to 'write what you know,' painters obviously paint what they see. Swedish painters see a lot of snow, sailboats, cows, and a whole lot of blondes with creamy white bosoms overflowing their low-cut milkmaid dresses. As for the gods and flying babies with the bows and arrows, the artists must imagine those creatures during the long, cold winter nights.

Don inspected the works carefully and mentioned that they were indeed the kinds of imagery that his wife was partial to. I cringed when he started, and breathed a sigh of relief when he said 'my wife' instead of inadvertently dropping an 'Ellie' bomb. That would have signalled the cavalry, and we weren't quite ready for that. For one thing, there were only eight paintings on display instead of the expected 11. There was still the matter of the missing trio.

'They're south, in anutter state,' Murgolo said. 'If you wantem, we can getum.'

'How far?' I inquired.

'Close enough. Steelers country,' he danced, alluding to the Pittsburgh Steelers NFL football team. 'You ain't a Cowboys fan?'

'No way. Giants and Jets all the way,' I responded, referring to the local franchises.

Since we had the most valuable paintings in the batch on hand, it made sense to move ahead and deal with the Pittsburgh connection later. I took out my bare bones portable inspection kit, a simple jeweller's loupe, and gave the oils a quick going-over. I couldn't get too detailed because I was supposed to be goon muscle, not some dainty artsy-fartsy fairy. The array all appeared to be legit as to aging and styles.

We announced our satisfaction, and the Jersey boys immediately started hammering me for the money. I reminded them that the deal was that I'd only bring half, $25,000, to this meeting, and would get the rest shortly thereafter if all went well. In fact, I interrupted, giving them more bad news, I only had that one ten grand stack on me. I'd have to get the remaining $15,000 from the limo. They nodded in agreement, by now fully accepting that they were dealing with a cautious, trigger-happy, horse track degenerate bodyguard.

I descended the stairs, leaving Don alone with the gang. He wasn't too happy about that, but I figured he'd be okay because I was carrying all the cash. The only wrinkle would be if someone had the notion of turning it into an ad-libbed kidnapping. That was possible, but my instincts told me they would be more than happy to unload the troublesome paintings, take the money, and disco bop off.

Down at Hoover's limo, I shooed the human flies off the hood, and retrieved the money, all while a couple dozen low-level eyes observed my every move with great interest. I sensed that the kids knew something was about to go down, and they weren't going to miss it for the world.' Don't any of you rug rats go to school?' I wondered, genuinely curious.

'Teacher work day,' an angel with a dirty face informed, solving yet another mystery.

'Just our luck,' I muttered to myself as I headed back inside. By that point, I'd traded greetings and smiles with the pretty receptionist so many times we were practically dating. I similarly acknowledged the toothache set waiting painfully in the lobby, then climbed upstairs with the money.

Back in the literal den of thieves, I counted out the bills for all to see. For supposedly big-time mob associates, they were a little too enamoured of the green piles. Once the final hundreds were tabulated, I stuffed the wads back into my jacket pocket, which caught them off guard.

'I've got to go get the rest and arrange for a special pickup vehicle for the paintings,' I announced. 'We can't carry them around with us all day. That would be stupid. You'll get it all at the same time.'

As expected, they began to grouse. They naturally wanted me to leave the cash behind. I secretly signalled to Don that it was time to drop the E-bomb before this latest deliberation got nasty again.

'Yep, Ellie is sure going to like these,' he said. 'Ellie really loves those winter scenes. I can't wait to see Ellie's face when I bring them home.'

We killed some time talking about the specific paintings while waiting for the doors to be busted in. Nothing happened. Don and I both dropped additional E-bombs, and the only activity was the hum of the dentist's drill downstairs, and the moans of the customers in the waiting room. The situation was not good. We were in a dicey neighbourhood surrounded by young Turk mob associates itching to make their bones, and I was carrying $25,000 in cash. Not the best of circumstances. Don and I started sweating and trying to suppress our panic.

When it became apparent that the troops weren't coming. I told the gang that I need to go out and make the call to get the rest of the money, and order the truck. They handed me a phone. 'Not here. Gotta do it on a clean line,' I insisted. 'This can't be the first time you've done your acts here.' They groused some more, but being mob associates, they knew what I was saying. All business in gangland is done on payphones.

As happy as I was to escape the tension, it wasn't easy to abandon my mentor a second time, especially under those trying circumstances. I didn't have a choice. Something had gone wrong, and we were in dire Scandinavian straights. I quickly dashed downstairs, swept through the painful lobby, and shot out the door. My new mission was to locate one of the shadows parked nearby and verbally tell them it was time to get moving.

I searched the streets around the house. Unless the FBI had suddenly started recruiting nosey 10-year-olds, there was nobody around. I jogged to a business area with a deli and gas station and spotted a vehicle that looked promising. Edging closer, I noticed a young man and woman inside. Since there were very few female special agents, I wrote them off.

Ducking into the deli, I grabbed a payphone and dialled the Newark FBI. I informed the woman who answered that I was an undercover agent in an emergency situation. Thankfully, instead of thinking that I was a nut, she passed me to a supervisor who knew the score.

'Hey, we're dying out here!' I screamed. 'We dropped the code word a dozen times, and nobody came. You're going to get us killed! Don's still in there alone!'

'Okay, okay, calm down,' he said.' We'll be right on it.'

'Wait five minutes. Let me get back inside.'

'Okay. Don't worry. I'm in touch with our team. We'll be there for you. We got your back.'

Yeah, right, I thought, slamming down the receiver. They didn't have my back, front, or side. Thoroughly miffed, I jogged the two blocks back to the house and had barely walked into the downstairs lobby when I was jumped from behind and knocked to the floor. My first thought was that it was a double cross, and Don was either dead or being held hostage. I then heard someone say 'FBI' as people began pouring into the place, roaring up the stairs. Among the arrivals were the young man and woman I'd spotted in the car on the street. Guess the Jersey office was an equal opportunity employer.

My girlfriend the receptionist was naturally beside herself, standing with her hands on her face, totally freaking. The toothache-sufferers were also freaking, but there was nothing I could do. I had this big goon Irishman on top of me manhandling my body like I was the Zodiac Killer. After he handcuffed me and jerked me off the floor, I turned my head and whispered out of the side of my mouth, 'Take my gun.'

'What?'

'I'm armed. Take my gun,' I repeated emphatically, believing that I was schooling a raw recruit. With that, my keeper freaked, shouted 'He's got a gun!' then started pounding me about the chest trying to locate it. I suddenly realised that the guy had no clue that I was the undercover agent. He thought I was art thief Nuncio Goombah, armed and ready to shoot it out with the FBI!

Locating the weapon, he ripped it out of my holster so hard that the back of the hammer cut a bloody gash across my chest, and ripped my borrowed Gucci shirt nearly off my back.

A second agent joined in on the fun and started bullying me as well. I hesitated for a moment, sighed, then dropped the next depth charge. 'Uh, I've got another one. Ankle,' I whispered.

'What?'

'Ankle,' I repeated, figuring by now these rookies might catch on that I was one of them.

'He's got another gun!' they shouted, then proceeded to knock me down again and rip it off my leg. While laying on the floor, I glanced up and saw the dentist dragged out in cuffs, dressed in his scrubs, all but carrying a water pick in his restrained hand.

What the hell's going on? I thought, sucking up the dust from the floor. I'd been 'captured' a dozen times before, and was destined to be cuffed 50 or more times in the future—often by cops and FBI agents who didn't know I was a good guy—but this was by far the roughest treatment I've ever experienced.

Upstairs, the G-Men were similarly manhandling Murgolo, the Travoltas, and the dentist's black sheep uncle. Don, on the other hand, was taken with restraint and dignity. They obviously made him for a veteran FBI boss. He would later say the difference in the treatment we received was poetic justice for leaving him alone with the goons not once, but twice.

Outside, the mob of street urchins were getting the show of their lives. They could hardly contain themselves, and kept skittering dangerously underfoot. Since we weren't using local police as backup, we didn't have enough manpower to seal off the street and contain the sugared up little twerps. They didn't know what the hell was happening, but knew it was Big Excitement and were determined to experience it up close. I heard some of them trying to sort out who were the good guys and who were the bad guys, a problem the arresting agents were obviously having as well.

When the others appeared outside, I angrily cursed Murgolo, the bad uncle, and the Travoltas for setting me up. Since I was ripped, dirtied, dishevelled, and bloodied, I figured I might as well lay it on thick. They protested their innocence, but with me looking ravaged, while they looked untouched, even the smallest fry on the street would have fingered them for the snitches.

After those dramatics, a Jersey supervisor sorted us out and separated Don and me from the others. Before we left, I warned whoever was 'seizing' Hoover's limo to be careful about the brakes. The young agent was so eager to touch the god Hoover, he only half-listened. He nearly had a major accident on the way to the field office, jutting the historical vehicle's big black nose into an intersection when the tank refused to stop on demand.

At the Jersey office, I showed my scars and asked what was up with the stomping? My esteemed co-workers laughed as usual and suggested that I vigorously complain to my boss in New York. Make sure you rip the Irish lug who beat up on you,' someone said. 'Maybe you should suggest that he should be fired.'

No dummy, I smelled a rat and started investigating. Sure enough, my arrestor was none other than Jim Dooley, my supervisor's son. When I mentioned it to the elder Dooley a few days later, again displaying my now scabby wound, he just howled and reminded me that agents showing preferential treatment to a fellow agent during an arrest can tip off the crooks and put the agent's life in danger.

While that was indeed true, I countered that his son didn't have to perform open-heart surgery on me with the back of a .38 Special's hammer. Dooley thought that was hilarious.

Meanwhile, the search of the dentist's house turned up some bonus gems. The follow-up crew discovered a Chinese statue from the Ming Dynasty (1368–1644) entitled *Kaun Yan*. The foot-high artefact traced back to a million-dollar theft the previous year at the Caramoor Museum in Katonah, New York. The *Kaun Yan*, worth $10,000 back then, was one of the few objects from the robbery that remained at large.

Shortly thereafter, one of the Murgolo gang gave up the location of the remaining Swedish embassy paintings down in Steelers country in return for consideration on his pending legal situation. We alerted the troops to the south and they picked them up without incident.

That still left one remaining big red loose end—Ronnie von Klassen. If my instincts were correct, he may have been the original thief. After huddling with the prosecutors, it was decided that to protect the Listerine Kid, and to build a stronger case than the toothless 'conspiracy to transport stolen property,' we'd take him down on the weapons charges. To do so, we needed to have our NYPD cousins perform the honours. We went to the proper city precinct, Midtown North, brought them up to speed, and warned the sergeant in charge that Ronnie was a dangerous character who hated Jews and cops.

'Oh, he does?' the sergeant reacted. 'Wait here.'

The next thing we knew, this 6-foot-2-inch, 300-pound police captain comes rumbling out like a T-Rex. 'Who is this perp who hates Jews and cops?' he bellowed.

'Meet Captain Rosenberg,' the sergeant introduced with a smile.

'Mind if I go out on this one myself?' the captain asked.

'Love to have you along, captain,' I said with a laugh.

Before we left, I mentioned Ronnie's plan to toss his guns out the window if the cops ever came.

'We'll take care of it,' Captain Rosenberg assured.

It turned out that Rosenberg and his men were well aware of Ronnie V. He had been going around to area Jewish delis at lunchtime, cursing the diners and spewing racial slurs. Ronnie had fouled their beat long enough, and the local boys in blue were eager to take him down.

A heavily Jewish team of officers and detectives poured into his building, banged on the door, and eventually busted it in. 'You the guy who's telling everybody you hate Jews and cops?' Rosenberg said when Ronnie was cuffed. 'Well I'm Captain Rosenberg, and you're under arrest.'

As feared, they didn't find any of the weapons in the apartment. Captain Rosenberg told me not to sweat it, and pointed to a trio of uniform cops approaching us carrying brightly coloured plastic laundry baskets.

'We caught 'em, captain! Just like you said!' one of the young officers proudly announced.

I couldn't believe it. The captain had stationed his men with baskets in the alley outside Ronnie's kitchen window. The guns came raining down 16 stories, and the patrolmen scooped them out of the air.

The adroit aerial display was only the beginning of Ronnie's troubles. I noted at the end of my accompanying arrest report that he had called the Italians 'spaghetti heads'. His judge just happened to be a veteran jurist named Mario di Capelletti or something like that.

When I read the report on the stand during the trial, the judge stopped the proceeding dead and asked me to 'repeat that last statement.' I did, with relish. The judge, his teeth clenched, shot Ronnie daggers with his eyes, thanked me, and asked me to proceed.

The trial of the Jersey six had some headline-making moments as well. Halfway through, the gang's flamboyant attorney tried to negotiate a deal with the prosecutor to enable his clients to go free or get lenient terms, in exchange for agreeing to help him shake down the Swedish government for a $50,000 reward for returning the paintings.

The US Attorney was outraged, calling it blackmail. He reported it to the judge and obtained an order to have the six re-arrested and their bail doubled, which for most of them was from $50,000 to $100,000. (The dentist and his tenant, our babysitter Joe, were considered to have played lesser, 'guilt by association' roles and had been given lower bonds.)

The wily attorney, Robert Weiswasser, skated, cleverly arguing that the money would only be used to pay his client's justifiable legal fees, and that word of the reward might lead to the recovery of additional stolen paintings.

Following that flare up, the suspects either pleaded guilty or were convicted, including Ronnie the Red, and were given probation or short terms.

After the legal cases cleared, the eleven 'Swedish national treasures' were returned to the new Swedish ambassador, Yngve Möller, helping to smooth over the shaky relations between the U.S. and Sweden. 'They are priceless to us,' said Swedish press attaché Lars Lonnback. 'We are truly happy that the police have done a good job in recovering the paintings.'

Interestingly enough, a great deal had changed in the world since Tommy Joe Listerine first gave me the tip a year before. Nixon had resigned over the Watergate scandal and could no longer vent his rage at the Swedes.

America was pulling out of Vietnam, so the Swedes were no longer calling us war mongering oppressors. Charlton Heston had a new stunt double, just in time to help him continue to escape the grubby paws of those 'filthy apes,' while waging new battles against *Soylent Green* and *Earthquakes.*

To top it off, the blondes, the wine gods, and Cupid's cousins were back on the walls of Ambassador Möller's refurbished residence. All was right with the world.

.16.

BOUGUEREAU AT THE BORGHI

SOME OF THE most dramatic undercover cases receive little media attention because they are too successful. Odd as that may sound, it's unfortunately the way the mass media operate. I'm referring to heists that are intercepted and prevented before the thieves have a chance to pull them off.

While these are often the most satisfying from a law enforcement standpoint—it can't get better than stopping a crime before it happens— the press take a ho-hum attitude. They prefer the more entertaining cops and robbers chase and shootout.

To understand this, think about the 9/11 terrorist bombing in New York. That received probably the greatest media coverage in US history. It has also led to reams of post-event criticism and scrutiny of the FBI, CIA and other law enforcement agencies.

In contrast, since 9/11, the government has periodically announced that similar terrorist plots were prevented through intelligence, the infiltration of terrorist cells, and/or good old fashioned police work. These stories wind up buried on the back pages of the newspaper, and are rarely mentioned for more than a single day.

No burning buildings crashing to the ground, no visuals for *News at Six*!

That's a shame because I think all would agree that preventing a disaster is preferable to cleaning up after one. It's just not nearly as dramatic.

If the media took the time and interest in fleshing out some of these interception events, they might find that they are actually overflowing with enough action and intrigue to fill a book or movie, much less a news story.

A prime example is a series of art heists I blocked in the early 1980s attempted by a mixed gang of Italian and Irish mobsters.

It started with an Irish fence named Danny Kohl who operated out of a cluttered antique shop on 76th Street and Third Avenue, walking distance from the FBI's New York headquarters. Danny 'Old King' Kohl, a short, wiry, weasel of a coke head, was a wannabe 'Westie', but he lived on the East Side. The Westies were an extremely violent Irish gang that terrorised the West Side of Manhattan. They operated under the umbrella of Gambino Family Mob Boss of Bosses, Paul 'Big Paulie' Castellano, the Don John Gotti assassinated in 1985 to begin his reign.

Among other things, the Westies had hit men who would take their victims' bodies to an apartment above a bar in Brooklyn and hack them up, *Sopranos* style, in the bathtub. The resulting bloodbaths were so grisly that the sticky red body fluid sometimes dripped through the cracks in the floor and down the pipes into the apartments below. Nobody ever complained.

The Westies were also heavily into cocaine, both dealing and snorting. They were so blitzed, the word was that one of their under bosses owned a large green parrot that had a $200-a-day habit.

Danny Kohl was the Westies eyes and ears on the East Side, alerting them to any lucrative activity or easy score he felt they might be able to profit from. He had his little corner of the world wired with a web of workmen, waiters, hotel bellhops, maids, delivery men, and anybody else who could tip him off to something of value. They also fed him a steady supply of the normally discarded carbon copies of credit card transactions, the old school method of identity theft.

When he wasn't playing scout for the Westies, Kohl made his living robbing and burglarising the storage rooms of the various Manhattan auction houses, and pilfering from the merchants all around him.

Down the block from Danny, an old Italian craftsman known as Mr Micheletti ran his own tiny antique shop. It was a frequent target for Kohl and his minions, and the guy was fuming about it. In his prime, Micheletti had been a respected painter and art restorer for the Carnegie Mellon University Art Gallery in Pittsburgh. Now, he was the art world equivalent of a broken down, punch drunk fighter, too blind and shaky to work the brushes, and too weak to fend off robbers and taunting children.

Fed up, he contacted the police, and eventually the FBI about the weekly thefts. Most blew him off, but I noted his address and saw it as an opportunity to get next to Danny Kohl and put him out of business. In addition, there had been a recent rash of crude, smash-and-dash robberies of local galleries, museums and antique shops, and I suspected Danny was behind them.

I set myself up as Mr Micheletti's new assistant, Tom Murray, and began puttering around the dusty shop, struggling to keep my distance from the guy. He had a habit of chewing raw garlic cloves, which he had convinced himself was the key to a long, healthy life. Maybe so, but the man stunk so bad you couldn't get near him. He reeked of garlic oil, from every pore. The overwhelmingly healthy smell was amplified by the fact that his claustrophobic shop was only about seven feet wide and 30 feet long. It was nearly impossible to get away from him.

Sundays were easier on the nostrils, as that was the day Mr Micheletti spent in Greenwich Village pampering stray cats with dozens of cans of white tuna. The felines didn't seem to mind the garlic.

Eventually, I wandered down the block for some fresh air and to bump into 'King Kohl', portraying myself as a kindred Irish spirit. He asked me what I was doing hanging around with 'that rotting corpse.' I indicated with a wink that I was running hot art, artefacts, and antiques through the old man's shop, the same way Danny was using his store. To prove my point, I came in one day and flashed an array of Picasso, Chagall, Rembrandt and Miró drawings and etchings that I'd borrowed from a nearby gallery. Suffice it to say, Danny was impressed. With his cocaine habit, he was always interested in new revenue streams.

Warming to me, Danny confessed one afternoon that he was behind the recent smash-and-dash robbery of a Degas bronze sculpture of a young ballerina from the Kennedy Galleries. The Degas, worth about $50,000 then, was a good investment. In 2004, another Degas bronze of a dancer, *Petite Danseuse De Quatorze Ans*, sold for $9.2 million.

Danny had pulled the profitable heist by walking into the lobby, smashing a display case, grabbing the little girl, and sprinting out.

'I can't move it,' he lamented. 'Everybody says it's too hot. This Degas bastard was some kind of master.'

I informed Danny that his troubles were over. I would find him a buyer within days.

Back at the FBI shop, I recruited our resident special agent mobster, Mike Popolana, a central casting gangster type who looked like Robert De Niro from *The Godfather II*. His cover was that he was an old country Sicilian hood like the 'Pizza Connection' gang, and therefore wasn't affiliated with any of the five domestic mob families. That meant he was a free agent who couldn't be verified, or exposed, by one of Danny's bent-nosed friends.

Next, we had to acquire some disposable cash that could 'walk', meaning it was to be a clean sale with nobody busting in to make an arrest. Danny would be allowed to keep the money, just like Jacques did in the Rembrandt case, because it was an ongoing investigation that had barely begun. We weren't ready to pull the plug.

I explained our dilemma to the insurance company, and they gladly ponied up $4,000 to avoid having to pay a $25,000 policy. (The bronze, like most art, was grossly underinsured.) We gave the money to 'Popo', dressed him in his pin-striped gangster suit, shaved a channel through his rug of jet black Italian body hair to tape on a wire, and sent him calling on Danny 'Old King' Kohl.

The Irishman and Italian got along famously, so much so that Danny felt compelled to give him special advice on what to do with the valuable ballerina. 'This kind of art you gotta get out of the country,' Danny warned. 'You can't put it in Macy's window during the Thanksgiving Day parade.'

We were rolling on the floor of the surveillance van with that one. The world famous, star-studded, giant-balloon festooned parade was indeed a few days away, so Danny's concerns were genuine.

'Don't worryaboutit,' Popo assured. 'This baby's going straight back to the island where it belongs. No parades back home in Sicily.'

Popo counted out the money, grabbed the ballerina, and breezed out the door. Seconds later, Danny shot out behind him to give the good news to his pusher. The insurance company's $4,000 went right up Danny insatiable nose. I couldn't help wondering what Degas might have thought about that transaction.

I dropped by Danny's store the next day and he was all smiles and praise. Because I had come through for him, he let me in on a big secret. 'Get your guys ready, because I've got a good one coming up. Like the Degas, only bigger and better. I got a line on a half-million Boogyroo that's candy, man, just candy.'

'No kidding? That's great!' I said. 'Just let me know when it's ready and I'm sure Popo or one of his associates will be back visiting again.'

In truth, I was winging and flinging because I had no idea what he was talking about. He could have been baiting me with a phoney artist to see if I knew my stuff. I dashed back to the office and began cracking open my various Who's Who of Great Artists books, trying to translate 'Boogyroo' into something that would come up with a hit. From the sound of it, however botched the New York Irish pronunciation, it had to be French. Boogy was probably Boug or something. Scanning the Bs, bingo, I nailed it. Bouguereau, which was pretty darn close to 'Boogyroo'. Crap, I thought, now feeling a bit embarrassed. This cokehead knew more about art than me.

Flipping the pages, I studied up on the artist. Adolphe-William Bouguereau was a 19th century French classicist who studied the previous generations of Renaissance masters and followed their tradition of vivid realism. He focused on history and mythology as subject matter. As with the leading portrait artists, some of his painting are so vivid and perfectly detailed they look like modern colour photographs.

Although successful during his life, Bouguereau's career was the typical roller coaster between praise and criticism, and was subject to the trends, whims, and 'next big thing' of the times. The hipper modernists and impressionists who followed did to Bouguereau what the Beatles did to Pat Boone, Eddie Fisher, Frank Sinatra and Dean Martin, blowing them off the charts into squaresville. As with so many artists, he was never fully appreciated until long after he died, and his style of classic painting staged a retro comeback.

Today, Bouguereau's best oils are approaching $2 million. Back in the 1980s, I guessed that the mysterious piece Danny Kohl was after could be worth as much as a quarter million.

Now that I had the scoop, I was faced with finding a rectangular needle in a giant New York haystack. Who in town had Bouguereaus that were within Danny Kohl's radar and reach, and were sloppy about their security? I called around and was told that the Borghi Gallery on 51st Street, near Park Avenue, Rockefeller Centre, and the magnificent St Patrick's Cathedral, specialised in 19th century French realists and might have some. It was a long shot, but I decided what the heck, I'd blow a fin on a short cab ride over there. Worst comes to worst, I could always duck into St Patrick's and say yet another prayer for that missing Picasso, *The Man With the Purple Hat*, then stroll to Madame Tussaud's Wax Museum to see if it was hanging behind the lifelike figures of Jack the Ripper or Elvis.

When I arrived, I glanced inside the picture window and noticed a large, five-by-three-foot oil painting of a woman at a farm well that looked very much like the Bouguereau's in the books. Nah, I thought. It can't be this easy. I went inside, flashed my badge, and introduced myself to owners Mark Borghi and his attractive sister. The knowledgeable siblings inherited the gallery from their father, who had the foresight to set up a branch in Riyadh, Saudi Arabia, at a time when the oil rich Arabs starting trying to outdo each other with their art collections. After some routine small talk, I inquired about the painting on display out front.

'That's a Bouguereau,' Mark said proudly. 'It's a real find.'

It was an unreal find. All my senses screamed that this was the one Danny Kohl was targeting. It was perched in a perfect place for a smash-and-dash, right out of the front window.

'We have information that it's going to disappear any day now,' I warned.

The Borghi kids stared back at me like I was dipping into Danny's white powder.

'That can't be,' Mark insisted, a bit haughtily. 'We have the best security money can buy. The paintings are secured.'

That gave me pause. Danny indicated that they had a cherry that was ripe for the picking. He was too crafty not to have checked out the alarms. There had to be a kink in the set up.

I asked Mark if he wouldn't mind summoning his security man. He agreed, made a call, and the guy quickly appeared. We went over the details. Within minutes, Danny's flaw jumped out at me. The alarms were wired to the backing and the stand, but not the painting itself. This was done, apparently, to make it easy to change the display. The set up seemed logical because a thief in the gallery would have to pull it off from behind, which would set off the bells and alert the monitoring company. However, a smash and dash artist coming in through the front could simply lift it forward and tiptoe down the street.

In essence, it was a quarter-million dollar lottery ticket sitting there naked in the window, begging for somebody to set it free.

Mark apologised for his umbrage and quickly replaced it with something pretty, but decidedly less valuable. It was just in the proverbial nick of time. The next day, Danny wasn't his usual euphoric self.

'You know that Boogyroo I told you about? We went to get it last night and it was already gone. Somebody musta bought it or something. Pisses me off.'

'Damn those legitimate buyers,' I countered, trying to cheer him up.

'They're always getting in our way.' Danny only half laughed. 'Ah, don't sweat it,' I went on. 'There's always another one out there.'

I didn't have to tell Danny that. Shaking off his bad mood, he quickly hit an Upper East Side Lutheran Church, looting it of a 17th century, Manchester Wool tapestry depicting an ancient battle scene. Danny fenced the $30,000 weaving dirt cheap to a shop far enough away that I felt it was safe to immediately go in and snatch it back. I had a sore spot about church thefts, the lowest of the low, and didn't want the rug to end up in Riyadh with one of Borghi Senior's customers. I figured that even if the owner complained, Danny would think that somebody merely recognised it from the news reports and dropped the dime. Besides, Danny already had sucked the money up his decaying nostrils, and was looking to finance his next snort.

As the Christmas holidays approached, Danny started telling me about the 'job of a lifetime' he had in the works. Little by little, he coughed up the astounding details. They had discovered an apartment house that shared a wall with a ritzy art gallery. A few nights a week at 2am, his boys had been unscrewing the entire cluster of mailboxes, sliding them out, and chopping away at the subsequent hole to clear a path in the little alley between the walls that would eventually enable them to crawl in and out. They'd then put the mailbox back in place, so nobody was the wiser. It was reminiscent of the prisoner in Stephen King's short story and movie, *The Shawshank Redemption*, hacking away chip by chip at the area behind his pin-up poster of Rita Hayworth.

With so much of New York's infrastructure tacked together as described, and nothing specific said about the particular gallery or its specialties, I knew I'd need help figuring out this mystery. By then, I'd endured enough full frontal blasts of old man Micheletti's garlic breath to have hung around long enough to bust, squeeze, and turn some moles inside Kohl's gang. One gave me the low down on America's latest 'hole-in-the-wall gang.' The target was the Raphael Gallery at 1st and 57th Street.

I strolled over to check it out. Everything was as described, complete with the apartment building next door with the steel mailbox cluster that showed obvious signs of tampering. I could see why the gang needed to hack away behind it because the box was small and narrow, containing 30 or so letter-sized slots. Unless they had a child or midget with them, the typical pot bellied, mutton stew gobbling Irish burglar didn't have a prayer of getting through.

Next door, the Raphael Gallery was chock full of smaller artefacts like coins, sculptures, statues, silver tea sets, candelabras, antique jewellery, and other relics. There were also stacks of Oriental and Persian rugs, which are easy to roll up and cart off. The place was overflowing with the precise commodities Danny preferred to fence because they were far easier to sell and scatter into the wind than a cumbersome van Gogh.

The informant advised me a few days later that the night crew was having problems quietly widening the path with the tools they were using. They had thus decided to bang through with sledgehammers on the night of the heist. That was set for 24 December, just before the stroke of midnight. Yep, Christmas Eve.

I can attest first hand what a brilliant strategy that was. Fired up and gung ho, I went to my bosses and tried to recruit a team to stake out the place. Everybody, I mean everybody, shunned me like I had leprosy. Even the normally eager beaver clerks aching to be special agents took off when they saw me coming.

'Come on guys, this is Ol' King Danny Kohl,' I begged. 'I've been working this case for months. This is the break I've been waiting for!'

It all fell on deaf ears. I was told to go hassle the local cops who had to work that night anyway. The leprosy must have been showing on my neck and hands because the NYPD wanted no part of a pie-in-the-sky Christmas Eve stakeout either. I made such a pest of myself the precinct captain finally let me borrow a pair of night watch detectives, which I knew would either be grumpy old timers, someone who screwed up and was in the captain's doghouse, or the medically grounded weak and wounded set suffering from bad tickers, stress related mental breakdowns, alcoholism, or excessive weight. They were forced into the wretched holiday duty on a rotating basis every five years or so.

Back up is back up, so I thanked the captain and put the plan in motion. On Christmas Eve, I arrived around 11pm and met my team. I wasn't expecting Dick Tracy, but I still wasn't prepared for what emerged. Two decrepit geezers limped out like walking corpses. They appeared weeks away from walkers, and months away from going six feet under. Their moods were the only thing worse than their physical condition. The creaky pair were expecting to serve their time inside a warm station house watching *It's a Wonderful Life* on television. Instead, they had to venture out into the 20 degree night on some absurd stakeout with an FBI prick.

I was almost ready to call the whole thing off, then I thought about all the precious, irreplaceable relics and artefacts the Irish goons were going to make off with that night unless we stopped them. Even if nobody else cared, I did. The ancient artists deserved better than that.

So off we went, me in my Federal car, and the Ghosts of *Hill Street Blues* Past in their beat up unmarked police vehicle. I gave them a radio so we could keep in touch, told them where to park, and bought them each a large cup of coffee so they wouldn't nod off.

Fortunately, we didn't have to wait long. As the clock struck midnight, along came the bad guys, slowly cruising around the block. Instead of arriving in a bright red sleigh driven by flying reindeer, they were steering a battered green Dodge with Jersey plates. After a few passes, and failing to either see, or give a crap about the two old goats, they parked and lumbered out.

A terrible thought crossed my mind. Dangerously outgunned, we were going to have to sit there, an FBI agent and two NYPD detectives, and watch some heavily armed Neanderthals loot an art gallery. And there was nothing we could do because there was no way we were going to be able to summon an appropriate SWAT team on such short notice on Christmas Eve.

I was about to throw in the towel when I noticed something through the door. As the goons went to unscrew the mailbox and lift it from the wall, they set their weapons in the middle of the floor. The armaments stood erect, as if held up by magic. I knew of no guns that could balance on their stocks like that. I grabbed the field glasses and focused in. The vision filled me with renewed energy. They weren't automatics. They were sledgehammers with sawed-off handles, just as the informant had said.

Back on track, I radioed my team that the eagles had landed and they were proceeding to bust through the wall. The plan was to wait until they made it inside and started carting out the goods before we pounced. That way, some wily attorney couldn't claim they were just doing construction renovations.

The gang hammered and hacked, but nothing happened. They failed to disappear from one room and reappear in the other like Raymond Burr in Alfred Hitchcock's *Rear Window*. They kept hitting steel girders and fortified cement. Apparently, the hundred-year-old building was made of tougher stuff than they expected. One of the gorillas tried to squeeze through the hole as it was, but couldn't make any headway. Frustrated, they stormed out the door and headed for their car.

'Let's get 'em, now!' I ordered, hitting my bubble gum lights and siren. The gang spotted me, sprinted for their vehicle, and squealed off like a rocket. We radioed for assistance, but by the time the skeleton crew of Christmas Eve squad cars fell in with us, the burglars were long gone into the maze of the city.

We ran a check on the license plate. Naturally, the car had been stolen. Ol' King Danny Kohl had escaped again.

I never did bag the little weasel. The NYPD Vice Squad busted him before I could hone in on another burglary. I was lucky they didn't grab me as well, as I'm sure they were watching us the whole time. It wouldn't have been the first or the last time different branches of law enforcement crossed paths.

None of that mattered to Danny. The exact pedigree of white hats cuffing him made little difference from his perspective. Actually, the state drug charges carried tougher sentences than anything I was trying to pin on the guy. He was convicted and dispatched to Riker's Island for a nice long visit. The hard time cleaned him up, and that may have proved to be his undoing. When he was released, he thought he could snort like the old days. Bad decision. The word was that the old euphoric high he so longed for while behind bars was too much for his newly cleansed body. His 'rush' was a series of violent convulsions that allegedly killed him. Either way, he hasn't been heard from since.

Despite not shutting him down personally, I was able to make one last interception in 1982 thanks to Danny. Not long after he went inside, the informant in his gang that I'd cultivated tipped us off to an elaborate plot to hit a bank somewhere in the area. The source didn't know which one, but knew the address of one of the robbers, and said they were going to use CB radios. We prepared a response team and monitored the police scanners at the designated time.

The target was the Citibank branch near the Queensborough Bridge on 59th Street. As it turned out, five heavily armed men were already inside the building, having been let in at 5am by a pair of crooked security alarm company employees. They waited until the staff arrived, took them hostage, overpowered the unsuspecting guards, forced the manager to open the safe, and proceeded to stuff pillowcases with $400,000 in cash. We immediately picked up their trail via the CB radio broadcasts and shadowed them to the address the snitch gave us.

I grabbed a discarded box of empty oil cans off the street and fell in behind one of the robbers, who was carrying his cash-laden bag over his shoulder like Santa Claus. We both lugged our loads into the rundown building, me pretending to be bringing in something as well so I could get a fix on the precise apartment where the bad guys were huddling.

The SWAT team was called to assist with the arrests because of the serious heat the gang was carrying. Before our equalising muscle arrived, two different men left the apartment, jumped inside a station wagon, and took off. Three of us dashed to our cars and went after them. When we received word that the SWAT team landed, stormed in, and arrested the five remaining men without incident, we pulled our autos in front of and behind the two escapees and took them down at gunpoint. They turned out to be the inside guys, the alarm company workers who had exited the bank before the robbery.

Citibank, the brass in DC, and even the media lauded us for our fast action. After all, it did involve a completed robbery, lots of weapons, sexy SWAT guys, and best yet, an old-fashioned cops and robbers car chase.

Lots of visuals for *News at Six*!

. 17 .

JOHN GOTTI'S HENCHMEN STRIKE OUT WITH PICASSO'S MISTRESS

*B*Y THE 1990S, my long sojourn in Oklahoma hiding from the thundering hordes of 'Pizza Connection' mobsters back East had taken me farther and farther away from the art world. Manets, Titians, Chagalls, and the like weren't exactly dotting every wall in the Sooner State, so that left little to steal.

It wasn't like I was sitting around twiddling my thumbs. There was certainly no shortage of Federal crimes in Oklahoma. They were just the more routine scams, graft, political corruption, and vice.

Along those lines, Oklahoma was deeply involved in the Pell Grant scandals that resulted from the much-abused government trade scholarship programme. That was a festering mess FBI field offices all over the nation had to clean up after bogus schools started popping up like camps during the Gold Rush. The Okie variety were long-haul truck driving centres that recruited bums, winos, the homeless, friends, and relatives in order to soak Uncle Sam for as much as $50,000 per 'student'; none of whom were taught to steer a skateboard, much less shift a big rig. With the swindle blazing out of control, we were left to painstakingly infiltrate the schools, gather evidence, and shut them down one by one before the operators ran off with the money.

Oklahoma proved to be rife with crooked politicians as well, although their scams were higher scale. The cadre of wheeling, dealing, kickback-loving, and trough-dipping state and Federal representatives, commissioners, senators, and governors, known as the 'Dixie Mafia' (even though they were more Western than Southern), kept us busy as well.

In between were the age old 'human weakness' crimes of drugs and prostitution that proliferated around Oklahoma City because of the wealth of military installations in the area. Tinker Air Force Base, home of the AWACS radar jets, was 10 miles from town. Fort Sill was a quick 40-minute drive, while airmen from Vance Air Force Base could make it to the bright lights in a little more than an hour.

Where there are soldiers, there will soon be strippers and hookers. And where there are a lot of soldiers, and not enough strippers and hookers to serve them, the ladies will be recruited from neighbouring states, and/or imported from faraway countries. That can get messy when the girls are shipped in against their will from places like Asia, and are forced into sexual slavery.

Soldiers, strippers, and prostitutes go hand-in-hand with organised crime and drugs. Organised crime and drugs invariably lead to even more political corruption, along with violence and murder. Thus, a single 'gentleman's club' opening with 'We're a legitimate business!' fanfare on the edge of town can quickly turn into an entire red-light district teeming with crime and grime of every stripe.

The FBI generally doesn't get into vice issues, but when a local police department becomes overmatched, and the crimes extend beyond the state with the arrival of women from the Orient, drugs from South America, and mobsters from Brooklyn, the agency is compelled to step in.

Seedy as the work can be, there is a bit of nostalgia from the bureau's standpoint. When J. Edgar Hoover took over the then Bureau of Investigation in the 1920s, the only notable Federal statutes were the interstate transportation of stolen vehicles and the Mann Act, which involved taking women over state lines for sexual purposes. Since then, the Federal statutes have multiplied like minks, but sometimes things have a way of spinning right back to the beginning.

The Lion King-like 'circle of lowlife' was precisely what happened with me as well, because the Oklahoma sex dens were about to jettison my gumshoes and magnifying glass right out of the sleaze and put me back on the more familiar turf of hunting a Picasso. A Picasso, ironically enough, that was drenched in mystery, vice, and its own sexual intrigue.

It began in 1992 with the Valley of the Dolls strip joint that popped up on the east side of Oklahoma City. The 'look-but-no-touch' pole dancing palace only satiated the soldiers for a while, and soon the Paradise Massage Parlour hung out a shingle nearby. The body rub emporium was definitely hands-on, including off-the-books erotic massages (hand jobs and blowjobs) and straight-out prostitution (everything else). It was operated by a veteran madam, and by a group of retired Air Force non-coms, or non-commissioned officers, who had the connections to import the brown-skinned, black-haired island girls from the Philippines and Taiwan to give the soldiers that overseas feel. Some of the ladies were just teenagers.

Despite the importations, we were advised that we weren't on solid footing regarding the Federal statutes. If the Asian women were now residing in Oklahoma, the Mann Act might not apply. I solved the problem when I determined that the erotic massages were paid for by credit cards with headquarter banks in different states. That gave us our in.

The local cops worked the sex angle, going in undercover and arranging for the erotic massages and off-site prostitution hook-ups. We mostly focused on the drugs. In the course of the investigation, I determined that the Number-Two lady at the massage parlour was a cute, shapely redhead from Texas who was a demure bank teller by day, and a lesbian she-devil named Linda Lovegrind by night. I resurrected my art dealer persona, went to the marbled financial institution, and quietly requested a discreet sit-down in the bank's cafeteria with the double-dealing cowgirl. I gave her my art world spiel, then told her I knew about her 'other job' and said I was in the habit of giving big parties for buyers, and might need some white powder and brown girls to spice up the festivities and get the clients in a buying mood.

She nodded that she understood. We traded phone numbers, then agreed to meet for dinner at a nearby Applebee's Restaurant after work. I then repeated my business offer, and she suddenly transformed into Mother Teresa, claiming that the massage parlour was legit and drug-free. Yeah, right. Tell that to *Ripley's Believe It or Not!* She was obviously spooked. I was a stranger and she was smartly acting with caution. This time, I nodded that I understood. She needed somebody to vouch for me.

A well-known bar owner in Norman, Oklahoma, had helped us in the past. He agreed to call Ms Lovegrind and back my story. That did the trick. She phoned me and agreed to broker a small cocaine deal to begin our relationship. We met behind the parking lot of the massage parlour in broad daylight. I gave her $500 for an 'eight-ball,' one eighth of an ounce. Back at the office, I handed the contraband to Floyd Zims, the special agent destined to take custody of Oklahoma City bomber Timothy McVeigh, and in the process, have his photograph splashed around the world. Zims tested the coke in the lab and proclaimed it 'good stuff.'

Zims and crew busted Ms Lovegrind, and squeezed her to assist us in building the legal case required to shut down her employers.

In the course of the investigation, Ms Lovegrind volunteered to her control agents that she had been farmed out to Las Vegas one weekend and, after rubbing some New York wise guys the right way, heard them talking about a 'ten-million-dollar Picasso' they were trying to move.

My eyebrows nearly shot clear off the top of my head with that revelation. Could this be the long lost *Man With the Purple Hat*, the huge Picasso that had been missing from the Jasper Galleries in Houston since the 1970s? The same painting that aliens had seemingly beamed out of a locked and sealed truck trailer? (See Chapter 4) I naturally jumped on this, coming out of the undercover shadows and reintroducing myself to Ms Lovegrind. She was initially cold, with good reason as I was the cause of all her current misery. Eventually, she agreed to call her girlfriend in Las Vegas, another day / night working girl, and have her pass my phone number to the entrepreneurial mobsters.

A few days later, the undercover phone rang. A gruff-sounding palookas with a New York accent wanted to know if I was the 'Da guy who buys art?' Indeed I was. I gave him my background, said I was out west doing business with Texas and Oklahoma oil barons and their art-loving wives, and confirmed that I was extremely interested in what he might have. Picking up on my accent, we started reminiscing about New York. We knew a lot of the same people, places, and restaurants. FBI agents and mobsters invariably do.

From what I picked up, my new friend 'Roy' was in Las Vegas hiding from the fallout of the conviction of Gambino family mob boss John Gotti, a man I had tailed on many occasions. The infamous Teflon Don had finally been brought to his knees when he had a squabble with his right-hand man, Sammy 'The Bull' Gravano, and put a hit out on him that we intercepted. We were able to use that information to turn Gravano against him. In a historic trial, Sammy the Bull took the stand and ratted out his legendary boss, ending Gotti's colourful reign.

With both Sammy and Gotti gone, and the Feds loaded down with crystal-clear wiretaps of the Gambino's myriad criminal dealings, the family was in turmoil. Many of the made men, friends, and associates headed for the hills until things cooled off, including my new pals in Vegas, Roy, 65, and his son Steve, 41. Needing cash to finance their life on the run, they were eager to deal some art.

Roy called the next day and told me they were ready to roll. 'The goods are in Phoenix. We hafta go dere,' he informed me.

'Why Phoenix?'

'Because dat's where it's at.'

'Dat' was good enough for me. I phoned my buddy Reno Walker from *The Gunsil* case (see Chapter 11) and told him we were back in the art business. He said to bring it on.

'It's always an adventure when you're in town, Tom,' he chuckled.

Roy wouldn't reveal much about the painting, but what he did say dampened my spirits. It was a smaller work of a woman, not a chopped-up man with a purple hat. Still, a Picasso is a Picasso, and the wacky abstract cubist trailblazer, who many still brand a total con man, was quickly pushing his way into the rarefied air of the greatest masters of all time. Three years earlier, his *Les Noces de Pierrette* had sold for $49 million. Eight years later, his *Femme aux Bras Croisés* would prove that was no fluke by selling for $50 million. Four years after that, all reason would evaporate during a frenzied session at Sotheby's. Pablo would set the all time record as the purple-infused *Garçon a la Pipe* broke the bank for an astounding $104 million.

With numbers like that floating around, we had to make this look really good. Even President Bush's Rolex, which I borrowed from the treasury again, and J. Edgar Hoover's aging limo, weren't going to be enough. No, we needed something that would blow them away.

I just happened to know precisely what. The new FBI director, William Sessions, was a CEO-type who had taken to tooling around in a private Sabreliner jet that cost the taxpayers the price of a medium-range Rubens. I figured we could give the public a little value for their purchase by putting the Sabreliner to better use.

Dialling DC, I officially made the request to the proper official.

'Are you crazy? I mean, have you lost your mind out there in the sun? You desert dipwads aren't taking the director's jet! Don't even think about it.'

Since there's more than one way to skin the cats back at the Puzzle Palace, Reno and I began calling in favours. I'd worked with the new Organised Crime chief, Mike Wilson, on the ABSCAM political corruption case, and reminded him how we used a fleet of planes on that one (See Chapter 3).

'All we need is one this time,' I argued. 'Background prop. In and out. Piece of cake.' Wilson laughed and said he'd try to arrange it. The next thing I knew, the Sabreliner was on its way to Phoenix.

I dialled Roy and told him when and where to meet me. Sessions' jet would be touching down at a small executive airport in Scottsdale, a ritzy bedroom community east of Phoenix. We'd meet there in the cosy terminal, reconvene on 'my jet,' and he could show me the Picasso on board.

'After we do our business, I'll take you for a cruise over the Grand Canyon,' I baited. They were certainly up for that. So was I!

Roy was so excited about how things were progressing, he finally revealed what he had. It was *La Mujer*, an abstract portrait of Picasso's stunning mistress of the 1940s and early 1950s, artist / poet / author Françoise Gilot. Perfect, I thought. A hooker tipped us off to gangsters who were holding a painting of a controversial Spanish artist's hot young French piece on the side. *La Mujer*, indeed.

Gilot, noted for a sweeping mane of dark, tousled hair, was 40 years younger than Picasso. She lived and studied with the artist for nine years while he was separated from his wife, ballerina Olga Koklowa. The May/December couple had two children together, Claude and Paloma. The budding artist wrote a book about their relationship, *Life with Picasso*, published in 1964. She later hooked up with famed polio vaccine doctor Jonas Salk, who married her late in his life. (Gilot's oils have recently sold for as much as $30,000.)

Hitting my files, I determined that *La Mujer* had been stolen nine years before by a skilled cat burglar who hit the ritzy, sky scraping Manhattan apartment of a dashing Spaniard, a man-about-town named Joaquin Alvarez Montes, the Marquis of Montréal. The pricey pad, in the swank, 58-storey Galleria building on 117 East 57th Street, was on the 42nd floor.

Montes' family claimed to have been given the 26-by-30 inch portrait by Picasso himself, a fellow Spaniard who lived most of his life in France. Picasso's gift came as thanks for the Montes family's help transporting some of his politically minded family members out of the country during a period of civil unrest prior to the 1939 takeover by Franco, Spain's long time leader.

With that history, and the titillating sexual aspect, *La Mujer* had to be worth a fortune. Certainly worthy of an appearance by William Sessions' prized wings.

It was mid-December, so it was lovely, not blisteringly hot, in the Arizona desert. A Chamber of Commerce day greeted me when I arrived: sunny, clear, about 68 degrees. I was dressed to sting, wearing an updated 90s version of my old art-pimp suit with thinner pinstripes, a much thinner tie, and Bush's Rolex, which I was starting to feel very comfortable with. I carried a large Gucci briefcase that held my art inspection tools, along with an embedded sound transmitter to record the conversations. Although I was in the Old West, I left the six-shooter at home. This was a first contact with alleged gangsters, and I had adequate backup. Plus, there was nothing said about bringing money, which we agreed would be half a million dollars if the painting looked good.

The Sabreliner arrived and taxied near the terminal. It was certainly impressive. It was also clean, meaning it didn't have a logo of the United States on the tail, or a picture of J. Edgar Hoover. The pilots, special agents themselves, assured me that there was nothing inside of that nature as well.

Roy and gang arrived on time. The first thing that struck me was that he looked like Picasso! Could this case get any weirder?

Picasso's goombah look-alike was an upbeat old guy, five-ten, slightly bent over, with thinning grey hair. The Las Vegas life was already taking hold because he was casually dressed in a golf jacket and open-collared shirt. The pinky ring and pointy shoes were the only signs of his back-East ties.

Roy's son Steve was a taller, thinner version of his dad minus the happy disposition. The unexpected third man, Brian, was probably the Phoenix contact who had the painting. He was a tall, handsome, athletic-looking man who sported a thin blue warm-up jacket and a worried expression. Brian was carrying a roll of brown paper that I was hoping was not the Picasso. Rolling multi-million dollar works of art like a Britney Spears poster from the local record store is about the worst thing that can be done to them. It cracks and frays the paint, among other atrocities.

After our introductions, I motioned them out to my plane. The old man was loving it. He remained upbeat and personable, while his son and Brian continued to play the bad cops.

We climbed the stairs and entered the jet. It was actually my initial time inside, so I had to hide the fact that I was seeing it for the first time. A preview might have been smart because it was smaller and more confined than I had anticipated. That meant I'd be dealing with these mopes within knife range. Thankfully, there really was nothing inside that identified the jet with Sessions or the FBI.

When I asked about the painting, Brian started to unroll it.

'Oh my goodness,' I said. 'That's it? Who told you to roll it up? That's terrible.'

Brian, who was already in a sour mood, didn't respond kindly to the criticism. Ignoring him, I explained that even when rolled, it should be done face in instead of face out, the way they had it. Face in kept one's grubby fingerprints off the master's work. As I scolded, it dawned on me that after 20 years of chasing, tracking, and studying masterpieces, I had transformed into a snooty art dealer.

The trio blamed the prior owners, and promised to put anything else they ever came across on the proper display stretcher. Roy remained upbeat. He laughed heartily when I broke the tension by commenting on how much he looked like Picasso. As on the phone, we got along splendidly.

Without the proper stretcher or mounting, Brian and Steve had to hold the corners to allow me to see the work. It was a nice piece. Picasso's lover girl apparently restrained him from going too far with his wild abstracts and making her look like a mutilated freak. One can only imagine those arguments. Inspecting it closely, I received a strong sense of the master buckling under his feisty girlfriend's nagging, walking the tightrope of maintaining her image of beauty while trying to sneak by the discombobulated abstract cuts he so loved. The one big eye, bone-thin body, and flowing lion's mane of hair were no doubt her demands. The messed-up other eye, blackout shadings of half her face, and wildly coloured jacket were probably Picasso's touches. (Some of Picasso's other drawings and portraits of the beautiful Gilot are free of all abstract qualities.)

It was a delightfully expressive work, one that epitomises the cliché that 'a picture's worth a thousand words.'

Was it authentic? That's always hard to say with Picassos because of the almost childish quality of his abstracts, added to the fact that he produced more than 22,000 works during his life, spanning myriad media. Picassos are some of the most forged, duplicated, and stolen artworks in the world. Even the best experts can be fooled.

'Picasso could draw upon various styles throughout his life,' confirms Picasso expert Ron Johnson, Professor of Art History at Humboldt State University in Arcadia, California. 'He could work in more than one mode at the same time. There are a lot of fakes out there for any well-known artists. Next to drugs, art theft is the most profitable crime out there. It's big business.'

That I knew. I also knew about the maddeningly divergent styles of Mr Picasso. I had taken the wife of the previous FBI Director,

William Webster, on a tour of New York City museums and galleries once, and we both paid particular attention to the many Picassos we encountered. In addition, I'd studied them extensively prior to the California forgery case, and during the Jasper theft, so I was well acquainted with Pablo's wild and crazy genius.

This one looked pretty good, much better than the fake of the king in California I'd exposed a few years earlier. The age, paint, and technique appeared to be on the mark. Yet something about it nagged at me. Something didn't quite match up with the paintings I'd studied. The creative, unrestrained sweep seemed to be off. Was this because it was a copy, or because Picasso himself was restrained by his strong-willed mistress who didn't want her eyes and nipples reversed? It was impossible to determine with the equipment I had at hand.

It didn't really matter on the surface because there was no way we were going to let a half million walk. That would be like handing them the keys to Sessions' jet and saying, 'See ya later.' No money was going to change hands because the sellers had made the critical mistake of bringing the work to my turf. They were cooked the moment they arrived with Ms Gilot. Still, with all the elaborate steps we had taken to secure it, it's always nice to be able to tell the media that what we rescued was the real deal.

As I was checking it over, Brian went on the offensive and began to test my expertise. He was peppering me with questions about the precise dates of Picasso's early 1900s blue period, rose period, and little-known purple period, along with other probes of that nature. I was too busy studying the canvas to take his queries seriously, so I barked that I'd been in the business for 20 years, and who was he to test me? He was actually doing the right thing by challenging my expertise, but I wasn't going to let him know that.

Brian was prepared to ignore my scolding and hone in some more, but my buddy Roy came to my rescue. He reminded Brian and his equally frowning son about my background, tools, and especially, the attention-grabbing private jet. After that, the younger men shut up.

'So how'd you guys come to get hold of this?' I inquired.

Roy was now happy to tell the story. He said everybody thought it had been stolen, but the truth was that 'This Spanish Count guy' got in deep to the tune of a million or more with 'the boys' in Vegas, and had used the painting to cover his marks. The sensational story of a 'human fly' cat burglar scaling up 42 stories stuck to the wall like a lizard, banging through a utility room, punching through the bathroom, and lifting the Picasso had been a fabrication, he said, howling at the far-fetched tale.

This was news to me. The police reports and media accounts I read had solid evidence of a sticky-fingered master thief slithering his or her way in through the walls. It was hard to determine what the truth was, but the gambling debt story sounded likely, especially coming from the mob guys who were in possession of the traded goods.

Actually, if I knew my mobsters, both stories sounded likely. The Count probably mentioned that he would use the Picasso to pay off the loan. Before he could retrieve it, the goombahs made a few calls, dispatched the wall crawler, and grabbed it. That way, they had the painting, and still had the Count on the line for the outstanding debt to collect. It was double or nothing, mob style.

Roy went on to claim that the Count himself had stolen it, but I knew that wasn't true, unless they meant he had taken it from his family?

My mind flipped back to yet another version of the story outlined in the files that provided some possible clarification. This account suggested that the original cat burglar, or someone he or she sold the painting to, was the one with the gambling problem. The thief or buyer subsequently used it to pay off the debt. The story of the craps shooting Spanish Count on a bad roll, sweating it out in a back room when he couldn't pay his debts, may have merely been the sexier tale.

A man promoting this account went so far as hiring an attorney in 1989 to negotiate *La Mujer*'s reappearance in return for a reward. The attempt fizzled over verification issues, and the fact that nobody had stepped forward to offer a reward. The painting was not insured.

They were all intriguing twists, but none were critical at that moment. Roy went on to mention the trouble they had encountered trying to sell such a famous piece, and I assured them that my buyers would see that as a plus, not a minus. 'Worst comes to worst, we can always sell it to the insurance company. They'll be happy to drop a half million to get back the five or so they probably paid.'

I'd winged the comment because, as mentioned, there was no eager insurance company trying to recover their lucrative payout. Brian failed to expose me on that whopper.

Feeling cramped, I told the trio that the pilots had to refuel the jet for our trip to the Grand Canyon, so we should get some air outside and loiter around the terminal. Brian took the Picasso and gently rolled it back up, grudgingly promising to put it on a stretcher at the first opportunity.

Roy and I continued our spirited conversation, mostly about the Little Italy area of New York in and around Mulberry Street. We'd both experienced the culinary delights of the hot spicy scungilli (conch meat) at Vincent's, the veal scaloppini at Luna's, and the canoles at Ferrari's—all best eaten during the annual San Genero Festival. He also mentioned all the wise guys he had shared a plate of pasta with, including noted art lover Carmine 'The Doctor' Lombardozzi of the Gambino Family.

Just before entering the terminal, I turned and pointed to a double-humped mountain in the background. 'That's Camelback,' I explained. 'I have a client who likes to climb Camelback. There's a trail weaving up the side of Camelback that people climb all the time. Some do it every morning before they go to work. Can you believe that? Up and down Camelback. That's all you hear about here sometimes. "Let's go climb Camelback. Let's go climb

Camelback. Let's go climb Camelback." They call it that because of the two humps that look like a camel's back.'

Any guess what the code word was?

We'd barely entered the building before the troops were on us. Reno Walker, the 6-foot-6-inch strapping cowpoke of a special agent, was all over Brian, taking the Picasso and securing the brute that appeared to be acting as the father/son team's muscle. The remaining agents jumped the rest of us.

'What's going on here?' I protested.

'You're being arrested for the interstate transportation of stolen property,' one of the agents informed. 'Is that your jet over there?'

'Yeah, why?'

'We're going to have to seize it.'

I went ballistic, as any legitimate businessman would over losing a prized aircraft. 'Get my lawyer. Now!' I demanded. 'You can't take my jet. You have no right. I'm a legitimate art dealer. I'm going to sue you all. You'll all be on the streets holding up signs, begging for work!'

I was raising such a ruckus that the others couldn't get a word in. The Feds dragged me outside, then took the trio away in separate vehicles. When they were gone, I inquired about my Grand Canyon trip.

'No can do, Tommy,' one of the pilots said, preparing for take-off. 'We just received a call. Willie wants his wings back ASAP.'

That stunk. Once again I'd put my neck on the line for goodness, justice, and the abstract American way, and I couldn't even get a little canyon flyby in return?

Adding insult to injury, the wine-coloured Toyota Land Cruiser the trio arrived in was nearly out of gas, the needle sitting on rock-bottom empty. I had to dig into my own pocket for $3.20 just to get it to the FBI impound lot.

As so often happens in the art sleuthing game, the confiscation and arrests merely kicked the insanity into a higher gear. We'd barely made the trumpet-blaring announcement of the successful recovery when the flak began boomeranging. Rumours started flying that the Picasso was a fake. Some clever reporters contacted the usual snobby experts, and the starched set were falling over themselves giving the thumbs down. At the official press conference displaying the recovered 'masterpiece' the authenticity issue completely overshadowed the crack undercover work. Hours before, the harried Phoenix media relations official asked me how to handle the probing mob.

'Tell them the FBI's not in the business of authenticating paintings, just recovering them,' I said, which was basically true. 'It's up to others to take it from here. Fake or not, it has value, and the value means a crime was committed when it was stolen, and when the suspects attempted to resell it.'

Safely back in Oklahoma, the controversy nagged at me so much I continued to investigate. It turned out the *La Mujer* we recovered was indeed the painting taken by the cat burglar from the Marquis' apartment. However, according to the family attorney, it was an expensive, expertly commissioned copy of the original, which the Marquis' family had safely tucked away in one of their many mansions back in Spain.

The snobby experts immediately challenged this account as well, and even questioned the noble family's story of acquiring it by helping Picasso's relatives. 'You'd be amazed how many fakes have the same story,' John Richardson, author of *A Life of Picasso,* huffed to the *New York Observer.* 'It's all bull. The painting is a roaring fake. I would have thought that anybody with experience with Picasso would've spotted it instantly!'

Well, excusssssssssse moi!

From my perspective, the fact that the painting wasn't real made for a more deliciously twisted tale. If the gambling story was true, that meant the Marquis was going to use a duplicate to clear his debt while hanging on to the original. The leg breakers, in turn, stole it from him before he could spring his plan. In essence, everybody was playing three-card monte, screwing each other first without anybody knowing they had taken a big one up the chute.

'I've been here 15 years and I've heard every story in the book,' summarised Virgilia Pancoast, director of the International Foundation for Art Research, an organisation which tracks stolen paintings. 'I have yet to see a work of art that was used in lieu of a debt that was authentic.'

Funny line, but that wasn't entirely correct. There was that bookie from Yonkers mentioned in a previous chapter that had a house full of them, all legit. And while my master con man adversary Harold von Maker, from Chapter 13, didn't use his purloined Jackson Pollock to clear a debt, he certainly used it to create one. Von Maker put it up as collateral to secure a $75,000 bank loan.

As a final insult, the media scrutiny revealed that the Marquis himself was suspiciously missing from the list of royalty and nobility in Spain's all powerful blue book, *Titulos del Reino y Grandezas*. At least not under that title. He was, however, listed as Vizconde de Miralcazar, a nobleman of lower rank. With title inflation running rampant in America, the count probably figured 'Marquis' sounded better to the gullible girls squeezed inside those painted-on pencil dresses at Studio 54 and the Galleria's Atrium Club.

That wasn't the last of it. Roy turned out to be a guy named Al Mauriello, but the rest of his story about the Gambino connection was apparently accurate. He had served time in the 1960s and 1970s for selling heroin and cocaine.

At his hearing, he loudly and repeatedly proclaimed that the proceeding was an outrageous abuse of his civil rights, so much so that it reminded me of Woody Allen's famous lines from the movie *Bananas*: 'This trial is a travesty. It's a travesty of a mockery of a sham of a mockery of a travesty of two mockeries of a sham.'

The craziness didn't end there. Brian looked so lean and athletic because he was a noted former professional athlete, ex-Oakland Athletics Major League Baseball pitcher Brian Kingman. The news of his arrest enabled the media to trot out the fact that Kingman was the last pitcher in pro-baseball history to lose 20 games in a season, going 8-20 in 1980. No wonder Brian was in such a bad mood.

To make matters worse, Kingman argued that he had no idea the Picasso copy was stolen. The Mauriellos were just baseball fans he met through another friend in Las Vegas. They had told him the painting had been used to pay off a debt.

I couldn't dispute that. It was the same story 'Roy' had told me. Kingman had obviously done his homework on Picasso, and was hammering me to make sure I wasn't a charlatan. He was released after the arrest and advised to scram.

The incident hardly fazed the Mauriellos either. Their charges were dropped from Federal to state. After receiving the standard probation, they went about their business.

As for me and that troublemaking Spaniard Pablo Picasso, this latest roller-coaster ride did nothing to dissuade me from renewing my eternal Inspector Javert search for *The Man with the Purple Hat*.

It's merely one of the unfinished 'cold cases' that still eats at me. Two years earlier, there was this truckload of masterpieces taken from a Boston museum ...

.18.

No Boston Tea Party at Isabella's

ON 18 MARCH 1990, as Boston's boisterous St Patrick's Day parties were winding down to a green beer hum, two men dressed as city police officers pulled off the biggest art heist in United States history.

Since then, the ice-cold case has grown into one of the most frustrating mysteries imaginable. Who were the thieves? Who, if anyone, were they working for? Why did they take what they did— 11 assorted artworks worth an estimated $200 million in 1990 dollars—and leave behind a wide array of historic masterpieces that might have doubled or tripled the value of their haul?

Most of all, where are those 11 irreplaceable paintings, drawings, and etchings today, and why hasn't a single one surfaced in nearly two decades? You can imagine how this one eats at me.

In the early morning hours of the day in question, a dark-haired pair of alleged Boston patrol officers, each sporting what were later believed to be fake moustaches, knocked on the office door in the rear of the internationally famous Isabella Stewart Gardner Museum, at 2 Palace Road, Boston, Massachusetts. They informed the security guard who greeted them that they were responding to a call regarding a disturbance in the compound, apparently caused by a marauding group of celebratory teenagers. The story was a ruse to get inside, initially not for the reason that later developed.

The visitors, dressed in authentic police hats and coats adorned with shiny silver badges, asked the security guard if anyone else was working that morning. He responded that his partner was making the rounds in the expansive building. The cops asked him to summon the second guard. When he arrived, the officers announced that they had a warrant for the first security guard's arrest, and proceeded to handcuff them both.

'Gentlemen,' the officers announced once the guards were secured, 'This is a robbery.'

The security guards were taken to the basement, where they were separated, then elaborately trussed-up with duct tape around their hands, ankles, mouths, chins, and heads. The robbers even taped over the handcuffs, blocking the keyhole. Two additional pairs of handcuffs were produced. They were used to secure the guards to structures in the basement.

Throughout the ordeal, the soft-spoken, apparently unarmed robbers asked the guards if they were comfortable, and if any of the bindings were causing excessive pain. They then took the men's wallets, removed their driver's licenses, and informed them that they now knew where they lived. The implication being that the security officers should not go out of their way to help in the subsequent police investigation, or else.

'Don't tell anybody anything,' one of the robbers said with a slight Boston accent. 'If everything goes right, you'll get a nice reward in a year's time.' (No such gift was ever reported.)

The Gardner museum had an elaborate computerised tracking system that noted the time various doors were opened. From the records, the robbers arrived at 1.24am, and spent 24 minutes securing the guards. After that, they immediately travelled to the second floor Dutch Room Gallery in the maze-like building to begin lifting a very specific group of paintings off the walls. They took Vermeer's *The Concert*; Rembrandt's *A Lady and Gentleman in Black*; Rembrandt's *The Storm on the Sea of Galilee*; Rembrandt's *Self Portrait* etching; and then two quizzical works, Govaert Flinck's *Landscape with an Obelisk* that for centuries had been attributed to Rembrandt; and even more inexplicably, a drab, 10-inch Chinese bronze beaker known as a *ku* from the Shang Dynasty dating to 1200–1100 BC.

The oil paintings ranged in size from the two large Rembrandts; *Lady* and *Storm*, checking in at 4.3-by-3.6 feet, and 5.3-by-4.3 feet respectively, to the tiny Rembrandt etching, which was little more than a postage stamp at 1 ¾ -by-2 inches.

A fourth Rembrandt, a larger and more valuable self-portrait, was anchored tightly to the wall and offered resistance. When the crooks finally pried it down, they realised that it was painted on wood, not canvas, and couldn't be cut from a frame and rolled up. They had to leave it behind. Ruffled and insulted, the great master sat across the room, 'watching' as the rest of the event transpired.

After that mixed bag, the duo went to the Short Gallery on the other side of the room and honed in on five extremely quizzical Degases: *La Sortie Du Pesage*, a pencil and water colour on paper; *Cortege Aux Environs de Florence*, a pencil and wash on paper; *Three Mounted Jockeys*, a black ink, white, flesh, and rose wash on paper; *Program for an Artistic Soiree;* a charcoal on white paper; and *Program for an Artistic Soiree II*, an unfinished version of the previous work.

The above selections have had experts shaking their heads for decades. With the almost-unlimited quantity of priceless oils available to them, including Titian's *The Rape of Europa*, which itself might be worth $300 million alone today, why did the thieves ignore the Raphaels of the world and select this bizarre collection of pencils, washes, charcoals and inks from a prolific artist like Degas who flooded the market? Those particular Degases are mediums, which can sometimes be purchased for mere thousands on slow days at the neighbourhood auction house, even from such a notable master.

Aside from being lesser works, the Degases were all small, none larger than 12-by-9 inches.

As if to send a message, or to display an odd sense of humour, the robbers made another astounding choice, taking a bronze, gilded, 9-by-7-inch metal eagle known as a 'finial' from the top of a Napoleonic flag jutting out of a case. The relic is so insignificant it's usually not included in the list of stolen works—which actually totalled 13 when figuring in the *ku* and the finial.

The Gardner Museum offered the thieves more than 2,500 pieces of ancient art, including oil paintings, sculpture, furniture, manuscripts, books, silver, photographs, textiles, artefacts, and relics, some dating back 30 centuries, and the pair took a weathered flagpole ornament?

After those head-scratchers, the robbers returned to the first floor Blue Room and made a more logical selection, Manet's *Chez Tortoni*, a small, but traditionally more valuable oil on canvas that was 10 ½ -by-13 ½ inches. Normally, there were Corots, Courbets, and Delacroixes in the Blue Room, worth up to $2 million each, but they were out for renovation.

Having their fill—and leaving more than a billion dollars worth of historic masterworks behind—the duo left the building one at a time at 2.41am and 2.45am, exiting separately for reasons only known to them. The computer records indicated that the pair never bothered to venture to the third-floor galleries where the prized Titian, the Raphaels, and countless other Italian masterpieces hung untouched. Were they unaware that the Titian was up there—in 'The Titian Room?'

Because of a quirk in the otherwise elaborate security system, the theft wasn't discovered until the morning shift of guards arrived at 8am. They found the security station unmanned, so they called the police. The late shift crew was then discovered hog-tied in the basement. Although the alarms had engaged, and times were recorded when the works were removed, the museum had only internal signals that did not alert an external police or security company. That notification was supposed to have been accomplished by the manual pressing of a 'panic button' at the main security desk. By neutralizing the security officers at the start, the knowledgeable robbers had eliminated outside intervention.

When the arriving police and security guards checked the facilities, they learned that the thieves had taken the video from the surveillance recorder, turned the first floor camera away from the security desk, and tore off and removed a computerised printout that reported all the alarm and door engagements.

A disk that held the printed information remained, as did the computer's internal hard drive. That enabled investigators to simply reprint the information that was taken.

It was also determined, to everyone's horror, that some of the paintings, including Rembrandt's *Storm*, and *Gentleman* had been cut from their frames and stretchers and probably rolled up, which would cause the ancient paint to crack and flake. (A Vermeer, stolen in Brussels in 1971, was not only rolled up, but the thief sat on it in a cab, all but destroying it.)

Taken as a whole, the theft was puzzlingly schizophrenic. On one hand, there was an extensive knowledge of the Gardner's security operation, a solid understanding of art when considering the first three primary targets, and a cleverly devised plan that worked without a hitch. In contrast, there were the baffling subsequent selections, the weird secondary artefact choices, and the confusing attempt to blot out the computer records by taking a printout, but not the disk containing the information.

Were the thieves geniuses or dunces? How could they be simultaneously both? Or, was there a specific agenda involved that no one has ever figured out?

What about the festive date chosen for the headline-grabbing event? Was the Irish holiday selected in deference to Isabella

Stewart Gardner herself, a globe-trotting party girl who opened the grand museum in 1903 on New Year's night?

Even more intriguing, was this a theft that eliminated all the crass monetary values and returned to the very crux of art itself? Meaning, were the thieves working from a childlike Christmas list of things someone simply saw and liked during a casual trek through the museum?

To expand upon that theory in a more fanciful way, it almost appeared as if the robbers were the loyal servants of a very wealthy child, someone like the ancient kings who ascended to their thrones while still pre-teens. If not royal, then maybe a Mini-Me version of Ian Fleming's Dr No from the early James Bond movies.

As *Star Trek*'s Mr Spock would say: 'Fascinating.'

The media brought out their biggest headlines, reacting to the intrigue, the drama, the $200–$300 million figure, and the famous names involved. Putting Vermeer, Rembrandt, Degas, Manet, and even Napoleon in the same sentence makes for a star-studded cast.

As expected, for the general public at least, Govaert Flinck was like the answer to the routine multiple choice question, 'Which name doesn't belong in this group?'

Flinck, a 17th century Dutch technician, was a student of Rembrandt who copied his style so well that many of the Rembrandts in the world are actually Flincks. Even after being included in such lofty company, his paintings aren't wildly popular and sell for five figures when they occasionally appear on the market.

Which begs the question: did the thieves really want a Flinck, or did they fail to read the inscription and think it was another Rembrandt? If they were limited by time and carrying ability, why did they choose Flinck over Titian?

Or, did they simply like the painting? The *Obelisk* was an angry, red-hued, desolate landscape that looked like it would have made a better background for Rembrandt's *Storm* than the one Rembrandt himself chose.

The Flinck dilemma aside, the robbery remained huge international news. Everybody was shocked and horrified—everybody except award winning *Time* magazine art critic Robert Hughes, who stuck up his nose and produced one of the classic art snob dismissals of all time. Positioning himself as the ultimate authority, the best-selling author ripped into the thieves as Neanderthals, the media as ignorant troglodytes, the museum itself for caring a whit about such mostly insignificant pieces, the museum's condition, the museum's security, the police, the French, greedy art auction houses, and even the great artists themselves for producing so much inferior junk.

'At most,' he sneered, 'only two of the works stolen from the slightly frayed but beloved museum, built as a re-creation of a Venetian palace in 1903, have real significance in art history. Rembrandt's *Storm* is his only sea piece, and the Vermeer, *Concert*, is, well, a Vermeer: a sublime patch of silence and visual harmony washed in pearly light, one of only 30 known works by the master. The other 'Rembrandt' painting, of a husband and wife, is probably by one of his pupils; the French works—one by Manet and several by Degas—vary from slight to trivial.

'It seems quite clear that the thieves had very little idea of what to go after, since the glory of the Gardner Museum is its Italian paintings, starting at the top with Titian's *Rape of Europa*, regarded by some as the greatest single Italian Renaissance canvas in the US … This was more the Gang That Couldn't See Straight.'

It went on like that for two gloriously snooty pages. Hughes questioned the monetary figure given, suggesting that it was wildly inflated by the police and museum. (He did value the Vermeer at $70 million, and greatly undervalued Rembrandt's *Storm* at $15 million. The total value of the haul today is said to be between $300 and $500 million.)

Warming up, Hughes insisted the clumsy thieves wouldn't even be able to reap a 5% fence fee based on his low figure, and cackled that the paintings weren't insured, so the crooks couldn't ransom them to an insurance company. (Covering such an extensive collection as the Gardner's would have cost $3 million a year—more than the museum's entire operating budget.)

Hughes then used the theft to get on his high horse and rail against one of his pet peeves, the commercialisation of art and the frenzy created by such auction houses as Sotheby's and Christie's.

'Is there a moral to this event? Only the obvious one: that we owe it to the sanctimonious, inflated racket that the art industry has become. The theft is the blue-collar side of the glittering system whereby art, through the 1980s, was promoted into crass totems of excess capital. Sotheby's and Christie's tacitly recognised this last week, when ... they volunteered the $1 million in reward money ... a touching PR gesture, like a cigarette company giving money to a cancer ward.'

Whew! Tell us how you really feel, Bobby! The article was so blistering, I literally had to toss the magazine down. It all but burned my hands.

'The worldwide volume of art thefts is now epidemic,' Hughes truthfully declared near the end.

The funny thing is, I couldn't disagree with most of what the immensely knowledgeable Hughes scathingly wrote. The first two Degases, for example, were once slapped together inside a single frame. And poor Mr Flinck's haunting landscape didn't even warrant mention by the esteemed art critic.

Regardless, I certainly wouldn't have expressed it in such a haughty manner. Hughes spoke of the lesser Rembrandts, the Manet, and all of the Degases as if they were a third-grader's Mother's Day finger paintings. He saw nothing in the robbers but ignorance and stupidity because their choices didn't match what his loftier, more intelligent and studied ones would have been.

This is where I disagree. It's my belief that these thieves, either by their own devices, or working from a specific list, took exactly what they wanted, right down to the silly little eagle on Napoleon's flag. Similarly, they left exactly what they didn't want, which included

Titian's menacing Rape that even Hughes would have to concede would have been impossible to sell on the open market, and almost as difficult anywhere else.

So again, the question remains: were the robbers Hughes' knuckle-dragging, blue-collar unsophisticates, or was there a method to their madness? There was only one way to find out. Track down the paintings, scoop up the thieves or their agents, and ask them.

To that end, I was summoned to Boston on the Monday after the weekend robbery. Walking through the museum, and reading all the reports, I came across two curious items that were potentially revealing. There was a five minute period just prior to the thieves' arrival in which the computer system was dormant. From 12.39am until 12.44am, the machine recorded no activity. When the system reactivated at 12.44am, alarms indicating a glass break and a fire went off on the fourth floor, a residence area where, according to the computer, the thieves never ventured. The readings were checked by the security guard, deemed a malfunction, and the alarm reset.

That kind of pre-theft distraction was the calling card of both the Irish Republican Army, a band that was noted worldwide for art thefts dating back decades, or its rival loyalist group, the Ulster Volunteer Force, which was starting to follow suit. What was the IRA/UVF doing in America, one might ask? Was this really America, might be the best answer. Boston, like so many US cities, is filled with ethnic pockets that are deeply rooted in the culture and politics of the 'old country'. Boston is so Irish even some of the Italians speak with a brogue. The city has long crawled with IRA and UVF agents, either hiding out, recruiting, lobbying, or raising money for the cause.

Boston's notorious Irish 'Winter Hill' mob, headed by the FBI's Top Ten Most Wanted fugitive James 'Whitey' Bulger, has at times wielded more power than the traditional Patriarca Italian Mafia that supposedly controls the city from its headquarters in Providence, Rhode Island. Whitey had strong IRA ties, along with compromised law enforcement officers inside the Boston police department, and, unfortunately, Boston's FBI office. The deadly mob boss, who didn't go on the lam until 1995, could have easily given his IRA pals a pair of authentic Boston police uniforms—or even arranged for a duo of legitimate cops on his payroll to pull off the heist.

Four years earlier, as mentioned in Chapter 14, Martin 'The General' Cahill, a Dublin mobster with loose ties to the UVA, hit the famous Sir Alfred Beit collection at Russborough House in Blessington, Ireland. This was the same palatial 18th century Palladian mansion/museum, robbed by the IRA a decade earlier. Cahill's gang used a glasscutter to make a hole in a large French window, opened the shutters, deliberately set off the alarm, altered it in some manner so it wouldn't go off again, then hid outside in the grass as the police and security checked it out.

Once the coast was clear, they returned and lifted 18 paintings worth $40 million, including a Vermeer and the usual Rubens, Goyas, and Renoirs, along with the same exact Gainsborough, *Madame Baccelli*, that the IRA had grabbed 12 years earlier.

If this was now the IRA, UVF, or any other similar political, paramilitary, or terrorist group invading our shores—or more specifically our museums—it didn't bode well for the future.

The matching modus operandi in each case was the alarm tripped within an hour of the thieves' entry. In the Gardner heist, however, there was no indication of how an accomplice could have entered the building clandestinely and scurried to the fourth floor undetected prior to the robbers' official entry at the main security station 40 minutes later. There was, however, an employee who failed a polygraph, quit his job, and didn't bother to return for his last pay cheque. The person denied any participation in the robbery, and no connection beyond his highly suspicious behaviour was ever established.

Residents celebrating St Patrick's Day in the area reported seeing a medium-sized, light-coloured vehicle parked near the museum from 12.30am to 1.15am. Two men were inside that fitted the description of the 30-something robbers. The first was about 5-

foot-10, medium build, shiny fake moustache, short dark hair, with square gold-framed glasses. The second man was taller and heavier, about six-foot-one, 200 pounds, with 'puffy' collar-length black hair and the same type of fake moustache. They were not, however, described as wearing police uniforms—at least not then.

Continuing my on-site inspection of the castle-like museum, I wondered anew why the grand Titian wasn't taken, and why the ku and finial were. It again seemed like part theft of the century, and part fraternity prank. Looking closer, I noticed a small dent in the wall above the now finial-less Napoleonic flag. The crooks had banged the eagle against the wall in the process of yanking it off, possibly damaging it. That was telling. Not only were they determined to take the curious item, they apparently had a hard time doing so.

From a psychological profiling perspective, I reconsidered the possibility that the culprits were real cops. They had acted with the confidence and gumption of men who had worn the badge and blue uniform before, and knew the respect the symbols commanded. A notation buried in a file mentioned that the pair each wore standard black police radios on their hips, live transmitters that crackled with authentic police activity, including the array of codes dispatchers use to designate particular crimes.

The 'cops' additionally acted like men who knew their way about a crime scene investigation lab. The FBI CSI types went over the place with a fine-toothed computerised comb and came up with nothing, not a fingerprint, footprint, hair, DNA sample, clothing fibre, nothing. The duct tape was the kind that can be purchased anywhere on the planet with no tracing codes. The handcuffs, surprisingly enough, were nearly as prevalent, available everywhere from security supply stores to S&M sex shops. The robbers operated completely off the CSI radar—a neat trick considering that the security guards said they weren't wearing gloves.

If the suspects had outfoxed the lab techs because they were indeed real Boston Blues who knew the score, what a hornet's nest this was going to be. Either way, the disguise was an extremely effective ruse.

'The policy has always been that you don't open that door in the middle of the night for God,' said Lyle Grindle, who headed the bolstered security after the theft. 'Why on this one night they opened the door, no one can explain.'

I can. Police officers can be intimidating. They don't react kindly to anyone failing to 'obey my au-thor-re-tiii,' especially security guards who are viewed as inferior.

The speculation circled back around to Bulger and/or Ireland's notorious General. Was Cahill in town? That was easy enough to check and dismiss, unless he was travelling under an alias, which he wasn't known to do. In fact, like most mobsters, he was mostly provincial and territorial. Plus, there was no indication that his previous art robberies had brought him anything but the same grief his predecessors quickly discovered—no buyers stepping forward to take a chance on anything so well-known. Jewellery and extortion, two of Cahill's more profitable commodities, were much easier to convert into cash. I just didn't see the guy hopping the pond to come to America to steal more headaches.

Whoever was responsible, the key to solving it was the same as always—follow the money to the oil. More precisely, the attempt to convert the oil, ink, pencil, and charcoal into money.

The law enforcement strategy was for everybody to pound their informants. That was especially true of me as my sources were directly connected to the art world. The problem was, the $1 million reward had them all salivating. Nobody was going to give up their lottery ticket by admitting they didn't know anything. Most didn't even wait until we called, jumping on the phone and informing us that they 'might' know something. All they needed, they kept repeating, one con man after the other, was a little up-front flash money to get the ball rolling. The grifters were hustling up a storm as fierce as the one in Rembrandt's missing sea painting.

Needing a new, 1990s identity to deal with them, one that wasn't overexposed, played out, or on the Sicilian Mafia's hit list, I wheeled Thomas Bishop into the restoration shop and emerged as super 1990s art dealer Thomas Russell, international man of money and action. I put out the word far and wide that I was in the market for Vermeers, Rembrandts, Degas and Manets, baby! I'd even be interested in paying top dollar for a Chinese ku, or a French finial once waved by a general with a severe short guy's complex. That is, if anybody out there just happened to have any of those things.

While waiting for the leads to filter in, I hit the files and read everything I could about New England art thefts. Some of the cases I knew well, like the Fogg Museum coin heist from decades, and chapters, past (see Chapter 9). I also took refresher courses in the techniques of Rembrandt, Degas, Manet and Vermeer in case I had to start inspecting the rash of forgeries that often materialise after a sensational theft. I noted with interest that Vermeer was a tavern owner with lots of kids, two things that probably were instrumental in keeping his production numbers so low.

Of all the tips that flooded in, only three or four were deemed worth pursuing. One pointed to a noted Boston fence who was spreading the word that he had a bead on the Gardner art and could broker the deal. I phoned him as Tom Russell, shady art dealer extraordinaire, and listened as he tried to work me for a $20,000 finders fee—paid up front. Since he had some credibility with the Boston agents, I fought the urge to drop an F-bomb on him. We agreed to have a sit down at a ritzy Pier 4 restaurant, my treat. When the time came, he never showed. We wrote it off as another attempted hustle.

The unusual no-show was the beginning of a disturbing trend. One of the local agents had some solid contacts with the IRA, and nothing came through with them either. Another Boston agent was in tight with Bulger, who was actually a long-time FBI informant dating back to when he was a street punk. That extremely rare inside connection nonetheless failed to produce any worthwhile information.

I was starting to get a really bad feeling about what was going on in Boston—on both sides of the law. With such a wealth of informants, including a top mob boss, how come nobody knew anything about such a major theft? Where was the traditional 'mob blessing' required to operate in someone's territory?

That question wouldn't be answered until a decade later. In 1999, a Federal investigation headed by Judge Mark Wolf accused 18 Boston FBI agents and supervisors of handling informants in an illegal manner. That set off one of the worst scandals in bureau history. Special Agent John Connolly, the man closest to Bulger, was subsequently convicted in 2002 of one count of racketeering, two counts of obstruction of justice, and one count of making a false statement to the FBI. He was found innocent of the even nastier charges of leaking information that led to the deaths of three informants.

'Today's verdict reveals John Connolly for what he became, a Winter Hill Gang operative masquerading as a law enforcement agent,' branded US Attorney Michael J. Sullivan. Connolly was sentenced to 10 years in prison.

Connolly's supervisor, John Morris, confessed to receiving a series of payoffs, and to leaking information to Whitey about police investigations. He was granted immunity for testifying against Connolly.

Suffice it to say, the informant tips coming into the Boston field office regarding the Gardner theft were no doubt being finely screened. It may also explain why a legitimate source may not have even bothered calling, and why my fence stood me up. It's only natural to assume that one of the main functions of a police officer or a special agent on the mob's payroll is to tip them off regarding the activities of undercover agents.

On the positive side, the lead investigator who caught the case and worked it for more than a decade, Daniel J. Falzon, was a squeaky-clean kid of 26 whose father, Frank, was a well-respected San Francisco police homicide detective. Falzon was completely out of the loop of the older Connolly and his group of long-time cronies, and was never suspected of any foul play.

'It wasn't a task, it was a passion, and still is,' Falzon told a reporter in the late 1990s, echoing my own sentiments on a career spent tracking masterpieces. 'You get involved in something like this, it's part of your life. It's part of you.'

As time passed, the lid on what happened at the Gardner Museum closed tighter than a Scotsman's wallet. In response, the tips became as fanciful as my idle speculation that the thieves may have been working for some foreign child king who had randomly picked out pretty pictures and objects from the museum like he was in a candy store. Along those lines, we were told by someone with an Aristotle Onassis/Jackie Kennedy complex that the theft was done on behalf of a Greek tycoon who wanted the art as a gift for his new high-society girlfriend. That lead went nowhere.

Another wild goose chase took me back to Canada, a place that was noticeably missing from my list of favourite bordering countries ever since the fiasco at the Montréal jail detailed in Chapter 9. This time, I was dispatched to Toronto to meet with this Little Caesar character with a French accent, an Edward G. Robinson–looking yoyo who claimed, see, to have an in, see, with the guys who have the goods, see. Little French Caesar set up a meeting with the guys, see, and they didn't show either, see.

You could take the undercover agent out of Boston, apparently, but you couldn't take the leaky mess that was the Boston office out of the undercover agent. I was lucky to have survived.

The next wild goose led me to New York, where this giant Bubba Smith–looking African American guy tried to sell me a painting purportedly by Samuel Finley Breese Morse, the man who invented the Morse code. I didn't even know Morse was an artist. If he was, and this was legitimate, he was a bad one. The painting was garbage. Bubba said he'd only tell me about the Gardner theft after we did the Morse code deal. Right. And we'd do *The Da Vinci Code* deal after that.

'What hath God wrought!' Morse's first dots-and-dashes message on the telegraph, seemed to sum up this sinking ship of a case. (Morse was indeed an artist of some note.)

After a few weeks of this run-around, I again sensed that something was terribly wrong in Boston, and that nothing was going to get done as long as I stayed there. I retreated to Oklahoma, and worked my national and international sources without having to report to the nosey Boston supervisors.

I narrowed my suspects down to a pair. The first was a man named Brian Michael McDevitt, a noted con man who had attempted to rob similar paintings from the Hyde Collection in Glens Falls, New York, a decade earlier. McDevitt, who was living in Boston at the time of the Gardner robbery, had devised an elaborate plan for the New York caper. He and the night manager of the Queensbury Hotel where he was staying, Michael Brian Morey, dressed themselves in Federal Express uniforms, hijacked a Federal Express truck, kidnapped the female driver, knocked her out with ether, and headed to the Hyde. The express mail carrier ruse was going to be their cover to get inside the museum.

The scheme was foiled when they became stuck in traffic, and the Hyde closed before they could get there. Police officers responding to the vehicle theft found an elaborate diagram of the museum in the truck, along with 14 pairs of handcuffs, duct tape, medical tape, and sharp instruments the pair admitted would have been used to cut the paintings from their frames.

Convicted of unlawful imprisonment and attempted grand larceny, they spent less than a year in jail.

McDevitt, who fitted the description of the larger of the Gardner robbers, except for his thinning red hair, was brought in and interrogated. He naturally denied it. His alibi for the night in question bounced, and he refused to take a polygraph. When brought in, he was discovered to be clean-shaven for the first time in eight years. His easy-to-identify bushy red beard was gone, and his short red hair could have been muted under a 'puffy' dark wig.

An extremely interesting tid-bit in McDevitt's file was the fact that he was a flag aficionado. In the mid 1980s, while attending the University of Massachusetts, Boston, McDevitt spearheaded an effort to raise money, purchase, and display more than a hundred flags around the institution to reflect the diversity of its student body.

That sure sounds like a guy who, in mid-robbery, would have taken the time to try and filch a Napoleonic flag and its capping finial.

Still, other than a pile of compelling circumstantial evidence, we had nothing that enabled us to hold him.

Afterward, McDevitt ran to California, where he juiced his resume, set himself up as an award-winning television writer, author, and movie producer, then somehow talked his way into the lofty position of Chairman of the Grants and Foundations Committee for the Writers' Guild West.

As far as I know, however, he has never made any attempt to sell a painting taken from the Gardner theft. Either he has extreme patience, he immediately dumped them off to a discreet wealthy buyer, or he wasn't involved but half-wanted us to think he was just to play with our heads.

My second theory spins back around to the IRA or UVF. If they did the job, the paintings more than likely ended up overseas. From there, they were either sold in Japan, or to someone in one of the Arab nations, to help finance Ireland's never-ending angst over English rule.

My suspicions didn't stop Special Agent Dan Falzon and company, including my old friend Harold Smith working independently of Lloyd's of London, from chasing their own flocks of geese. Twice, civilians spotted what they were certain was Rembrandt's *Storm* in private homes, one in Boston, and the other in Japan. Both turned out to be legally owned copies of the popular work. *The Storm* had hung in the same spot in the ruffled Japanese collector's house for more than 40 years.

Infamous cat burglar Myles Connor from the Woolworth Estate heist (see Chapter 12) jumped into the fray and dicked investigators around for years. Languishing in prison for trying to move paintings taken from Amherst College's Mead Museum in 1975, Connor and various associates insisted they knew who had pulled the Gardner caper. Connor and crew would be happy to help in return for their freedom and the reward, which had leaped to $5 million. Although it was the standard tired old hustle—I need to get out to track down the paintings, and I could use some up-front cash as well—the fast-talking feline was heeded because of his history of New England art thefts, and the oh-so-elaborate tale he wove.

The master thief, himself the son of a hardworking police officer, put it off on two good pals named Bobby Donati and David Houghton. Connor went so far as to say he and Donati had cased the Gardner museum 15 years before, and had determined that it was ripe for the plucking. Slick as a greased cobra, Connor had the insight to mention offhand how much Donati was taken with some 'worthless bird' sitting on a Napoleonic flag, a comment that had investigators salivating. The crafty former rock musician, who was an avid reader of art books and magazines, had no doubt picked up that little tid-bit in one of the news reports. He failed to mention, however, that the thieves had tried to steal the whole flag, but couldn't remove the screws from the case.

When it was pointed out that Donati and Houghton didn't fit the robbers' description, Connor deftly sidestepped the issue by claiming the two thugs hired even lower-level thugs to be their front men.

Not very likely.

The story, however well played, contained an even bigger hole, this one the size of the Grand Canyon. Both Donati and Houghton were ghosts, having conveniently died of 'natural causes' within two years of the robbery. Houghton was taken down by illness.

Donati's sliced and diced corpse was found tied in the trunk of a car, the victim of a mob disagreement. Wags quipped that of the two, Donati's bloody demise was the more 'natural' way guys in their line of work move on to the next dimension.

From Connor's perspective, it couldn't have worked out more perfectly. There's no patsy like a dead patsy.

When investigators refused to give Connor what he wanted, he merely re-baited the hook and cast the line again. He had an associate on the outside take a news reporter to a secret warehouse outside Boston and show him what was said to be Rembrandt's much reproduced *Storm on the Sea of Galilee*. The reporter was even allowed to take flakes of paint that were raining off it like dandruff, a description that mortified Gardner officials.

The chips were initially deemed authentic, which had everyone in a frenzy, and enabled the tipster to con the Gardner museum, he claimed, out of $10,000 in walk around money. (Museum officials have never confirmed or denied the assertion.)

The Boston FBI, however, said 'Not so fast.' They asked Connor's boy, William Youngworth, for a small show of good faith. Bring them one of the minor works, a Degas ink, the ku, heck, even the much-maligned Flinck, and they'd sign on. It was a triviality considering the $5 million reward and $100 million Vermeer.

A triviality that queered the deal, or scheme, or con job. Neither Youngworth, nor Connor—in or out of prison, then or now—have ever complied. Nor have they provided any useful information. (Connor did sell his 'I was the mastermind!' story to Hollywood, but the movie has yet to be made.)

A Scotland Yard informant and New York antiques dealer with the unlikely name of Michael van Rijn, no relation to Rembrandt van Rijn, surfaced in the new millennium with his own wild tale. Van Rijn, a man I was familiar with from past cases, made the same routine noise in *Atlantic Monthly* magazine in 2001 about knowing who did it, where, and why. When pressed, he claimed to be in fear for his life, then quickly hopped across the ocean to a wormhole in London.

It was one similar frustration after another, a quagmire I was more than happy to leave to the uncooperative and compromised Boston field office. I did feel for Special Agent Falzon, as it was the kind of nagging case that can sour one's career right from the start.

'With all the people we know in and out of prison, we've never got a quality piece of information that indicates this is it, this is who did it,' Falzon lamented years later. 'We've had everybody and his brother say they know who did it, and none of it has led to anyone going to prison or any of the art going back on the walls.'

Following my first retirement in 1994 at the still-spry age of 51 (I was later recalled before and after 9/11), I've continued to work this case, remaining in contact with four separate informants around the world. The $5 million reward makes it a worthwhile endeavour for anyone in the bustling art trade. Filthy lucre aside, it would be nice to, at the very least, recapture the Vermeer and Rembrandt's *Storm* for history's sake, if not to make *Time* magazine art critic Robert Hughes happy.

Speaking of Hughes' two 'significant' favourites, I received a solid lead not long ago that those particular masterpieces have been expertly duplicated, and were pawned off for big bucks to separate, Donald Trump–like corporate barons who believe they have the real thing. If those men would like to set the record straight, and maybe get a measure of revenge for being duped, they can call or e-mail my co-author, Dary Matera, no questions asked, at 602-351-8684, dary@darymatera.com.

That goes for anybody who may know the whereabouts of the Gardner paintings. This includes the original thieves. The statute of limitations for the theft ran out in 1997, meaning the two 'cops' are off the hook as long as they no longer have any of the art, or are actively trying to sell it. They could actually now collect the reward for assisting in the recovery if they play their cards right, a prospect that outrages both the law enforcement and art communities.

If the paintings are found in the possession of mobster-in-hiding Whitey Bulger, a budding treasure hunter can hit a $6 million quinella —$5 million for the art, plus the $1 million bounty for Most Wanted Whitey. (See Dary Matera's book, *FBI's Top Ten Most Wanted*, for details on that reward and tips on how to find Whitey.)

A positive that did result from the Gardner theft was the long-sought stiffening of the legal statutes dealing with art theft. As noted in the Introduction, and as detailed in action throughout this book, the weak 'transportation of stolen property' law more times than not resulted in thieves and fences getting nothing more than probation. That's not a bad risk when stealing a $100 million painting. A special 'Theft of Major Artwork' statute was passed in 1994 that called for sentences of up to 10 years for snatching museum art worth $100,000 and up, or grabbing something that is more than a century old. Ironic that it was passed the same year I retired.

Another optimistic aspect of the Gardner case is that unlike murder or most other crimes, where a case grows colder by the day, art theft recovery is timeless. Masterpieces like the Rembrandts, Rubens, Ter Borches, Picassos, and Tintorettos of the past chapters can be lost for decades, or even centuries, then suddenly pop up as if they'd merely been sunbathing on the Riviera for a spell.

Meanwhile, back in Ireland, the fun just keeps on keeping on. Thomas Gainsborough's *Madame Baccelli* was stolen for a third time in 2001, and recovered yet again. The same Bellotto, *View of Florence* was also taken and recovered in the three politically minded burglaries. The 'kick me' stamped Russborough House was hit a fourth time in 2002, when five paintings were grabbed, including two Rubens and yet another work entitled *Adoration of the Shepherd*, this one by Adrien van Ostade.

Thomas Gainsborough was an 18th century British portrait and landscape artist. One of his oils, *Portrait of Richard Tickell*, sold for $3.4 million in 2003. Bernardo Bellotto was an 18th century Italian from the Venetian school. Bellotto's best oils sell for around

$1 million. Adrien van Ostade was a 17th century Dutch master. His oil, *Peasants Dancing and Carousing Outside an Inn*, sold for $5.8 million in 2004.

On 18 August 1994, the once 'untouchable' Martin Cahill was gunned down by an IRA volunteer as he slowed down at an intersection near his home in Swan Grove, Ranelagh, on the south side of Dublin. The assassin was posing as a traffic planner. Two movies were made about Cahill's life: *The General*, starring Brendan Gleeson, and *Ordinary Decent Criminal*, staring Oscar winner Kevin Spacey. Both films covered Cahill's known art heists.

Back in Boston, the empty frames from the Gardner theft still hang in the museum, waiting for the lost sheep to come home. The effervescent Isabella Stewart Gardner, a frequently naughty society's child who lived *la vida loca* before it was cool, collected the valuables herself during her frequent trips to Europe in the 1880s. (Two of the museum's untouched oils, by Anders Zorn and John Singer, are commissioned portraits of herself.) Her will decreed that nothing would ever be removed from, or added to, her glass-ceiling, Venetian-style palace. That means the empty spots on the walls, and the dent from the eagle, will remain for all eternity until they are filled with precisely what was there before.

That should be the policy of all museums. The empty spaces should forever stand as enduring reminders of the beauty, and irreplaceable history, that's constantly chiselled away by growing legions of thieves.

EPILOGUE

*A*T MY RETIREMENT party in September 1994, I was given the standard gold watch. After wearing ex-President George H.W. Bush's gleaming Rolex Presidential for all those years, the functional Seiko was a bit of a letdown.

It would have been nice to ride off into one of Manet's glorious sunsets with the ol' familiar upgraded timepiece, but then again, they weren't going to let me fly away in William Sessions' jet, or roll down the road in J. Edgar Hoover's limo either.

Stuffy regulations and all.

Besides, those trappings of wealth were never mine to begin with. They belonged to Thomas Bishop, Robert Steele, Thomas Russell, and my other alter egos.

As I observed everyone happily celebrating the end of my career, it occurred to me that only Thomas McShane was retiring to a golden trout stream. Bishop, Steele, Russell, and the rest were being rubbed out, buried, and forgotten.

Such a realisation can often be traumatic to undercover agents. In the absorbing Arizona political scandal book, *What's In It for Me?* former mob associate turned undercover operative Joe Stedino movingly described the unexpected demise of his alter ego, Tony Vincent. Stedino had transformed himself into a powerful, high-living, cash-happy gangster who showered money on politicians willing to sell their votes for a casino gambling initiative. It was a role Stedino relished, a character that was everything he'd always wanted to be. One morning, in the midst of the wildly successful sting, Stedino discovered that his cover had been blown by a reporter jumping on a scoop.

'Whatever the journalistic intrigue, one thing was certain,' Stedino wrote, 'Tony Vincent was dead—murdered by the morning newspaper.'

I know the feeling. Although the demise of my alter egos had been less sudden, the result was no less painful.

The conflicting images of my schizophrenic existence were everywhere that festive afternoon in Oklahoma. My three children; Tommy Jeff, 17, Danielle, 15, and Marianne, 11, were there. They belonged to Thomas McShane. Aside from the occasional growing pains and wild oats sowing, they were mostly a joy. Their mother, however, was not present. We had separated four years earlier, and would be divorced two years later. The marriage fell victim to my multiple personalities.

My wife married Thomas McShane, a white-shirted, dark-suited, government attorney who was supposed to punch a clock from nine-to-five, pick up the kids from football and cheerleading practice, then come home for dinner. She had not married the 'art pimp' Thomas Bishop, the player who was up all night, always in the company of bad men, and often in the company of both good and bad women. She had not married Robert Steele, who hopped on jets at a moment's notice to track a stolen painting around the globe, unable to risk calling home, or to give any details as to where he was, what he was doing, when he was coming home, or even who he was pretending to be. She had definitely not married Thomas Russell, who shadowed and wiretapped some of America's deadliest and most vengeful mobsters, then testified against them in open court—a 'civic duty' that put her in constant fear of violent retribution.

Nothing new there. Undercover agents and broken marriages go hand in hand. It's a sad cliché, but bitingly true. The clandestine life is indeed hell on a relationship. I commend my wife for putting up with it, and me, for as long as she did.

The melancholy swept over me again that afternoon when I was presented with a replica sculpture of *The End of the Trail*, James Earl Fraser's war weary Native American warrior. It was an appropriate piece, and I appreciated my bosses and co-workers for making the effort to give me something artistic. Yet, the contrast was staggering. Bishop, Steele, and Russell had touched, felt, recovered, and been inspired by some of the greatest masterpieces the world has known, more than $300 million worth and rising by my last accounting—paintings that now adorn the walls of such places as The Louvre in Paris.

Thomas McShane? He was dispatched with a $100 watch, and a $50 copy of a plaster sculpture that sits in the Cowboy Hall of Fame in Oklahoma City.

Not that I'm complaining. Nor did I expect anything more. To the contrary: during most of my wild and woolly career, I felt like I was stealing my pay cheque. I wouldn't have traded all the adventures for anything. Those feelings aside, it was definitely a rather ironic moment.

Still, even as I painted on the happy smiles, I couldn't help feeling waves of sadness. One of my longstanding regrets is that I was never able to train a protégé in my special field and pass the black light 'torch' to him or her as Don Mason had done with me. I'd tried numerous times in New York to get someone interested, but frequent transfers, and the increased focus on terrorism, kept moving people around. That, and the fact that 25 years later, art theft remains an eclectic field that wasn't accepted as properly macho by the tight-knit G-Men fraternity.

My recruiting efforts were akin to Agent K in *Men in Black* telling Will Smith that he would have to give up his life as he knew it, including all his friends, lovers, and relatives, if he wanted to work for the government's secret space alien agency.

Complicating matters was the fact that my transfer to Oklahoma City jettisoned me from Manhattan's bustling art world. Any chance of finding and schooling a last-minute Agent J vanished with the move.

The FBI continues to work art theft cases, but despite the increasing scope of the crime, still only has a single agent specialising in it full-time. And this one works out of the Philadelphia office instead of art world central in Manhattan. That's all equally disheartening.

Near the end of the retirement party, as the last grains of sand were sliding through the career hourglass, I thought back to the day I started with the FBI 25 years previously. As detailed in the Introduction, I had to hit the ground running when two fellow FBI agents were ambushed and killed by a bank robber.

In contrast, my retirement, at least at that moment, was more in tune with General Douglas MacArthur, the idol of the whacky *Ben-Hur* stuntman from Chapter 15. I felt like an old soldier who had faded away like an ancient Renoir watercolour.

My mentor, Mason, went out with a splash in 1976. We had spent the previous year tracking a half-million dollar painting by 19th and 20th century Russian artist Wassily Kandinsky entitled *Leise Deutung (Soft Interpretations)* that was stolen from famed movie director Otto Preminger. It was snatched from Preminger's Fifth Avenue New York office by the advertising salesman boyfriend of his secretary. The case was especially interesting because Kandinsky was known as 'The Father of Abstract Art' and Preminger was the 'Father of Abstract Film Noir,' a style rooted in hard-edged, dark-themed German expressionism. (Kandinsky's best oils sell for $6 million today.)

After chasing it halfway across the planet, we finally located it in Basel, Switzerland, and grabbed it back. On the day he retired, Mason was able to present it to the great director at a flashy news conference.

'I can only say that I had completely given up hope,' an emotional and grateful Preminger said. 'Having this one back is like having an old friend return ... I feel safer now, knowing the FBI is watching me.'

Mason was equally moved. 'I can't think of a more satisfying way to go out.'

Me neither! Don always did have a flare for the dramatic.

As it turned out, my MacArthur-esque 'fade to black' was merely an illusion, a temporary blip on the radar screen of life. My 'retirement' would prove to be anything but a string of tranquil bass ponds.

The whirlwind post-FBI years actually began six months before I officially checked out. I was assigned to ferret out corruption in the Small Business Administration, and was given an office at the agency's Oklahoma City branch inside the Edward T. Murrah Building.

After I retired, I teamed up with an established area attorney to work on some civil suits involving the misuse of state pension funds. His office was two blocks from the Murrah building.

On the morning of 19 April 1995, I called the attorney, Bob Schick, and told him that I'd work from home that day. There was no special reason, I was just swamped with paperwork and had it spread out on my table. No sense packing it up and driving 10 miles to the downtown building.

Seven minutes later, I felt my apartment building shake. *What the heck was that?* I thought. The phone rang. It was a friend who worked for the Highway Patrol.

'Tom, a terrorist just blew up the Murrah Building!'

'What?' I said, disbelieving. 'That can't be. There aren't any terrorists around here. It has to be a gas explosion.'

'No gas. Terrorists,' he insisted.

I turned on the radio and heard a request for help, especially from those with trucks. I hopped in my pickup and rushed downtown. The building where my last official office had been was now in ruins. It looked like a giant machine had sheered off its face. Desks, chairs, and equipment were dangling from the exposed interiors.

Chaos reigned on the streets below. People were stumbling out of the structure, many injured, bleeding, and dying. I ran inside to help rescue the scores of others that I knew were trapped inside, but had trouble seeing anything through the smoke and dust. After a few minutes of blindly feeling my way around, everyone was ordered out. Word had spread that a second bomb was going to finish the job.

Outside, I rubbed the grit from my burning eyes and tried to regain my vision. Glancing to my right, I saw a policeman hand the dusty, bloody body of a limp toddler to a fireman. The big fire-fighter gently cradled it in his arms. A photographer snapped their picture, and the resulting Pulitzer Prize–winning photograph was destined to serve as the defining image of the terrible tragedy.

Gut-wrenching as the photograph was, the infant in the fireman's arms wasn't the only child who died that morning. There were 19 in all. I saw many of them as well.

Standing helpless in the shadow of the destruction, unable to get inside, I flashed back to a conversation I had near the end of the first day I reported to the Small Business Administration headquarters. I had heard children laughing, crying, and screaming for most of the morning and afternoon, and finally asked someone what that was all about.

'The day care centre is right across the hall,' she said. 'Modern times. Bring your child to work.'

Oh God no, I now thought, stricken by the horror of the vocal memory. *All those laughing little children ...*

When they finally allowed rescue teams back inside the building, it was apparent that that the firemen, EMTs, and trained rescue professionals had the masks, helmets, medical supplies, and other equipment needed to efficiently do the job. I'd only be in the way, or become a victim myself. I instead drove to St. Anthony's Hospital and helped unload the parade of wounded who needed to get inside for treatment. It was an exhausting, emotionally battering day as the bodies kept piling up, and the injured continued to arrive in waves. In all, 168 people died, and more than 500 were hurt.

Something occurred to me on the way home from the hospital that evening that gave me chills. I had opted for an early out, having put in my 25 years by age 51, four years before the mandatory retirement of special agents kicked in. It was a tough decision, one I wrestled with, but I eventually decided to get a jump on my second career as an attorney and private art theft investigator. If I hadn't made that decision, I would have been at my desk inside the Murrah Building that morning.

Similarly, if I had chosen to work at the law office that day, I would have been there when the windows and doors were blown in, and the glass was flying like shrapnel.

I later learned that my daughter, Marianne, had been scheduled to go on a field trip to the Oklahoma Academy of Music that morning, travelling a route that would have taken her and her classmates right by the Murrah Building at the time of the explosion. The trip was postponed at the last minute due to a transportation snafu (situation normal: all fucked up).

Only an incredible series of coincidences had kept me and my loved ones out of harm's way.

In the days following the bombing, I visited the many Iranian friends and associates I had made in Oklahoma City to assure them that despite the nation's intense anger, combined with widespread suspicion that Arab terrorists were behind the incident, the law would still protect them. I told them to let me know if they were hassled or threatened, and I'd intervene with the police.

As the world now knows, there were terrorists in Oklahoma City, but they weren't Arabs. They were a bunch of strange, anti-government, separatist crazies of the domestic variety. An ex-Desert Storm soldier named Timothy McVeigh blew up the building with a powerful homemade fertiliser bomb packed inside a rented van. McVeigh was captured, tried, found guilty, and executed. An associate of McVeigh, Terry Nichols, was sentenced to life in prison.

Oklahoma City was never the same for me after that. I hung around a few more years, then moved back to New York in 1997, partly to start a law office and art recovery business closer to the action, and mostly to get away from the painful memory of terrorists, disasters, and tragedy.

It wasn't destined to be one of my shrewder decisions.

In January 2001, I was recalled into service by the FBI to perform early and mid-career background re-evaluations on the current crop of special agents. The upswing in worldwide terrorist activity was straining the agency's manpower, while at the same time increased efforts were being made to scrutinise our employees. The goal was to avoid another Boston situation where agents were compromised by the mob or terrorists. The standard background checks were cut in half from every 10 years to every 5 to make sure the next Whitey Bulgers, John Gottis and Carlos Jackals of the world weren't seducing our weak links.

The object was to look for veiled signs of vulnerability, gambling debts, living beyond one's means, drugs, alcoholism, bigamy, DUIs, expensive women, hustling men, anything that would make an agent susceptible to, say, a sultry Russian, Italian, or Arabian prancing around naked in front of a window.

That assignment put me in New York on 11 September 2001, the latest day of infamy in American history. Arab terrorists hijacked four commercial airliners in Boston, smashed two into the World Trade Centre towers, and the third into the Pentagon building in

Washington DC. The fourth jet crashed in a Pennsylvania field when either the passengers rebelled, or the government shot it down. (Few remember that President George W. Bush gave the order to down it before it hit its expected target, either the Capitol or the White House. The government denies that it came to that, but conspiracy theorists have long felt otherwise.)

I was driving between my home near Kennedy Airport and my law office in Suffolk County when the first jet hit the tower. Like everybody else, I figured it was an accident. When another airliner crashed into the second tower 15 minutes later I, like everybody else, knew it wasn't.

For the next few minutes, as the horror again sunk in, I struggled with myself over what to do. Should I rush into Manhattan and try to help pull bodies from the rubble, or should I sit this one out and let the professionals handle it? I wondered if there was anybody else at that moment who had experienced Oklahoma City, and now were within miles of 9/11? What were they thinking? Could they, or I, go through the madness again? The waves of dusty, red stained victims stumbling out of the building like zombies, many taking their last breaths? The bodies and body parts scattered amid the debris to such a degree that human beings suddenly appear more machine than person? The children ...

From what I allowed myself to remember from Oklahoma City, the last thing the fire rescue officers needed were civilians stumbling around getting themselves injured, transforming themselves from Good Samaritans into additional victims needing care. In this case, that's precisely what would have happened. After burning for 62 and 101 minutes respectively, both buildings collapsed from the intense heat of the fiery jet fuel.

Between the crash and the implosion, nearly 3,000 people died, including 403 fire-fighters, policemen, EMTs, paramedics and other emergency responders who came into the building after the explosions—as I would have. The figure, while tragically high, was not the 25,000 to 50,000 that can fill the towers at any given time, the numbers terrorist Osama bin Laden was probably shooting for.

In the end, I decided to stay away. Experiencing one such tragedy in a lifetime is more than enough. If I felt for a second that I could have made a difference, that I could have rescued one person, I'd have been there in a heartbeat. My rational mind intervened and told me that adding an art sleuthing FBI agent to the death toll wasn't going to change history, or make a difference.

Following 9/11, I shifted over to the joint NYPD/FBI terrorist task force, which really brought back memories because I had addressed the first meeting of the merged group in 1986. Back then, in the 'good ol' days,' the terrorists were mostly radical domestic groups like the Black Liberation Army, Puerto Rican independence groups, and fading 1960s holdovers like the Weathermen and Students for a Democratic Society. For the most part, they preferred sit-ins and marches to mass destruction. When they did feel the need to blow something up to get attention for their cause, they virtually always did it after-hours when the buildings were empty in order to minimise the loss of life.

Internationally, the Serbians, Croatians, IRA, Palestinians, and Libyans were causing trouble, but they operated almost exclusively overseas.

Those days were now tragically gone.

This time around, my function was to screen the retired NYPD detectives and officers with top secret Federal security clearances who were returning into the fold to battle the foreign terrorists invading our nation.

When things settled down, I thought about how fortunate I was to have made the career choice that I did. While other FBI agents were hunting vicious terrorists, violent bank robbers, murderers, serial killers, rapists, greedy businessmen, crooked politicians, and child molesters, I was hanging with Rembrandt, van Gogh, Renoir, Manet, Degas, Titian, Cassatt, Pollock, and their uplifting fraternity.

My co-workers faced a constant stream of violence and ugliness, while I sought to restore beauty and history.

When my peers located their prey, they came face-to-face with the dregs of humanity. When I found mine, I was awed by the best creations of humanity.

Even when our worlds crossed, when a cutthroat gangster got hold of a classic masterpiece and held it for ransom, the situation was different. It was as if being in the presence of such stunning images of our world's past moved and mellowed the hardest of criminals and put them on their best behaviour.

When a trap was sprung and the art thieves were pounced upon by the Feds, none of these lifelong bad guys ever resisted arrest, or chose to fight or shoot it out. They all went quietly into one of van Gogh's *Starry Night*.

I'll never forget the emotion that swept over the violent, hardcore career criminal, Johnny Rio, from Chapters 1 and 2 when he finally had to part with Rembrandt's *The Rabbi*. You just don't see that with child molesters and mass murderers.

G.K. Chesterton, the early 20th century English author of *Charles Dickens* and scores of other books, wrote something once that has always stuck with me: 'In the beginning there was art for God's sake. In the Renaissance, there was art for man's sake. Beginning with Impressionism, there was art for art's sake. Now, unfortunately, we have no art, for God's sake.'

The sardonic Chesterton was conveying his disdain of modern techniques, but I view the quote differently. I see it as an indictment of the glaring lack of protection and security by museums, society's guardians of priceless historical art. If the world's museums and galleries don't tighten their sanctuaries, and the courts don't further beef up the laws pertaining to art theft, there won't be anything left but Chesterton's despised modern art.

Another favourite quote is one by the English poet Lord Byron: 'A drop of ink can make a million think.'

It's my wish that the many drops of ink it took to produce this book will help in the recovery of those masterpieces that remain missing, and enable them to one day return to their rightful owners. An art thief's greatest offence is severing the public's critical link to its vividly portrayed cultural heritage, and preventing future generations from enjoying the vision of those who came before. That is an unpardonable sin.

Degas once observed that a good painting was like committing the perfect crime. It's a clever line, but one that should not be misinterpreted. The theft of one of these allegorical 'perfect crimes'—however well planned and carried out—should never be confused with the genius of the object purloined.

When I travelled across Europe in 1977 with US Attorney Peter Murphy, searching for the thieves who had raided a Spanish church and stole the Serra brothers' *Scenes From The Life of the Virgin*, (Chapter 14), I peppered him with questions about his job. I'd always wanted to put my legal training to use, and told him I was contemplating becoming a prosecutor.

'Are you crazy?' he exclaimed. 'You have the greatest job in the world! You'd be nuts to leave it.'

You know something? He was absolutely right.

INDEX

A

Abdul Enterprises 54, 56
Abrahams, Montréal Detective
    Kenny 146, 152-154
ABSCAM 5, 57, 59, 65, 86, 98,
    148, 165, 180, 288
Acquaviva, Nicholas 257
Adams, Nathan M. 2, 37, 150
Adoration of the Shepherd, 102,
    319
After the Hunt 199
al-Fassi, Mohammed 165-167,
    171, 172
Alford, FBI Agent Susan 162,
    164, 169, 171
Amor Som Bacchus 248
Anfossi, Antonio 91, 93
Ann 221

Arp, Jean 212
Atlantic Monthly magazine 317
*A Japanese Vase Filled with Red
    Roses* 204
A Lady and Gentleman in Black
    301
A Life of Picasso by John
    Richardson 296

B

Barreiro, Tony 161
Battle Ensign 189
Bazé, Paul, Curator, Leon
    Bonnat 5, 37, 38
Beit, Sir Alfred, owner of
    the Beit Collection,
    Russborough House,
    Blessington 224, 244,

308

Bellotto, Bernardo 319

Benton, Thomas Hart 117, 205,
208, 211

Bielefeld, Ted 201

Bild newspaper 8, 9

Black Liberation Army 330

Boat in Early Morning 221

Boggs, Frank Myer 214

Bonanno Family 14, 160

Bonhams Auctioneers 15

Borghi Gallery, New York 274

Boston Museum of Fine Arts
11, 197

Bouguereau, Adolphe-William
6, 117, 273-274

Bremen Museum 77

Bronfman, Samuel 15

Brooklyn Bridge 135, 220

Brown, Special Agent Bobby
109

Brueghel, Pieter 206, 214

Bryant, Billie Austin 12-13

Bulger, James 'Whitey' 307,
310-312, 319

Burgomaster Six 3, 9

Burnham, Bonnie, and
Connie Lowenthal
of the International
Foundation for Art
Research (IFAR) 120

Bush, President George H.W.
62, 117, 244, 287, 289,
321, 329

C

Cahill, Martin 'The General'

244, 308, 310, 320

Campbell, Assistant US
Attorney Susan 80, 198

Capone, Al 126, 133, 136

Captain Rosenberg 264-265

Caramoor Museum, Katonah,
New York 264

Caravaggio, Michelangelo
Merisi 173

Carlo, Charles 'Chuckie' 17,
19-20, 42

Carlson, Donna and Gil
Elderman of the Art
Dealer's Association of
America (ADAA) 120

Carnegie Mellon University
Art Gallery, Pittsburgh
270

Caserele, Dominic 45-46, 59

Cassatt, Mary 68, 117, 205,
330

Castellano, Gambino mob boss
Paulie 94, 269

Catlin, George 199

Cézanne, Paul 139, 141, 148

Chagall, Marc 117, 158, 271

Chapman, Mark David 180

Chase, William Merritt 54,
117

Chateau Villa 82

Chez Tortoni 302

Christie's Auctioneers 61, 63,
232, 306

Christ Child Enthroned 77

Christ on the Cross 3, 9

Chubb & Son Insurance 187,
194

Coe-Kerr Gallery, New York 196
Colombo Family 14, 46, 134-136, 203
Congo the chimpanzee 15, 16
Connolly, ex-Special Agent John, associate of Whitey ulger 312-313
Connor Jr, Myles 196
Cook, Christopher M. 176
Coolidge, Cassius 56
Corallo, Anthony 'Tony Ducks' 46
Corot, Jean-Baptiste-Camille 117
Cortege Aux Environs de Florence 301
Couse, Eanger Irving 131
Cox, FBI Aagents Terry, and Fred Berins, Ed Murphy, Bill Roemer, Larry Kennedy 238
Cox, Warren E. 218-220, 238
Cronkite, Walter 39
Crucifixion 205, 207
Cuyp's Cow 241
Cuyp, Aelbert 241

D

D'Avanzo, Lewis 'Louie' Vincent 125-128, 133, 135-136
Dalí, Salvador 106, 212
Daly, FBI Agent Thomas 198
Daumier, Honoré 124
Davies, Arthur 212
da Vinci, Leonardo 63, 75, 81, 118, 225
Deer Island, Maine 221
Degas, Edgar 158, 166-167, 169, 170, 211-212, 271-272, 301, 304-305, 311, 317, 330, 332
Delacroix, Eugène 302
Dennehy, Special Agent Mike 54-55, 180
Dewing, Arthur S. 140, 149
De Besche, Hubert 248
de Kooning, Willem 176
de Laboulaye, Francois 39
de Vlaminck, Maurice 141
de Young Museum, San Francisco 25
Dillinger, John 3, 41-42, 110
di Capelletti, Judge Mario 265
Donati, Bobby 316-317
Dooley, Operations Supervisor John 255, 263-264
Dove, FBI Agent Jerry 112
Draskulla 248
Dresden Museum 71, 76
Dubois-Pillet, Albert 114, 128-129
Dubuffet, Jean 176-177, 181
Dugdale, Dr Bridget Rose 224, 244
Dürer, Albrecht 77

E

Edward T. Murrah Building 325
Errichetti, Angelo 57
ETA, (*Euskadi Ta Askatasuna—* Fatherland and

Freedom) 224

F

Fabritius, Carel 212
Faidit, Jacques 7-14, 28
Falzon, FBI Investigator Daniel J. 312-313, 315, 318
Fantin-Latour, Henri 204
Fasolino, Gennarino 'Jerry' 17, 19-21, 23, 31, 33, 37-38
FBI 1, 6-7, 9, 12-19, 20, 22-24, 31, 35, 37, 39, 41-42, 45, 47, 48, 51-53, 55, 57-60, 62, 65, 68-69, 72, 80, 84, 86, 101, 103, 108, 110, 112, 114-115, 119-120, 122, 126-129, 132-133, 141, 146-148, 151, 153, 155, 159-160, 162, 165, 170, 179-185, 189-190, 192, 195-196, 198-200, 213, 219-220, 226, 229-230, 235, 238-239, 244-245, 261-262, 268-271, 278, 282-283, 286-287, 290-291, 295-296, 307-309, 311-312, 317, 319, 324-325, 328, 330
FBI Truck Hijacking Squad 65
Femme aux Bras Croisés 63, 287
Fleischman, Lawrence A. 44, 59, 64
Flinck, Govaert 301, 304
Flynn, Special Agent Eugene 91, 108
Fogg Museum, Harvard University 136

Fordham Law School, New York 12
Franzese, Sonny 46, 136
Fraser, James Earl 323
Freeh, Assistant US Attorney Louis 160
Frick Museum, New York 173
Fuller, Special Agent Myron 46, 56

G

Gainsborough, Thomas 141, 224, 244, 308, 319
Gambino Family 22, 39, 125, 269, 294
Ganci, Joe 'The Whale' 230
Gandolfo, John Joseph 'Johnny Rio' 13, 15, 18-19
Garçon a la Pipe (Boy with a Pipe) 63
Gauguin, Paul 171
Gentleman 301, 303
Gerry, Samuel Lancaster 199
Giacometti, Alberto 176, 181
Gilmore, Bob, and Horst Drewnoik, co-Chiefs of the FBO Brooklyn/ Queens Organised Crime Squad 126-127
Gilot, Françoise 288
Giuliani, Rudy 125, 128
Glassman, Israel David 109
Good, Supervising Agent John 49, 56-57, 59, 65-66, 91, 129, 329
Gore, Allan, author of *King of the Pickpockets* 119-120

Gotti, John 'The Teflon Don' 6, 22, 94, 125, 180, 269, 286, 287
Goya, Francisco 3, 224
Grabach, John R. 176-177, 181
Grandma Moses, aka Anna Mary Robertson Moses 5, 114, 123, 131, 188-189, 199
Gravano, Sammy 'The Bull' 286
Grindle, Lyle 310
Grogan, FBI Agent Benjamin 112

H

Haag, George 87-91, 93, 241
Hagen, Tommy 174
Hammer, Dr Armand 116-123, 125, 128, 136
Hammer Galleries, Manhattan 116-123, 125, 128, 136
Hanlon, Special Agent John 96-97, 99, 109, 112
Harris, William 16
Hartnett, Don, FBI Buffalo Organised Crime Chief 30-31, 39
Harvard Magazine 139, 156
Harvard Widener Library 141
Hassam, Childe 117, 199
Hearst, Patty 16, 43,
Hearst, William Randolph 16, 43, 117-118
Helmick, Howard 188-189, 191, 196
Henner, Jean Jacques 117-118

Henri, Robert 68, 204, 221
Hill-Stead Museum, Connecticut 95, 98
His Favourite Meal 191
Hohenschwangua Castle 202
Home Sweet Home 199
Hoover, J. Edgar 13, 16-17, 31, 41-42, 112, 121-122, 129, 147, 189-190, 226, 230, 249-250, 252, 255, 259, 263, 284, 287, 289, 321
Houghton, David 316
House of Tasha 17, 22-24, 26, 33, 35
Howard, Bernie 'The Dirty Little Coward' 180, 188-189, 192, 203, 213, 215, 240
Hughes, Robert, art critic 192, 305-307, 318

I

Interpol 6, 8-9, 13, 25, 60, 62, 68, 119, 217, 228
IRA (Irish Republican Army) 224, 244, 307-308, 311, 315, 320, 330
Isabella Stewart Gardner Museum, Boston 300

J

J. Paul Getty Museum 11
Jackson, Harry 7, 176-177, 181, 183, 194, 205, 297
Jackson Pollock, Paul 194, 205,

297

Jason and His Teacher 212

Jasper Museum, Houston, Texas 36

Javert, Inspector, of *Les Misérables* 69

Johnson, Professor of Art History at Humboldt State University, Arcadia, California, Ron 291

K

Kallstrom, Former FBI Chief Jimmy 126

Kandinsky, Wassily 324-325

Kaun Yan 264

Kennedy Galleries, Manhattan 44, 122, 232, 271

Kimon 149

Kingman, Brian 297-298

Kirchick, Allen I. 144-145, 148, 155-156

Klötzke, Michael Jurgen 8-11

Knapp Commission 218, 220

Kobelt Airport, Wallkill, New York 50

Kohl, 'Ol' King', Danny 68-69, 269-274, 276-277, 279

Koklowa, Olga 288

Kregelstein, Walter & Francis 109

Kuhn, Special Agent John 127

L

Lady 10, 43-44, 52-53, 301

LaGuardia Airport, New York & New Jersey 48, 126

Lambardozzi, Carmine 'The Doctor' 221

Landscape with an Obelisk 301

Lang, Special Agent Jerry 72

La Cosa Nostra 61

La Dame a la Toilette 82

La mere de l'artiste 211

La Mujer 288-289, 294, 296

La Seine au quai St Bernard 1885 114, 129

La Sortie Du Pesage 301

LeBec, Robert 2-11, 13, 28

Leger, Fernand 176-177, 181

Leigh, William R. 199

Leise Deutung (Soft Interpretations) 324

Leone, Vinnie 'The Human Fly' 203

Lèon Bonnat Museum in Bayonne, France 2

Les Noces de Pierrette 63, 287

Levine, David 214, 221

Levine, Jack 214, 221

Le Lion 211

Le Petit Pont 114

Life and Works 212

Lloyd's of London 6, 113, 120-121, 128-129, 136, 315

Lombardozzi, Carmine 'The Doctor' 203, 217, 294

Louvre 3, 10, 33-34, 103, 323

Lucchese Family 46

Lynch, Hammer Galleries Curator Richard 118-

123, 128-132

M

MacArthur, General Douglas
  252-253, 324-325
Madame Baccelli 244, 308, 319
Madonna 225
Magnalina Family 20, 39
Manet, Edouard 96, 212, 302,
  304-306, 311, 321, 330
Mann Act 284
Marin, John 221
Marsh, Reginald 212
Mason, Don, FBI art theft
  pioneer 1, 13, 19, 58,
  141, 143, 187, 189, 196-
  197, 239, 249, 323-325
Matisse, Henri 117, 139
Matix, William 112
Mauriello, Al 297
Mawn, Special Agent Barry
  128-132, 134, 162
Maxwell Galleries, San
  Francisco 206
McCarthy, Special Agent Jack
  56
McCrary, Special Agent Gregg
  21-23, 26-27, 31
McDevitt, Brian Michael 314-
  315
McGowan, Detective Inspector
  John 86
McLaughlin, Michael 91-94
McShane, Thomas, aka Thomas
  Bishop, aka Robert
  Steele 12
McVeigh, Timothy 285, 328

Meador, Joe Tom 80
Mead Museum, Amherst
  College, Massachussetts
  316
Metropolitan Museum of Art,
  New York 11, 75, 95,
  120, 142, 174, 207, 227
Metsu, Gabriel 224
Michelangelo (Buonarotti) 75
Mika, Special Agent Richie
  127
Miller, Alfred Jacob 199
Millet, Jean Charles, grandson
  of 19th Century French
  Barbizon master Jean
  François Millet 9
Mills, London FBI Bureau
  Chief, Darrell 244
Miró, Joan 117, 166-167, 271
Möller, Yngve 248, 266-267
Mona Lisa 10-11, 36, 63, 65,
  225
Monet, Claude 5, 11, 68, 82-83,
  91-92, 94, 110, 117, 130,
  157
Montes, the Marquis of
  Montréal Joaquin
  Alvarez 289
Montréal Museum of Art 141,
  145, 156
Moran, Percy 212
Morey, Michael Brian 314
Morgan, J.P. 117-118
Morse, Samuel F.B. 199
Munch, Edvard 225
Murgolo, Phil J. 251, 256-258,
  262-264

N

Nadjari, Knapp Special Prosecutor Maurice 218

National Art Institute of Madrid 227

National Gallery of Art, Washington DC 220

Neuschwanstein, the 'New Swan' castle 202

Newsday magazine 176-177

New York Museum of Natural History 36

New York Observer 296

New York Times 95

Nichols, Terry 328

O

Oceanberg's Seven 95-96, 110

Of the Nature, Weight and Movement of Water 118

Olarte, Gloria 94

Oluluma, Marianne 202

Operation Tepee 1, 17, 21, 31, 35, 37,-38, 41

P

'Pizza Connection', The 159

Palmer, Edward 53, 59

Pancoast, Director, International Foundation for Art Research, Virgilia 297

Paris Police Nationale 6

Parrish, Maxfield 212, 214

Peasants Dancing and Carousing Outside an Inn 320

Pell Grant scandals 282

Pepperdine University 158

Persico, Carmine 'The Snake' 14

Petite Danseuse De Quatorze Ans 271

Picasso, Pablo 5-6, 10, 12-13, 36-37, 59, 62-69, 82-83, 91-92, 94, 117, 139, 157, 166-167, 169, 212, 271, 274, 284, 286-296, 298

Pisano, Salvatore 133-134, 136

Platt, Michael 112

Poerstel, Special Agent Jack 22, 23, 26, 27, 30, 31, 39

Popolana, Special Agent Mike 271

Portrait of Anne 68

Portrait of a Man With Red Cap and Gold Chain 25

Portrait of Doctor Gachet 114

Portrait of Lady Johanna Quadacker Bannier 44

Portrait of Madame Cordier 205

Portrait of Richard Tickell 319

Portrait of Titus 2

Portrait Presume Achille Degas 211

Powell, Special Agent Dick 162

Preminger, Otto 324-325

Presentation in the Temple 102

Program for an Artistic Soiree 301

Program for an Artistic Soiree II 301

Purvis, Melvin, top FBI Agent 155
Putzel III, Henry 'Pete' 211

Q

Quedlinburg Treasures 80
Quitting the Mob 136

R

Raguideau, Gilbert 61-62
Rain, Charles 199
Rape of Europa 301, 305
Raphael 75, 276
Raphael Gallery, New York 276
Reader's Digest 2, 8, 37
Reasoner, Harry 39
Reed, Christopher 87-88, 139
Regan, Martin G. 141, 156
Reilly, Patrick 175, 178
Rembrandt Committee 25
Rembrandt Harmenszoon van Rijn 1-3, 5, 7, 11-13, 15-17, 19-21, 25-30, 33-37, 39, 45, 47, 60, 69, 75-76, 115, 117, 139, 144, 158, 166-167, 186, 197, 236, 241, 271-272, 301, 303-305, 310-311, 315, 317-318, 330-331
Remington, Frederic 6, 188, 199, 212
Renoir, Pierre-Auguste 15, 68, 76, 117, 139, 324, 330
Reverend McKinstry 199
Rinaldi, Detective Sergeant John 86

Rockwell, Cleveland Salter 199, 212
Rockwell, Norman 199, 212
Rosenberg, Art expert Mr 207-208, 210, 264-265
Rouault, Georges 68
Rubens, Peter Paul 3, 5, 12, 44-45, 51-52, 57, 60, 64, 94, 97-98, 102-104, 106, 110, 139, 141, 158-159, 212, 224, 288, 308, 319
Russell, Charles M. 6, 188, 199, 311, 321, 323

S

Sabloski, Ron 54-56
Saltimbanque Seated with Arms Crossed 63
Samson and Delilah 45, 98, 178
Sangello, Special Agent Jim 182
Sangillo, Montréal Detective Pierre 146, 152
Sargent, John Singer 117
Sarro, Robert 101-105, 108
Sartori, Toni 19-20, 33, 37
Sartori, Toni and John 19-20, 33, 37
Saturday Evening Post 189
Scenes From the Life of the Virgin 223
Schick, Bob 325
Schwartz, Martin, Esq. 207-210, 213
Scream 225
Self Portrait (Rembrandt) 301
Serpico, Frank 178, 218

Serra, Jaume & Pedro 223, 226-
        229, 232-233, 236, 239,
        241-242, 244-245, 332
Sessions, FBI Director William
        287-290, 292, 321
Shapiro, Philip 99-105, 108
Shore, Jeffrey 175, 178-179,
        181-183, 185
Shorski, FBI Supervisor Lynn
        78, 239
Sioux Indian Reconnoitering 199
Slacker Museum, Harvard 156
Smith, Lloyd's of London
        Adjuster Harold 113-
        116, 119-122, 124-125,
        128-129, 131, 133, 190,
        192, 199, 254, 313, 315,
        324
Smith, Special Agent Robin
        192
Smith, Xanthus Russell 113-
        116, 119-122, 124-125,
        128-129, 131, 133, 190,
        192, 199, 254, 313, 315,
        324
Sotheby's 63, 122, 142, 159,
        232, 287, 306
Spiel, Special Agent Bob 213-
        215
Starry Night 331
Stella, Frank 214, 220
Stern newspaper 9
Still Life with Fish 212
Storm 301, 303
Students for a Democratic
        Society 330
St Matthew Being Inspired by the

        Angels 34
Sullivan, US Attorney Michael
        J. 312
Sunflowers 114
Susanna 205
Symbionese Liberation Army
        16

T

Ter Borch, Gerard 44-45, 51-
        52, 57, 60, 64
The Concert 301
The Cotton Field 199
The End of the Trail 323
The Guitar Player 224
The Gunsil 176, 184-185, 287
*The Holy Family with St
        Catherine and Honoured
        Donor* 71
The Judgement at Cambyese 44
The Mail is Here 199
*The Man with the Purple Hat aka
        L'Homme a la Casquette*
        62
*The Marriage Feast of Jan
        Brueghel* 206
The Massacre of the Innocents
        45, 98
The Philadelphia Inquirer 198
The Rabbi 1-3, 5-7, 9-13, 15-16,
        18-20, 26-27, 31, 34-35,
        38, 40, 331
The Smoke Shield 199
The Sting Man, by Robert W.
        Greene 54
The Storm on the Sea of Galilee
        301

The Wave 221
Thompson, James 196
Three Mounted Jockeys 301
Timen, Frans 248-249, 258
Time magazine 10, 61, 125, 305, 318
Tintoretto, Jacopo 5, 69, 71-75, 77-79
Titian, Vecellio 71, 139, 144, 301-305, 307, 309, 330
Titulos del Reino y Grandezas 297
Todardo, Joseph E. Senior 37
Tommy Joe 'The Listerine Kid' 247-250, 266
Tortoriello, James Junior 108-109

U

Utrillo, Maurice 83, 92

V

Vaglica, Anthony 140-141
Valtat, Louis 214
van Derveer, FBI Agent Peter 146-147, 152, 154-155
van Dongen, Kees 211
van Gogh, Vincent 12, 61, 113-115, 117, 119, 121, 123-125, 128, 131, 133-135, 158-159, 162, 169, 171, 236, 241, 277, 330-331
van Ostade, Adrien 319-320
van Rijn, Michael 3, 317
Vase with Flowers 204
Velasquez 224

Venus with a Mirror 71
Vermeer, Johannes 76, 224-225, 301, 303-305, 308, 311, 317-318
Vervinter 248
View of Florence 319
Vinokur, Rajmond 72
von Harrach, Michael, assumed title Prince Michael Balthasar Karl Friedrich von Hohensiegen du Zunger und von Harrach, aka Michael Goldbaum 201
von Jawlensky, Alexej 176
von Klassen, Ronald 250, 257, 264
von Maker, Harold 200
von Maker, Harold, aka Prince Harold von Hohenloe, aka Dr Harold J. Maker, aka Peter Wertz, aka David Patterson 200, 203-207, 210-217, 220-221, 228, 297
Vuillard, Edouard 204, 211

W

Walker, FBI Agent Reno 184-185, 199, 287, 295
Walker, William W.A. 199
Warhol, Andy 15, 62, 129
Waterman Wood, Thomas 199
Weathermen 330
Webster, FBI Director William 39, 41-42, 57-58, 292
Weinberg, Mel 42-43, 46, 53,

228

Weiswasser, Attorney Robert
    266
Weitzman, J. Daniel 175-177,
    179, 181, 185
Wertmüller, Adolf 248-249,
    258
Wesselman, Tom 176-178, 181
What's In It for Me? by Joe
    Stedino 322
Whistler, James McNeill 114
Willard, Simon 198
Williams, Allison & Cliff 87-
    88, 94, 197-198
Williams, Lester 87-88, 94,
    197-198
Will Rogers Airport, Oklahoma
    City 13
Wilson, FBI Organised Crime
    Chief Mike 288
Witness Protection Programme
    42
Wolf, Judge Mark 312
Woods, FBI Pilot Eddie 48-50
Woolworth, F.W. 12, 187-188,
    191, 195-199, 316
Woolworth, Pauline, son R.
    Frederick, husband
    Norman B. son of Fred
    M. the cousin of Frank
    Woolworth 12, 187-
    188, 191, 195-199, 316
Wyeth, Andrew 6, 114, 117,
    189
Wyeth, N.C. father of Andrew
    188, 196

Y

Yamron Jewellery Store,
    Atlantic City 198
Youngworth, William 317

Z

Zhukov, Georgy 76
Zimbalist Jr, Efrem. from TV's
    FBI 155
Zims, Special Agent Floyd 285
Zorach, William 221
Zorn, Anders 248-249, 258,
    320

MORE NON-FICTION FROM MAVERICK HOUSE

THE LAST EXECUTIONER

MEMOIRS OF THAILAND'S LAST PRISON EXECUTIONER

By CHAVORET JARUBOON
WITH NICOLA PIERCE

CHAVORET JARUBOON WAS PERSONALLY RESPONSIBLE FOR EXECUTING 55 PRISON INMATES ON THAILAND'S INFAMOUS DEATH ROW.

As a boy, he wanted to be a teacher like his father, then a rock'n'roll star like Elvis, but his life changed when he joined Thailand's prison service. From there he took on one of the hardest jobs in the world.

Honest and often disturbing—but told with surprising humour and emotion—*The Last Executioner* is the remarkable story of one man's experiences with life and death.

Emotional and at times confronting, the book grapples with the controversial topic of the death sentence and makes no easy reading.

This book is not for the faint hearted—*The Last Executioner* takes you right behind the bars of the Bangkok Hilton and into death row.

To order this book go to www.maverickhouse.com

MORE NON-FICTION FROM MAVERICK HOUSE

CONFESSIONS

The Sexual Adventures of a Modern Irish Woman

By BILLIEGEAN with YVONNE KINSELLA

Over the last 29 years Billiegean has experienced a lot in life. She was expelled from school at 13, gave birth to a little girl at 17, battled with a drink and drugs addiction, worked as a pole dancer, a lapdancer, a strippogram and 'gave it loads' on a telephone sex line.

Over the years she has made tabloid headlines with her sexual antics, and in *Confessions* she is ready to tell some of the secrets that didn't make the papers.

As Ireland's most famous bad girl, Billiegean speaks frankly about sex and the modern Irish woman, and her outrageous romps with celebrities.

This is the first book to explore sexuality in modern Ireland and gives an insider's account of the country's growing adult entertainment industry.

It is a book not to be missed.

To order this book go to www.maverickhouse.com

FINAL WITNESS

MY JOURNEY FROM THE HOLOCAUST TO IRELAND

BY ZOLTAN ZINN-COLLIS WITH ALICIA McAULEY

The concentration camp at Bergen-Belsen is the scene of one of the world's largest mass murders. It was here that Zoltan Zinn-Collis was incarcerated as a five year old boy, along with his family and where, incredibly, he managed to survive the inhuman brutality of the SS guards and the ravages of near-starvation, disease and squalor.

Discovered by a Red Cross nurse who pronounced him 'an enchanting scrap of humanity', Zoltan was brought to Ireland and adopted by one of the camp's liberators, Dr Bob Collis. Having endured the physical and mental legacy of his childhood, now, aged 66, Zoltan is ready to speak.

This story is one of deepest pain and greatest joy, told with tremendous honesty and surprising sparks of humour. It is a story of how a young boy lost one family and found another; of how, escaping from the ruins of a broken Europe, he was able to rebuild a new life.

The triumphant story of this remarkable man's journey through the darkness of genocide will inspire anyone whose life has been touched by fear, suffering, and loss.

To order this book go to www.maverickhouse.com

MORE NON-FICTION FROM MAVERICK HOUSE

WELCOME TO HELL

ONE MAN'S FIGHT FOR LIFE INSIDE
THE 'BANGKOK HILTON'

BY COLIN MARTIN

Written from his cell and smuggled out page by page, Colin Martin's autobiography chronicles an innocent man's struggle to survive inside one of the world's most dangerous prisons.

After being swindled out of a fortune, Martin was let down by the hopelessly corrupt Thai police. Forced to rely upon his own resources, he tracked down the man who conned him and, drawn into a fight, accidentally stabbed and killed the man's bodyguard.

Martin was arrested, denied a fair trial, convicted of murder and thrown into prison—where he remained for eight years. Honest and often disturbing, *Welcome to Hell* is the remarkable story of how Martin was denied justice again and again.

In his extraordinary account, he describes the swindle, his arrest and vicious torture by police, the unfair trial, and the eight years of brutality and squalor he was forced to endure.

To order this book go to www.maverickhouse.com